BORDERLANDS

BORDERLANDS

Delia & Ferdinand Kuhn

MAPS BY ROBERT·W·GALVIN

NEW YORK : ALFRED·A·KNOPF

1 9 6 2

L. C. catalog card number: 62–8692

THIS IS A BORZOI BOOK,
PUBLISHED BY ALFRED A. KNOPF, INC.

FIRST EDITION

TO

J. L. K.

INTRODUCTION

THIS BOOK examines six remote border regions of Asia. They are Hokkaido, Japan's northernmost island; the Sulu Sea, including North Borneo and Mindanao; the Shan and Kachin States of Burma; the protectorate of Sikkim, a sample of India's Himalayan border; Afghan Turkestan, between the Hindu Kush and Soviet Central Asia; and, finally, the eastern fourth of Turkey to the Soviet and Iranian boundaries.

A reader may well wonder whether these lands have anything in common, or simply find themselves by chance between the same hard covers. An elephant and a whale happen to be large mammals, but this hardly entitles them to share a cage in a zoo. To someone who has not known these borderlands at first hand, they would appear no more comparable. They lie scattered all the way across Asia from the North Pacific to the Black Sea; their climates range from stinging cold to tropical; their people have had little or no contact with one another through the ages. One of the six belongs to a highly industrialized modern nation; the rest are only beginning to respond, in varying degrees, to the impact of Western technology and ideas. In our early acquaintance with the six regions, it did not occur to us that they might belong to the same genus of human society, or, for that matter, that we would want to write a serious book about them.

Only after reacquaintance on the spot did we find an affinity, if not a blood kinship, among them. It became gradually clear to us that these particular borderlands were like children of different parents who had been shaped by similar forces. We found that by training an X-ray camera on each of them in turn, we ourselves had gained a deeper understanding of all.

Here it may be useful to define a word. By a *borderland* we mean an area far from the center of political, economic, and social power in its own country, an area also close to someone else's political and cultural boundary. Adjoining a *borderland* one finds people of other faiths or races, and often different political and social systems as well. Many examples besides our own will spring to mind: Outer Mongolia, between the Soviet Union and China; or Alaska, facing Soviet territory across the narrow Bering Strait. What follows is by no means an inventory of all that meet our tests. Even in an age of jets and cushioned travel, two middle-aged writers would have to be made of steel to cover them all. We have simply taken a long, hard look at a few that we know from personal experience, and reported our findings.

The reader will discover at least three other common denominators among them, in spite of many differences. Each of our examples is cut off from the center of power in its own country, not just by physical distance but also by a failure of communication. The failure is two-way. The city men who rule the nation from a Western-veneered capital cannot hide their sense of superiority toward the people of the outlying regions, who are largely rural, often illiterate, and slow to change traditional ways. The borderlander, for his part, cannot hide his suspicion of the "foreigner" who comes from the national capital as governor, tax collector, policeman, or soldier, and who often looks like a colonial master. Between the two layers there is little understanding or sense of belonging to the same national community.

The gulf between urban and rural Asians is nothing new.

But the impact of the West appears to have widened it. Western influence rushes into Asian cities, but only creeps from the capitals into the farming areas, including the borderlands. When an Asian student returns to his own country from a university in Europe or the United States, is he better equipped to understand his own countryside? Having acquired Western tastes and techniques, he usually finds it harder to communicate with the farmers, and they, in turn, with him. Each nation is thus at least two nations: the few and the many, the modernized and the traditional. Each suffers from what Dr. Toynbee calls, in a somewhat different sense, a "schism in the soul." The widening of this schism is the most pernicious of the trends we have watched in the borderlands. It afflicts them all, even the most advanced, and we shall have to revert to it again and again in the chapters that follow.

All of our regions, secondly, share some of the handicaps of colonial status. Only three of them ever belonged to Western powers, yet all are in fact, if not in name, mere dependencies of their respective countries. What does this relationship mean? It means that they are, with one partial and surprising exception, primarily suppliers of raw materials to be processed elsewhere. It means also that they lag behind the rest of the country in roads, schools, and other mechanisms for moving ahead. The irony of the situation should not be missed. Some of the newly independent governments declaim in the United Nations against colonialism, but remain indifferent to colonial problems in their own back yards. Sooner or later they will have to finish the imperial tasks they inherited: to govern and develop their own outposts of traditional culture along their distant borders.

This brings us to a third common denominator: each borderland has natural and human resources which its country as a whole can ill afford to neglect or squander. When Asian governments draw up budgets or five-year development plans, they usually put the border regions low on their lists

of priorities. Perhaps this is natural, since population tends
to cluster near the national capital or commercial center.
Nevertheless, neglect of the frontier provinces is not only
economic but political folly. No nation can become united
or secure while its border peoples harbor grievances, or
while, as in one or two countries, they toy with separatist
ideas. It goes without saying that with the unity and security
of these Asian nations the United States is deeply, irrevo-
cably involved.

Such, then, are some of the threads that tie the borderlands together. The reader will recognize them as he moves
from the forests of Hokkaido westward around the arc of
Asia.

We might mention what took us to the borderlands in the
first place. During the 1950's we made seven long journeys
to Asia as reporters for newspapers and magazines. Bits and
pieces of our material have therefore appeared (in different
form) in *Collier's*, the *National Geographic Magazine*, and
other periodicals, and in *The Washington Post* and other
newspapers. Our work naturally began in the capital cities
and kept us there too long. Asian capitals may be centers of
information, but they tell little about their countries, and
with rare exceptions are disagreeable. After struggling with
the crush and clutter of these urban jungles we headed compulsively for open spaces. Sometimes the urge drove us to
the limits of the nation's territory, the edge of the blue yon-
der. The instinct was sound. Whoever makes the effort as
we did will find unexpected treasures, and memories to last
a lifetime.

Christopher Rand, an insatiable traveler in Asia, has written that American reporters tend to find the peoples of the
hills more appealing than those of the plains. To the second
part of the indictment, we plead not guilty: a city-bred
Indian in Calcutta, or an Afghan in Kabul, can be as engag-
ing as his country cousin in the hills. But the first part of the

accusation is true. The reader will sense that we have not escaped the charm of border peoples, nor the trap they unwittingly set for writers. We have found them nonconformist, proud, and generally slow to be pressed into a standardized modern mold. Moreover, most of the borderlands are comparatively empty; the so-called population explosion has not strewn its debris among them. Under their peaks and in their forests, surrounded by their solitudes, one can laugh at Walter de la Mare's lament of the 1920's that "there will soon be no wild and far for which to pine." It reassured us to find parts of these regions still "wild and far," with the look and the feel of pioneer lands.

But it is only fair to warn the reader: this will not be a tale of personal adventures. Like others who have written from odd corners of Asia, we might have filled our pages with border guards who blocked our way, with insects that ate us, and with the food we ate which laid us low. Who cares? After more than thirty years in the reporter's trade, it is our guess that the reader wants to get on with the story. We also assume that he wants to go deeply enough into these borderlands to know what they are like, and why.

Nor will this be a travel book. Greater travelers, from Marco Polo to Marco Pallis, have roamed our chosen areas and have left matchless records of their journeys. We cannot compete with them, and do not intend to try. Among them have been Germans, Frenchmen, Swedes, and Chinese, sportsmen, traders, naturalists, and spies. Long before the United States became a world power, Americans, too, showed up in sequestered parts of Asia: the missionaries who flocked to Armenian Turkey and northern Burma; the "general" from Pennsylvania who planted the Stars and Stripes on the Hindu Kush; the future President who poked into the Shan States in search of a fortune; the technicians and engineers who anticipated a Point Four program for Hokkaido by almost a hundred years. Of these half-forgotten figures we shall have something to tell.

But above all others, it was the British Victorians who pushed their way into the recesses of the East. No other people in history can touch them for sheer nosyness. Young James Bryce, climbing the peak of Ararat all alone; biologist Alfred Russel Wallace collecting specimens in savage Borneo; botanist John Anderson struggling up the Irrawaddy to find a new trade route to China; Lord Curzon strutting along the fringes of India, and a lesser traveler of the same name but of another family cataloguing the birds of the Turkish highlands—these have been only a few of a fearless, peerless breed. Not the least of them were Englishwomen who brushed off tigers and leeches and kept journals filled with Asian lore. It heightened our delight to tag behind these men and women of long ago, to compare our notes with theirs, to discover the border regions through their alert and expert eyes. Their writings are foundation stones of ours.

A final disclaimer: this is not primarily a book about trouble spots. True, five of our six borderlands face Communist frontiers; if they are not in trouble today, they well may be tomorrow. But whoever has read their history knows that border peoples have long lived with danger from predatory neighbors, long before Russia and China flew red flags. Besides, where is the haven of safety? What corner of the earth is not a potential trouble spot? Who knows where the lightning may strike next? Such riddles we gladly leave to news editors and commentators.

We hope these pages may be useful to them as background. Perhaps even scholars will find something of value here. For although scholars have dealt with each separate area, no one, to the best of our knowledge, has seen fit to relate them. In making the attempt, we have learned so much about the human scene that we would be misers not to share it with the general reader. So to the general reader we offer *Borderlands*.

D. K. AND F. K.

Washington, D.C., February 1962

ACKNOWLEDGMENTS

DURING ten years of journeying to Asia in search of information, we incurred more debts than can be acknowledged here. It would add too many pages to this book to list all those who gave us time, showed us kindness, and enlarged our understanding of the border regions. Although we remember each and every one, we must thank them collectively, and hope they will not think us ungracious.

A few in each country must be mentioned individually. First of all, there are those who opened borderland doors to us. In Tokyo, officers and staff members of the Japan Broadcasting Corporation (Radio N H K) smoothed our path in Hokkaido, particularly Mr. Yoshinori Maeda, the general managing director, and Miss Fumie Mizuhara. In Manila, President Carlos P. Garcia and Mr. José Nable enabled us to cross the Sulu Sea on the gunboat *La Union*, under the command of Lieutenant Simeon Alejandro. In North Borneo, the Governor, the late Sir Roland Turnbull, and his officials in Jesselton made us welcome everywhere in the colony. The Head of the Shan State, Sao Hkun Hkio, extended many courtesies in Taunggyi, and our good friend Mr. James Barrington, of the Foreign Office in Rangoon, helped at every turn. In New Delhi, Mr. T. N. Kaul and Mr. K. L. Mehta of the Ministry of External Affairs arranged permits to enter

Sikkim; in Kabul, Mr. Abdul Tarzi, the Minister of Tourism, made the north unexpectedly accessible; and in Ankara, Colonel Ahmed Yıldız and Mr. Orhan Mizanoğlu obtained the necessary military pass for our travel in the eastern provinces. For all these services we are grateful.

We received expert guidance within the border regions themselves. In Hokkaido it came, for example, from Mr. Masanobu Hasei of Sapporo, Mayor Ichiji Yoshitani of Hakodate, President Giichi Kamo and members of his faculty at the Otaru University of Commerce, and from Mrs. Yoshihiro Ozaki in Asahigawa. Those in Mindanao and Sulu who took trouble on our behalf included Mayor Cesar Climaco of Zamboanga, and Mr. Raymond Bowon of his staff; the Imam Ali Tahil of Taluksangay; and, in the city of Jolo, Mayor Arsad Sali, the Princess Putli Tarhata, and the Most Reverend Francis J. McSorley. Still fresh in our minds are the kindnesses of Mr. and Mrs. Michael Pike at Tenom, North Borneo, Mr. W. K. C. Wookey and Mr. G. L. Carson at Sandakan, Mr. Collin Wu and Mr. Donald Stephens at Jesselton, and the John Almans at Kent College in Tuaran. Among those in Burma who opened their minds, and sometimes their homes, to us were the Chief Justice of the Union, U Myint Thein, Sir Paul and Lady Gore-Booth, U Law Yone of *The Nation,* and U Sein Win of *The Guardian;* Daw Mi Mi Khaing and Mr. Timothy Slack of Kambawsa College, Taunggyi; U Shwin in Bhamo, and the late U Ko Ko Gyi of Mandalay, who guided us to the Chinese frontier and back.

We cannot forget the welcome of Mr. John Lall, the Chief Minister, and Mrs. Lall, who put us up—and put up with us —during our first stay in Sikkim. His Highness the Maharaja and his family showed us repeated courtesies there; so did the Political Officer, Mr. Appa B. Pant, and Mrs. Pant, and the Chief Minister in 1960, Mr. Baleshwar Prasad. And we remember, too, Mr. T. Sharab Gyaltsen's patience in shepherding us and letting us share his minute knowledge of the State. In Afghanistan, Dr. Korkut Kardes and Mme.

Kardes at Kunduz shed light on borderland problems, and Mr. A. W. Mackenzie in Kabul on the development programs. As for Turkey, we have many to thank, especially Mr. Niyazi Akı, former Governor of Erzurum and Kars; Dr. and Mrs. Lawrence Crowe and Dr. and Mrs. Marcus Weldon, of the University of Nebraska advisory group at Erzurum; and Colonel Yekta Ardor of the Turkish Signal Corps, who chaperoned us to Mount Ararat and the Iranian frontier.

In all six countries, members of United States government missions, from the ambassadors down, were helpful. This was no less true at the consulate in Sapporo (the only one in our borderlands) and at the headquarters of the military training team in Erzurum. American officials and soldiers will not expect us to name them here, but we should like them to know, one and all, of our appreciation.

Several busy authorities on specific areas were good enough to read the drafts of individual chapters: Dr. Rhea Blue, Mrs. Katherine W. Bracken, Dr. William C. Johnstone, Jr., and Mr. Ernest Sturc, all in Washington, D.C.; Mr. Morton Netzorg of Detroit, and Mr. John F. McDonald, Director of the American Cultural Center in Sapporo. We are deeply indebted to them for their comments and suggestions; they are not, of course, responsible for any errors that may have strayed into these pages. Warm thanks are also due to Mr. James J. Halsema, Mr. John F. Knowles, Mr. William Spengler, and Mr. Kenneth P. Sheldon for steering us to valuable sources we might otherwise have missed. We owe a special personal debt to our sons, Philip A. Kuhn and David A. Kuhn, who gave portions of this manuscript almost as much critical attention as if it had been one of their own.

CONTENTS

PLATES

Photographs are by the authors unless otherwise noted

MAPS

BORDERLANDS

1

Japan's Northern Island

A BORDERLAND IN DISREPUTE

> *How amazing it is that this rich and beautiful coun-
> try, the property of one of the oldest and most
> densely populated sections of the world, and in such
> near proximity, approachable on all sides by water,
> with harbors innumerable, should have remained so
> long unoccupied and almost as unknown as the
> African deserts.* —HORACE CAPRON

> *I have often wondered that any human being should
> live in a cold country who can find room in a warmer
> one.* —THOMAS JEFFERSON

WHEN a Tokyo commuter flips through his daily paper,
his eye will often light on an item of news from Hokkaido,
the empire's northern island. Usually the news is bad: a girl
frozen to death in the forest, a baby swallowed by snowdrifts, a train derailed in a blizzard. Between the long and
stormy winters, reports from the north may tell of crop failures and near-famine as in 1956; if not of nature's excesses,
then of man's, such as riots in Hokkaido's mines and factories, or the capture of a fishing boat and its crew in nearby
Soviet waters.

Calamity is no stranger to the Japanese; earthquakes,

fires, floods, and typhoons have struck all the islands through all the ages. But Hokkaido's troubles send a special kind of shiver down southern Japanese spines, a shiver that derives not just from the Japanese dislike of cold, but from a sense of dread. The reason is not hard to find. The name Hokkaido stirs the folk memory of a frontier: a few pioneer settlers on the northern rim of the Empire; a wilderness infested with bears, wolves, and a strange race of hairy men. This was, in truth, the Hokkaido of a hundred years ago. The image is almost wholly out of date, yet it persists. In the minds of most Japanese, Hokkaido remains wild, raw, and unfit for civilized living.

One must understand this public prejudice, for it is a clue to the island's history, its condition, and its prospects. It helps to explain why the Japanese worker in the overcrowded south closes his ears to job opportunities in the growing industries of the north; why the investor responds to Hokkaido's bid for capital with "I wouldn't put a yen there." When asked to detail his reasons, he replies that the place is too cold, too short of labor, too near the Russians, too far from markets. Such reactions in turn help to account for the island's sluggish progress, its fitful development, and its persistent neglect by the politicians in Tokyo. Although Hokkaido forms an integral part of one of the most highly developed nations, it suffers some of the handicaps of the underdeveloped. Its economy remains colonial, in that it serves Japan mainly as a producer of raw materials and a buyer of goods made elsewhere. Its status in Japanese society is that of a hewer of wood if not a drawer of water: the menial role of most of the borderlands we shall examine.

As a result, the rift between Hokkaidoans and "mainland" Japanese is deep, a rift in spirit as well as in space. Among the few who bridge it are the Japanese tourists—the hardy ones who come to ski on Hokkaido's slopes, and the more conventional summer visitors who can afford to escape the heat of the south. They have been attracted by a paid pub-

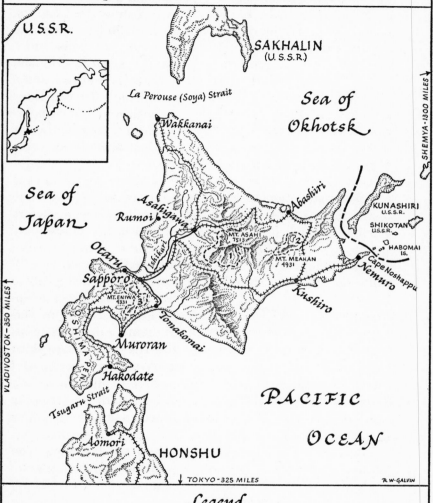

HOKKAIDO
Japan's Northern Island

U.S.S.R.

SAKHALIN
(U.S.S.R.)

La Perouse (Soya) Strait

Wakkanai

Sea of
Okhotsk

SHEMYA-1300 MILES

Sea of
Japan

Asahigawa
Rumoi
Abashiri

KUNASHIRI
U.S.S.R.

SHIKOTAN
U.S.S.R.

HABOMAI
IS.

Otaru
Ishikari
MT. ASAHI
7513

Sapporo
MT. MEAKAN
4931

Cape Noshappu
Nemuro

MT. ENIWA
4331

Kushiro

SHIMA PEN.

Muroran
Tomakomai

VLADIVOSTOK-350 MILES

Hakodate

Tsugaru Strait

PACIFIC

OCEAN

Aomori

HONSHU

↓ TOKYO-325 MILES

R. W. GALVIN

Legend

0   50   100   150   200 Miles

International Boundary –•— National Park Boundary ------
Main Railways ++++ Main Roads ——

NATIONAL PARKS
1-Daisetsuzan 2-Akan 3-Shikotsu-Toya

licity campaign that has sought in recent years to break the
evil spell and make Hokkaido popular. For persons who cannot avoid visiting the island on business, or to see relatives,
the rail and ferry journey from Tokyo is still a venture into
an unpleasant unknown. The night express speeds northward to Aomori, on the Tsugaru Strait that separates Honshu
from Hokkaido. Thirteen hours later, in the gray Aomori
morning, the passengers file onto an ungainly ferry as large
as a modern Dover-Calais steamer, with four high smoke-
stacks, two on each side. The intervening sea is no wider
than the Strait of Dover; the crossing of open water takes
only half of the four-hour journey. Yet the passengers might
be embarking on a vast and stormy ocean. Those at the rail
toss paper streamers to friends and relatives who have come
to see them off. A blast of the ship's horn sends visitors
ashore. Through loudspeakers on the decks, a cracked recording blares *Auld Lang Syne,* the favorite song of parting
in postwar Japan. The ship slides out into the bay toward the
white-capped strait beyond. Watchers on shore run alongside
it as far as the pier-end, shouting, waving, sometimes weep-
ing as if they would never see their loved ones again. Perhaps their emotion springs from the memory that this crossing can be dangerous; in 1954 the ferryboat *Toya Maru*
capsized in the strait, drowning 1,172 passengers and
spreading a seismic shock of horror through all Japan. More
probably, the emotion is just a throwback to the last century
when dangers as well as hardships accompanied emigrants
to the northland.

The transition from Old Japan does not last long. The
pointed hills of Honshu have not vanished before the ferry
is plowing along the Hokkaido coast, past fields that climb
high into the blue-gray hills. Soon the waves flatten. The
ship coasts into the semicircular bay of Hakodate, the one
old, historic city on Hokkaido, the gateway to a different
Japan.

How different from his imaginings, only a southern Japanese can say. In summertime, at least, Hokkaido shatters his picture of cold and misery. Japanese efficiency enfolds him as comfortably as in the southern islands. On the five-and-a-half-hour journey from Hakodate to Sapporo, the provincial capital, the train bears him northward as smoothly and smartly as trains at home. But he will notice differences soon enough as he looks out of the window.

In Old Japan, most farmers live in villages, as they do in Europe; in Hokkaido the southern Japanese will see farm homesteads scattered through the countryside, as in the United States and Canada. If he can distinguish one crop from another, he will identify fields of corn, oats, flax, and garden vegetables along with rice. Another curiosity will be the sight of cattle, sometimes a dozen, often only two or three; yet they make the Hokkaido landscape vaguely foreign, for in the rest of Japan dairying is a comparatively minor enterprise. Still another oddity, for a Japanese, will be the occasional barns and silos among spacious fields.

As his train slides through a town, an observant passenger will catch sight of houses with glass windows, sometimes of double thickness, in place of the rice-paper windows of familiar Japan. On one spectacular stretch of line, the train runs along the coast, where the ocean crashes against rocky cliffs. When the cliffs give way to gray beaches, the southerner notices fishermen's shacks that look shabbier, more dilapidated, than those he has seen in Honshu. Heaps of lumber behind the pulp mill town of Tomakomai, like slag heaps around a coal mine, remind a new arrival of the abundance of forests in a recent wilderness. Finally, at journey's end, a southerner walks from his train into Sapporo with a sense of strangeness. For the main street facing the station is long, straight, and 160 feet wide; the city is laid out in gridiron pattern, at first sight more like Omaha than Osaka.

If all this unsettles a visitor from Old Japan, it offers an American a momentary sense of coming home. Yet Westerners, too, will lose their stereotypes when they reach Hokkaido. From the time of Francis Xavier in the sixteenth century to that of Gilbert and Sullivan in the nineteenth, Japan connoted the swish of a geisha's silk, the tinkle of a temple bell, a cloud of cherry blossoms, the rustle of a fan. In the twentieth century this vision blurred and gave way to another: a beehive of thrift and industry. Hokkaido fits none of these images. It is neither quaint nor crowded. Here one can escape from the claustrophobia of Old Japan. Here, uniquely, one can observe a society of Japanese who are blessed with elbow room.

Because their island lies far from the center of Japanese power and against a political and cultural frontier, it constitutes a true borderland, as we define the word. In examining it, let us begin with the environment that gives Hokkaido, like other borderlands in this volume, a character of its own.

Maine in the Pacific

In all the world only nineteen islands are bigger than Hokkaido, or, if one leaves out five desolate and virtually uninhabited islands of the Arctic, only fourteen. It is slightly smaller than Iceland or Mindanao, slightly larger than Ireland. Photographed, as it was in 1960, from a space craft whirling above it, Hokkaido looks roughly diamond-shaped. The sea appears to have eaten a nick out of its eastern corner; a twisting peninsula, an inverted question mark, dangles from its western end. Cartoonists used to draw Hokkaido as the head of a Japanese dragon. The dragon's mouth spat bits of brimstone northeastward for more than 700 miles, in the form of the Kurile Islands. The arching neck was Hokkaido's southwestern peninsula; the body, the main Japanese island of Honshu.

Geographically and in a startling number of other ways,

Hokkaido resembles the State of Maine. In size the two almost match; in latitude and climate they are first cousins if not identical twins. The northernmost tip of Hokkaido protrudes as far north as Moosehead Lake; its capital city of Sapporo straddles virtually the same latitude as Maine's capital city, Augusta; its southwestern peninsula reaches beyond Maine as far south as Cape Cod.

Anyone equipped for the Maine climate, summer or winter, would be fortified for living in Hokkaido. In both places the summers are bracing, the thermometer sometimes hitting the high eighties by day and dipping into the fifties by night. But because of the cold current that washes Hokkaido's eastern coast, fogs are even more frequent and the sea even colder than on the coast of Maine. By mid-October the first snow has whitened the central mountains, carried by ever-icier winds from Siberia. By midwinter the western and central parts of the island are blanketed at least as deeply as northwestern Maine. The streets in some Hokkaido cities become trenches between white walls, and one-story houses in the country all but disappear as the snow piles up to their eaves.

Whoever has watched a sunrise light the dark forests in Maine could imagine in parts of Hokkaido that "I have been here before." And whoever has lived in the Maine countryside could hardly feel strange in the Ishikari River plain, with its barns and silos, its dairy cattle and potato fields. Almost half of Hokkaido's families make their living in the old-time Maine occupations of farming, lumbering, fishing, and canning.

The comparison is intriguing, but one cannot carry it far. Hokkaidoans outnumber the people of Maine by more than five to one. Each of Hokkaido's six chief cities is more populous than Portland, the Maine metropolis. The Japanese island also means far more to its nation's economy. It supplies almost a fourth of the seafood needed by the Japanese people, among the greatest fish eaters in the world. It grows all the nation's sugar beets, almost all the flax, and almost half the white potatoes; its cows provide a fifth of Japan's milk products; its forests yield two thirds of the plywood that Japan exports and two fifths of the newsprint needed to satisfy the rapacious demands of Japan's mass-circulation newspapers. Its miners dig almost a fourth of all Japan's coal. Industrially its chief role is that of a processor of raw materials. Since the 1880's Hokkaidoans have brewed a beer that still slakes thirst throughout Japan. In 1909 they began to mill steel girders with their scanty iron ore and plentiful coal. Flax into linen, peppermint into menthol oil, fish and fruit and vegetables into canned foods—these are among the processes that could, if developed further, lift the island out of its essentially colonial economy.

Hokkaido industry still starves for capital, of both the social and investment kinds. But there are compensations, one of them a money-making resource that gives Japan's wilderness island still another bond with the State of Maine.

The island has become a Japanese vacationland. In defiance of fear and prejudice, almost 400,000 Japanese from other islands flock there every year, chiefly in July and August when the humidity in southern cities grows insufferable. Many of them come on group tours paid for by their employers, who, in turn, deduct the cost from their taxable income. Conspicuous among other visitors are committee members from the Diet in Tokyo. In Japan, it seems, legislators feel a compulsion to inspect Hokkaido in the summer months, just as their counterparts in the United States find it hard to avoid committee assignments to the Caribbean in wintertime. Japanese visitors to Hokkaido spend almost $15,000,000 each year for *tatami*-floored hotel rooms, meals, and souvenirs.

Such vacationers seek what their kind seek everywhere: relaxation and a change of scene. For relaxation they spend hours soaking together in hot spring baths and pools, just as they do in Old Japan. In this respect, Hokkaido signifies

simply a home from home. But for change of scene, the
island provides a dramatic contrast. Here in the north one
can find space and solitude, if that is what one craves.
Plenty of wilderness remains as a reminder of the days, not
so long ago, when Hokkaido was a virgin land. Fortunately
for present and future generations of Japanese, three huge
tracts of mountains and forest are set aside, supposedly for
all time, as national parks.

[1]

Japan is no novice at making sanctuaries of its out-of-
doors. As long ago as 1873, soon after they had overturned
the feudal regime, Japan's young reformers designated certain beauty spots as parks for all the people. In the previous
year the United States Congress had voted to make Yellowstone the first national park. The idea, like so many others
from the West, won quick and eager acceptance among the
new rulers of Japan. The first Japanese parks, unlike Yellowstone, were either open fields in the cities or small patches
of scenic countryside. But foreign teachers, British and
German as well as American, persisted in preaching the
value of genuine parks, to conserve scenery and provide
breathing space for the cities. By 1961 Japan had twenty
national parks of varying types and sizes, of which three of
the grandest had been staked out in Hokkaido.

The most accessible of the three is the Shikotsu-Toya
National Park, a variegated preserve of volcanoes, hot
springs, lakes, and woods in the south central portion of
the island. Even by North American standards, this park
cuts a respectable figure, for it covers 381 square miles, a
tract as spacious as Rocky Mountain National Park in
Colorado. Like Yellowstone, Shikotsu-Toya offers freaks of
nature along with splendors. Its mile-long "Valley of Hell"
bubbles and stinks with geysers, fumaroles, and pools of
boiling mud. Gustave Doré might have used it as a model
for his engravings of the Inferno. Nearby, a brand-new

volcano obligingly displaced a farm to provide new excitement. In December of 1944, steam and lava shot up
through the winter stubble. The next summer an eruption
tore the fields apart. Foot by foot the debris rose, still
smoking, until by 1959 a true volcano had reached a
height of 1,337 feet. Named *Showa-Shinzan* ("New Mountain of the Showa era," the Hirohito reign) and labeled as
a national treasure, it keeps camera shutters clicking
throughout the tourist season.

Around Lake Shikotsu, the heart of the protected wilderness, Japanese could enjoy peace and solitude. But most
of them, like city dwellers everywhere, find nature and
noise compatible. A group of New Yorkers will take tran-
sistor radios into the woods at Bear Mountain; a group
of Japanese deep in the Hokkaido forests will eat, drink,
dance, and hold hands to the never-ending din of a loudspeaker. Do this, do that, the loudspeaker commands them;
you may do this, you may not do that; buy your tickets
here, your food there. At the lake shore itself, another
loudspeaker drowns the cries of the gulls and the lapping
of the waves. The vacationer could, but does not, escape.
To him, a Hokkaido lake is made for boating near the
shore, but not for swimming—it is too cold, he will explain, too deep, too dangerous because of rumored whirl-
pools. In the parks as elsewhere, a Japanese prefers indoor bathing, in almost scalding pools. An ideal day in a
Hokkaido park would contain a photogenic view, a stroll on
pine needles in the woods, and then, after the bath, a feast
on the crayfish and salmon trout which are among Hokkaido's delights.

The biggest of the three parks, the one with the highest
mountains, is Daisetsuzan, in the center of the island. Its
895 square miles make it about half the size of Montana's
Glacier National Park, or about three fourths the size of Yo-
semite. Here the Ishikari River has carved a spectacular
gorge on its way to the sea; a silvery waterfall, leaping

from a high cliff, attracts photographers as a piece of suet draws songbirds to a tree. Above the gorge, on the slopes of Mt. Asahi (7,560 feet), hikers can wander knee-deep in Alpine flowers. And in some places—unhappily not in all—they can find the forest primeval.

A typhoon, the same that capsized the *Toya Maru* in 1954, spread a trail of destruction through the Daisetsuzan wilds. So many trees were uprooted or snapped like matchwood that it took six years to saw up the fallen timber and truck it to the mills. During that time, the normal cutting within the park stopped. The typhoon scarred the landscape of Daisetsuzan almost as cruelly as forest fires defaced Glacier National Park. At the top of the watershed within the park, where some streams flow westward to the Sea of Japan and others eastward to the Pacific, a small, lonely figure of the Buddha perches on a stone column, beside the only road that crosses the park. Buses grind to a halt; passengers whip out cameras and file uphill to the monument. They focus, first on the column, then on one another, and sometimes on the inscription which, translated, says:

"To the souls of the trees that died."

[2]

Sentiment and thrift created Hokkaido's national parks, rescuing what remained of the island's wilderness. But the people who owned the wilderness before the Japanese were not so pampered. The Ainu, the prehistoric settler of the Japanese islands, survives—but just barely, and only in Hokkaido, his last refuge. That he survives at all is something of a miracle. His ancestors were slain or conquered and exploited even more efficiently than the North American Indian, and then belatedly freed and touted as a tourist attraction.

The Ainu baffle even the anthropologists. They refuse to fit into scientific or even pseudoscientific pigeonholes.

Once they were said to be Caucasoid, related to the
Caucasian "race," or forebears of Nordics who somehow
wandered to the Pacific and survived. Certainly the Ainu
could not appear more un-Japanese. They are powerfully
built, their bodies are hairy. Their men grow luxuriant
beards, so that any group of them faintly suggests a gathering of Civil War generals. They lack the fold in the eyelid
that makes most Japanese and Chinese appear slant-eyed.
Eyes deep-set and bright, high cheekbones as well as beard,
recall the Russian peasant as he was pictured and cari-
catured in tsarist times.

Is it any wonder that the Japanese find the Ainu peculiar?
A Japanese bows stiffly in greeting or farewell; an Ainu
strokes his beard. He does not share the Japanese passion
for marinating in hot water; like a Tibetan or an Eskimo,
he bathes seldom if at all. In appearance, manner, and
customs, and in what we call the arts of civilization, the
chasm between a Japanese from Tokyo and an Ainu is as
wide as that between a New Yorker and a Navajo.

Once the Ainu spread over most of what is now Japan.
They were roaming the forests of central Honshu, and
perhaps as far south as Kyushu, when the prehistoric ancestors of the Japanese crossed from the Asian mainland.
Decade after decade they rained their poisoned arrows on
the Japanese invaders, only to be pushed inexorably northward. The struggle went on intermittently for almost a
thousand years; sometimes it demanded extraordinary
exertions of the Japanese. By the start of the eighteenth
century most of the surviving Ainu, about 30,000, had been
penned up in Hokkaido, despised, despoiled, and cheated.
A smallpox epidemic is believed to have decimated them
in the mid-eighteenth century. By the mid-nineteenth,
only about 20,000 survived, living by hunting and fishing
and by selling deer horns to the Japanese who clustered
on the southwestern peninsula or around the coasts.

Virtually no pure Ainu are left on Hokkaido. Disease has

taken a continuing toll, and intermarriage with the Japanese has blurred their identity. By the end of this century the recognizable Ainu people may well have disappeared, like the woolly-haired Tasman Man who became extinct in 1875, or the great auk and the dodo. They will vanish leaving few traces of their stay. Since they evolved no written language, no Ainu literature will tell their story. Their songs, legends, customs, and ceremonies were recorded in 1961, but these will not fill the void. For there are few accounts of Ainu bravery in ancient times; the Japanese produced no Tacitus to describe the northern barbarians, no Caesar to chronicle the northern wars. Japanese artists and storytellers have left the subject severely alone. It is as if they found the very thought of the Ainu unpleasant. In this generation, Japanese film companies use the open spaces of Hokkaido as backdrops for westerns, which are endlessly popular on television screens. But they always use their own actors to portray American cowboys and Red Indians. In these Far Eastern westerns, the Ainu has no part.

The Reverend John Batchelor, a British missionary who lived among the Ainu in the last quarter of the nineteenth century, wrote of them as "a departing race." The word "departing" is apt, for it suggests the gentleness that sets the Ainu apart from fiercer primitive peoples elsewhere. Their exit will be as noiseless as the snuffing out of a candle. It was a candle that never threw much light beyond the Ainu circle, and it guttered sadly toward the end.

Perhaps sensing the tragedy, a Japanese tourist in Hokkaido gazes at the Ainu-on-display with a mixture of pity, distaste, and wonder. A few miles outside the modern city of Asahigawa, for example, sight-seers and their guides troop through one of the last remaining Ainu villages on the island. A museum entices them with weapons, carvings, costumes, and paintings of Ainu life. A chieftain with a beard and beetling eyebrows poses for their cameras.

In private conversation he shows intelligence and awareness. Until recently, he recalled in excellent Japanese, his people suffered many indignities.

"When I was a young man, working on the railroad," he said, "the Japanese in my work gang never spoke to me by my Japanese name. They called me 'Ainu!' The same used to be true of our children in Japanese schools. Now my people can get good jobs if they have some education. Our children go to the public school in the neighborhood, and one Ainu is a professor at Hokkaido University." An Ainu Association, formed in 1945, gives vocational training and scholarships and, incidentally, helps Ainu youths to find non-Ainu brides.

The chieftain used to rent his fields while he went hunting in the hills. The postwar land reform dealt him a blow, for it took away all his land except what he and his family could cultivate. In 1960 he was farming a small rice field and supplementing his income by whatever tourists were inclined to give him for posing for photographs. Children gaping at him in the museum will be able to tell their children: "We met a real Ainu." Future generations will know the Ainu only as a snapshot in the family album, or a tale that someone else has told.

[3]

There is more to set Hokkaido apart from the rest of Japan than its spacious emptiness, its gridiron-patterned cities and farms, its forests and parks and Ainu relics. The island again holds the uncomfortable position of being Japan's northern outpost. The Pacific War stripped Japan of Manchuria, Korea, Formosa, and the Ryukyu Islands. It also took away the Kuriles and southern Sakhalin, which had served as buffers between Hokkaido and Russian power. Since 1945 these have been Soviet islands pressing down upon Hokkaido, and the frontier runs through the middle of narrow waterways.

At three places in particular, the frontier has advanced so near that Russia has become a visible, brooding presence. On rare days when the sky is clear, one can just descry the outlines of Soviet land from a hill beyond Wakkanai, Hokkaido's northernmost city. From this fishing and canning port, the ferry used to leave for Sakhalin, the forested island, 600 miles long, only forty miles to the north. Japan had owned the southern half of Sakhalin since 1905; at the time of the surrender about 400,000 Japanese were living there, earning an uncertain livelihood from mining, logging, and fishing. The ferry runs no more. The flow of people and goods through Wakkanai has dwindled, and the city has fallen on evil days.

A second place where the boundary is palpable is the harbor of Nemuro, near Hokkaido's eastern tip. Fog shrouds Nemuro about half the days of June, July, and August, but when it lifts one can spy the profile of a mountain across the water. This is the Russian-held island of Kunashiri, the southernmost of the Kuriles. On August 14, the anniversary of the Japanese surrender, the booming of distant guns every ten seconds punctuates the sea gulls' cries. They are Soviet guns reminding the Japanese—if any reminder were needed—of Red arms within earshot.

Beyond Nemuro, where the Sea of Okhotsk meets the Pacific, Soviet claws come closest to pinching Hokkaido. A lighthouse at Cape Noshappu crowns a rocky hill, the limit of Japanese soil. In the lighthouse tower, one can focus a spyglass on a flagpole pointing up from a featureless shore only two and a half miles away. A Red flag on the pole proclaims Soviet control of the Habomais and Shikotan, offshore islands which had been part of the Hokkaido prefecture, and had always been Japanese. In 1945, at the moment of Japan's defeat, the Russians took possession of these islands, contending that they were part of the Kurile chain: a claim which the Japanese and their American conquerors stoutly denied. Stalin then proposed

that Soviet troops occupy the entire northern half of Hokkaido; President Truman refused. Once having fastened
their grip on the offshore islands, the Russians stayed.
By 1956 they were reported to have built a bakery, cannery,
and new piers on the Habomais and Shikotan, as well as
radar posts, power stations, and repair yards for their
patrol ships.

Soviet control of these islands has deprived Hokkaido
fishermen of rich crab and seaweed harvests; it has also
exposed them to new dangers in the treacherous waters
offshore. The northern straits, especially the channel between the Noshappu lighthouse and the Habomais, have
become traps for unwary skippers. Let a fishing boat be
caught in the swirling currents and borne across the halfway line, and it may be nabbed by a patrol boat lying in
wait along the Soviet shore. The losses of fishing craft have
been unending—during 1959, a hundred Hokkaido boats
were captured in this way. The fishermen know the risks,
but take them all the same. To them, as to their fathers and
grandfathers, these waters, rocks, and promontories were
always an open book, perhaps the only book they knew how
to read. Some of the captured fishermen are released after a
few days of questioning. Some are sent back in small row-
boats while their ships remain in Soviet hands. Some never
return.

To talk with one of the released fishermen is to peer
into the shadowed lives of hundreds. We found one, a sad-
eyed man of about forty, living in a village of paintless
wooden houses on a dreary coast. Strips of seaweed drying
on the sand, gray dunes stretching to a sky that is almost
always gray, a cold mist drifting shoreward from the sea,
the water near shore the "trembling, imageless mirror" of
Pierre Loti's northern ocean, the sea losing itself in the
distance ". . . only to become a vaporous mist—after that
nothing, nothing more, neither contour nor horizon"—such
is the setting of this fisherman's life at home. Storms and

fogs form the almost daily hazards of his life afloat. In villages such as his, one finds the seamy side of Hokkaido life, the drabness and poverty that feed southern Japanese prejudices against the entire northern borderland.

Answering questions on the beach outside his family shack, our fisherman spoke of his capture by the Russians. One foggy day, a Russian patrol ship loomed alongside his crab boat and signaled him to follow. He had drifted across the invisible boundary. The Russians guided him to a harbor where six other Japanese boats lay captive. On shore, in a dugout which had been an air-raid shelter, a uniformed Russian interrogated him with an interpreter. Why did you come so close? How many men do you have in the Japanese defense forces? Are you building any airfields, and where? What is the name of the lighthouse keeper? For nine days the Russians cooped him and his crew in the dugout. "They didn't treat me as badly as I expected," he said. But his wife and children at home worried, then grieved as if he were lost at sea.

One could expect this man and others like him to steer their craft toward bluer pastures. But, on the deep seas as in coastal waters, the island's fishing industry has been caught in doldrums that show no prospect of being blown away. Every mid-May, in a festival both proud and sad, the ocean fishing fleet sets out from the port of Hakodate. Waterfront streets and ships blaze with flags and streamers; families throng the quays to shout *sayonara* to their men whom they will not see for at least three months, perhaps not ever. The fleet heads northeast in packs of thirty-two, each ship with a crew of twenty, and each pack with a floating cannery manned by 200 men. Equipment as well as courage are not lacking. In August the ships creep home individually, to report a total catch sadly smaller than in the prewar or immediate postwar years.

Why? The explanation consists partly of the cycles of nature, partly of the firmness and growing power of the

Soviet Union. The Hakodate fishing fleet first scours the
Alaskan side of the Bering Sea, in search of salmon trout.
Gradually, its nets move westward toward Siberia, until
they are forty miles off the Kamchatka Peninsula. Here the
Japanese must stop. The fish that have eluded them escape
into the Sea of Okhotsk, where Russian fishermen lie in
wait for them. The survivors of the successive Japanese
and Soviet onslaughts then push up the rivers of Kamchatka to spawn.

Not only the area but also the time and the size of the
Japanese catches are limited by agreement with the Russians. Partly for conservation purposes, and partly to give
each a fair share, Japan and Russia negotiate quotas each
year. In 1958 the Japanese quota was 100,000 tons, in 1959
it dwindled to 80,000, in 1960 to 67,500, with a roughly
equal share for the Soviet Union. Japanese ships must get
out of northern waters by August 10, whether or not they
have caught their quota. When the salmon trout fishers
have returned and the ships have been repaired, they head
south to the Fijis for tuna, or to coastal Japanese waters
for mackerel. As for the coastal fishing grounds, these, too,
have ceased to be profitable. The warm currents around
Hokkaido have moved north in recent years, and with
them the herring, which now throng the territorial waters
of the Soviet Union rather than those of Japan.

Some businessmen and politicians hope that Japan will
regain the Kuriles as well as the offshore islands. They talk
as if the Soviet presence will vanish in a sudden wind,
like a Hokkaido fog. In the context of the 1960's they are
daydreaming. There was no evidence up to 1962 that
Hokkaido itself stood high on the list of Soviet priorities;
the few Russian agents arrested along Hokkaido railroad
lines in recent years had been bunglers, apparently of low
status in the Soviet apparatus of espionage and sabotage.
But the islands to the north, especially the Kuriles, belong
to Russia, and no amount of wishful thinking will return

them to Japan. Hokkaidoans, of all people, should be realists. For the nearness of Russia has influenced their island's history for almost 200 years, both hastening and hindering the development of the Japanese borderland.

Early Russian Contacts

If ever a historical development was the product of the unforeseen, it was the opening of Hokkaido in modern times. For more than a thousand years Japan had been content to leave its northern island a wilderness. In the early seventeenth century the ruling Shogun turned over the supposedly valueless property to a single clan, the Matsumae, as a feudal preserve. The few Japanese settlers in the island's far southwest were forbidden to move into the interior.

Northwest of Hokkaido, on the desolate Asian mainland, the first Russians arrived at the Sea of Okhotsk by the middle of the seventeenth century. In eighty years the trappers, traders, soldiers, and adventurers of the Tsar had pushed the Russian flag across Siberia, a distance one and a half times the width of North America.

Where would the Russians move next? If their pioneers had been named Cortes, Champlain, or Drake; if they had had behind them the cupidity and drive of Britain, France, or Spain; if easternmost Siberia had not been so far from the center of Russian power—can there be any doubt of the answer? Surely they would have sailed south to the island empire, a land so rich, according to Marco Polo's tale, that its ruler's palace was "entirely roofed with fine gold." Instead, the Russians chose to grope eastward to Alaska and southward along the coast of mainland Asia. They were seeking furs, not gold. They also wanted trade with China, and supplies to build up their straggling settlements in Siberia. Japan lay near their shores but beyond their desires.

A few dates will show the Russians' lack of enterprise when judged by the empire-grabbing standards of those days. Not until 1739, a whole century after the Russian advent on the Pacific, did their first ship sail southward past Hokkaido. It anchored off northern Honshu in a half-hearted and futile search for Japanese trade. Not until 1777 did a Russian ship actually land on Hokkaido, on the northeast coast near Nemuro. Both ships' captains tried to open commercial relations with Japan, then wrapped in its cocoon of isolation; both met firm refusals. A third vain attempt came in 1792, when a Russian captain returned castaways to Hokkaido; a fourth in 1804. The leader of the fourth expedition, Nikolai Rezanov, head of a chartered fur trading company, had to cool his heels for five months in Nagasaki, in polite but firm detention, before the Japanese ordered him out.

It was in this uneasy period, while Japan was still sealed against foreign contacts, that a small group of Japanese writers pleaded for a change in policy. One of them, greatly daring, named Toshiaki Honda, wrote *A Secret Plan for Managing the Country*. His book was a bugle call for catching up with the West, and especially with Russia. Among Honda's prescriptions was the rapid colonization of Hokkaido. "It must not be neglected," he warned. "If we abandon Ezo [Hokkaido] it will fall to foreign countries. The proper attention can keep it Japanese." Honda's only reward was a term in jail.

So far the Russian contacts with Hokkaido had been haphazard, hesitant, and peaceful. The Japanese could count themselves lucky that they had been facing so ir-resolute a neighbor, one that did not use cannon as wedges for commerce, as other European powers had done else-where in Asia. But now Russians showed that they, too, could shoot. On orders of the same Rezanov who had been cooped up in Nagasaki in 1804, though without the knowledge of the Tsar's government, two Russian naval officers directed the looting and burning of Japanese settlements on southern Sakhalin and on one of the Kuriles. Japanese guards were kidnapped and four Japanese vessels captured off the coast. This was in 1806 and 1807. The Russians were teaching the Japanese a lesson in the approved European manner. Panic as well as prudence marked the response of the Japanese. After the Russian raids, they strengthened their guards in the north, and resolved to permit no further intrusions by foreigners, on any pretext whatsoever.

At the height of Japanese vigilance, in 1811, an observant Russian naval officer named Vasilii Golovnin undertook an official mission to survey the coasts of the northern islands. Under a cloak of polite negotiations, the Japanese lured him ashore on Kunashiri, the southernmost of the Kuriles. Then their guards seized and roped him, together with six companions. They dragged the seven, like criminals, off to Hakodate and then to the feudal capital of Matsumae nearby. For more than two years the Russians languished, sometimes in wood-slatted cages, sometimes in more bearable quarters, in reprisal for the raids of four and five years before. Interminably they had to answer questions from Japanese officials, questions about themselves, about Russia and the Western world. For long months they despaired of ever seeing their homeland again.

Once, in May of 1812, Golovnin and four others escaped, and spent eight days wandering miserably in the hills of the Oshima Peninsula. Their courage was wasted. The Japanese caught and reimprisoned them. Release did not come until October 1813, when a Russian naval captain arrived with formal assurances that the raids had not been officially inspired. The Tsar promoted Golovnin, who had endured so much in Russia's service. Almost a century and a half later, the Soviet successors of the Tsars gave his name to the desolate outpost on Kunashiri Island where he had been captured.

The Golovnin story did not end with his release. Soon after returning home he wrote a book of memoirs, which was not only printed in Russia at government expense, but also translated into English and published in London. The book was a storehouse of information about Hokkaido for Russians and Western Europeans alike. Golovnin wrote without rancor toward those who had trapped and tormented him. He found much to admire in the Japanese and their society: their politeness and neatness, their intelligence and diligence, their curiosity about the world outside. But of Hokkaido itself, his picture was dark and forbidding. He could not help reliving his days and nights of hiding in the forests, "surrounded by enemies and wild beasts, wandering over a strange island. . . . Even now," he confessed, "I never look back without horror upon the frightful gulfs and huge rocks of Matsmai [southwestern Hokkaido] and millions of money would not tempt me to travel over them again."

He was the first European to penetrate the interior of the island; his testimony merited respect. Hokkaido, as he described it, was not worth the bones of a single grenadier. If "millions" could not tempt him back, why should Imperial Russia spend a kopeck on it? The leaders in St. Petersburg soon lost whatever interest they had had in the place. Emerging from a struggle with Napoleon, beset by unrest at home, they saw no point in forcing access to a distant wasteland and poking into a hornet's nest of Japanese.

Their designs on Hokkaido had never been as sinister as Japan supposed. In the ensuing four decades the magnet that attracted them in the Pacific was not Hokkaido but Sakhalin further north, the island that virtually blocked the estuary of Russia's Amur River.

Thus the prick of foreign interest no longer spurred Japan to colonize Hokkaido. The shogunate relaxed its watch. Not until the eve of the Crimean War in the 1850's did the Russians seriously plan a new expedition to open Japan to diplomacy and trade. But by then another foreign power had intruded to transform the Japanese scene and, indirectly, to wrench Hokkaido out of its seclusion.

Americans and Meiji Reformers

By the late 1840's a fresh breeze was blowing from a new direction. The Japanese islands lay on the shortest, or Great Circle, route of the clipper ships that carried Yankee cargoes to and from China. New Bedford whalingmen found the waters around Hokkaido spouting oil and profits. When steamers began to replace sailing ships, the Americans needed a port in that vicinity for coal, water, and refuge from North Pacific storms. Shipwrecked Yankees had been cast ashore on Hokkaido's coasts; seven of them had lain in prison for seventeen months before being released in southern Japan. Stories of Japanese prison cages trickled back to the United States, and horror at such "barbarism" added to the commercial pressure for opening Japan.

The overriding American interest in Japan was neither curiosity about a mysterious land nor a desire to tap the supposed riches of Cipangu, nor even a craving for expansion and glory, although all of these had tempted some of the mid-century politicians in Washington. The dominant motive was commercial convenience. For this purpose, Hokkaido was at least as useful as the Honshu "mainland." When Commodore Perry led his black ships into Tokyo Bay to force the Japanese to open their ports, it was natural for him to insist on at least one in Hokkaido as well as one in Honshu. The Treaty of Kanagawa (1854) gave the

Americans access to Hakodate, the southern port of Hokkaido, as well as to the smaller fishing port of Shimoda on the main island.

Steaming into Hakodate in May 1854 to inspect the newly opened harbor, Perry felt that his persistence had been rewarded. To one of his officers who had sailed the seven seas, the bay was "most spacious and majestic in its sweep, and for facility of entrance and anchorage it can scarcely be surpassed by any other in the world." Perry himself considered that this Hokkaido harbor was worth "fifty Shimodas."

To the Japanese in Hakodate, Perry's warships came as a visitation of evil. Local officials had not yet heard of the treaty. Townspeople had no way of knowing that the foreigners' guns would not fire on their flimsy wooden houses. American officers, peering through their glasses from the ships, watched as long lines of people and pack horses twisted away into the countryside. Merchants and householders were moving their belongings to safety.

The first official American contact with Hokkaido was, therefore, chilly. Nor did Japanese attitudes become warmer when American sailors came ashore and proceeded to bully local shopkeepers. Officials of the Shogun wished that these boorish foreigners would go home.

The Governor of the province sought to make Hokkaido unattractive. Hakodate, he told Perry, "is an outlying, remote region, and its population sparse and ignorant. . . . This place," he said, "is, as it were, no bigger than a pill or a speck, and the country in its vicinity is sterile, and produces almost nothing." Dr. James Morrow, the botanist of the Perry expedition, wandered into the surrounding country in search of specimens. Far from finding Hokkaido "sterile," he noted that there were "fruit trees of the largest and finest description—apples and pears, but principally pears." The Americans had seen only a corner of the Oshima Peninsula, the only part of Hokkaido where Japanese had settled in appreciable numbers. They had not even glimpsed the almost untouched country beyond: the forests, the mines, the river valleys that could be farmed.

Southernmost Hokkaido, at least, quickened its growth as Hakodate opened to foreign shipping. Townsend Harris's commercial treaty of 1858 led the way for Britain and Russia to follow. In a few years the fishing port transformed itself into a bustling town. The Russians had the good sense to station a Japanese-speaking consul there, a learned man, Iosif Goshkevich, who gave the people of Hokkaido their first acquaintance with photography, Western medicine, and other arts and sciences. The sight of American, British, and Russian warships became a commonplace, and the townspeople profited rather than panicked as each new ship steamed into their harbor.

For the first time colonists were allowed to break the fertile soil of the plain where the provincial capital of Sapporo now stands. Their access was by trail or flatboat; there was not a wagon road, not a wheeled vehicle, outside Hakodate and the few other coastal settlements. The interior was a fisherman's paradise. When inland settlement began, a single haul of 12,000 river salmon was not exceptional. The salmon trout ran from three pounds to twelve. On a few miles' stretch of a single stream, the Ishikari, 6,000 tons of salmon were caught and salted between August and November of one year.

The forests quivered with wild life. When the British consul ventured into the interior from Hakodate in 1860, he and his party were told to fire their guns to frighten away the bears. They had to keep wood fires burning for protection against the animals. In warm weather deer abounded everywhere; their most dangerous enemy was not man, not bear, but the Hokkaido wolf, weighing from seventy to eighty pounds, armed with deadly fangs, its feet three or four times bigger than those of the largest dog and thus able to chase its prey in deep snow.

But as man moved inland, the wild life of Hokkaido paid the usual penalty. Strychnine bait all but exterminated the wolves; as for the deer, Ainu arrows slaughtered tens of thousands of them in a single severe winter as they crowded the coast to escape snowdrifts. In Japan's far north, the wasteful tragedy of the American West was reenacted; game was massacred, and forests were slashed with little thought of conservation for the future.

Shortsighted though it was, the government did show curiosity about what lay beneath the Hokkaido soil. It took the unprecedented step of recruiting two American geologists, Raphael Pumpelly and William Blake, to survey the island's mineral resources. But it did not let them explore beyond the Oshima Peninsula. The Americans left Japan after a year, pessimistic about the prospects for the northern territory. They had accomplished little except to teach the Japanese on Hokkaido how to use explosives in mining coal.

[1]

Before scattered seeds of change could take root, the shogunate itself was swept away in the restoration and reformation of 1867. It made its last stand in a battle just outside Hakodate. The new regime brought the fifteen-year-old Emperor Meiji out of shadowy isolation at Kyoto, and in his name set about transforming the dilapidated Japanese Empire into a modern world power. The nations of the West had made themselves powerful, and the new rulers of Japan wanted the prescription. They wished to adapt it to their needs. Their purpose was not to remake themselves in the Western image. Their motive was not enchantment with Western ways; it was self-preservation. Unless Japan proved herself an equal, they reasoned, the nations of Europe might be tempted to conquer her or carve her up as if she were another China.

Both directly and indirectly, Hokkaido was to profit from

this purpose. Its strategic position was immediately recognized and its development given priority in an imperial rescript of 1869:

> Yezo [Hokkaido] is the northern gate of the Empire, beyond which lie Santan [the maritime provinces of Siberia] and Manchuria over the sea. True, there is a boundary between this country and the others, but toward the north it is so vague that foreigners dwell mixed with the native. After Hakodate is quieted, we intend to take steps to reclaim and people the island. Every suggestion to that effect is welcome.

Acting on this proclamation, the new government set up a Colonial Office, the *Kaitakushi,* and named a young southerner, Kiyotake Kuroda, as its vice-chairman and director. Its mission was to govern, to colonize, and to apply up-to-date techniques to the exploitation of the island —to keep it out of foreign hands, and to extend Tokyo's control to the far corners of an exposed and empty region. Here the new leaders were already beginning to borrow ideas from the imperial powers of Europe, the British and French for example, who had pushed roads, railroads, and telegraphs across trackless colonial territories in Asia so as to leave no vacuums for acquisitive rivals. The Emperor's intention "to reclaim and people the island" promised Hokkaido a new deal.

Kuroda merits more than a passing reference. In retrospect he towers over the modern history of Hokkaido, and we shall meet him again. He sprang from Satsuma, one of the two southern feudal clans which gave the new regime most of its farsighted leaders, much as Virginia had done to the early American republic. Trained as a soldier, Kuroda had an accurate awareness of Russia's strength compared to Japan's. On his first assignment for the Colonial Office he inspected western Hokkaido and Sakhalin to the north, both of which had been placed under his control. His verdict was that Sakhalin was too vulnerable, too remote, to be worth a serious effort. Japan, he decided, must concentrate its colonization in Hokkaido, where he saw both a need and an opportunity. The government took his advice.

Its next step was to send him to the United States at the end of 1870. With a German-American botanist named Louis Boechmer as his guide, he traveled far and wide seeking ideas, techniques, and talents for Hokkaido. He proved that he could swim in foreign waters. Far from being swept away by Western ways, this serious-eyed Japanese of thirty knew what he wanted for his northern island. Whatever he saw he appraised in the light of Japan's requirements. Sometimes he was too enthusiastic; but is not enthusiasm what every pioneer needs? Of Kuroda one can say truthfully that he combined vision with knowledge, and that he, more than any other individual, deserves the credit for the building of modern Hokkaido.

[2]

While Kuroda was sizing up America, the Meiji leaders made an imaginative and daring resolve: to create a system of compulsory schooling for all Japanese boys and girls. Their motive was not a liberal one; it was to tighten state control over everyone, to consolidate the power of the new regime. Yet their step was revolutionary. It not only predated anything else of its kind in Asia by a quarter of a century; it also put Japan ahead of Europe.[1]

The government began by issuing an act that enjoined every parent to "subordinate all other matters to the education of his children." But what kind of education should

[1] Scotland in 1872 was the first to undertake compulsory secular education. Switzerland followed in 1874, although some of its cantons had done it for many years. France followed suit in 1882, Norway in 1889, England in 1891. The United States had anticipated all others, but only in the Northern States, where free public school systems were everywhere at work by 1860.

the children get? Whom should the Japanese emulate? A survey of the various types of schooling in Europe produced a Japanese compromise: to take the highly centralized and standardized system of France, and to infuse it with some of the breadth and variety of the American curriculum. As its first superintendent of educational affairs, Tokyo imported David Murray, an American from Rutgers College in New Jersey.

Even before these bold decisions, Kuroda had been petitioning his government for schools on Hokkaido. He wanted to be sure that the new tree of knowledge would spread its branches all the way north to his island colony. Again he had his way. In this respect Hokkaido came to be unique among all the borderlands we shall discuss. From the beginning, the government made primary schooling for all children a cornerstone of its development policy. Soon, as we shall see, it also crowned Hokkaido with a college and then a university. It should not be imagined that the desert blossomed overnight into a garden of literacy and learning. For many years Hokkaido suffered from a shortage of secondary and vocational schools. But among their many just grievances, the islanders could not complain that their children were forgotten while those of Old Japan moved into the modern world.

Hokkaido was to profit, too, from Tokyo's plans to educate more of its youth abroad. Whereas the sons of Japanese aristocrats had gone to China for learning in ancient times, they now turned to the Occident. By 1871, 250 young men were studying in Western schools, at least half of them in the United States. These stalwarts deserve to be remembered. The first sizable group sent to the United States by a foreign government, they pioneered the educational gold rush that has since descended on American campuses from all over the world.

Since the new Japan was determined to educate girls as well as boys, it would need women teachers as well as men. From this need grew Kuroda's plea, promptly heeded by his government, to send Japanese girls to the United States to be trained for teaching in Hokkaido. Kuroda had already reconnoitered American women's colleges. So star-struck was this young reformer by the young American college women that he urged his twenty-four-year-old friend, Arinori Mori, the Japanese Minister in Washington, later the Minister of Education, to marry an American girl without delay. Mori balked at so sudden a move, but agreed with Kuroda about the worth of the women's colleges.

The government lost no time in choosing five daughters of Japan's elite, aged from eight to fifteen, to train as future teachers for the northern colony. It sent them across the Pacific with an official mission headed by Prince Iwakura, whose chief purpose was to persuade European nations and the United States to revise unequal treaties. On January 15, 1872, the mission ship *America* docked at San Francisco, and from it stepped the five girls. Two of them were destined to enter Vassar, and one, many years later, Bryn Mawr. Their winter crossing of the continent gave them a foretaste of what they might face in Hokkaido. A blizzard blocked the new transcontinental railroad, stranding them in the Salt Lake City of Brigham Young for almost three weeks. Carefully chaperoned in American homes in Washington and New England, the girls soon learned to manage crinolines as well as kimonos. They also learned to cope with the fresh shad, beefsteak, and ice cream which, as a visiting British clergyman reported, were staples of the Vassar dinner table in those days. None of the young women ever reached Hokkaido. The only one who put her teacher training to full use was Umeko Tsuda, founder of the women's college in Tokyo which bears her name.

To catch up with the West in technical skills, the Meiji leaders cast their net widely in Europe. For their silk mills they recruited British, French, Swiss, and Italian technicians; for their army, French officers; for their navy and lighthouses, British experts. A British naturalist and businessman, T. W. Blakiston, was encouraged to open the first steamship line linking Hokkaido with the main island; a monument to him stands at the summit of Mount Hakodate overlooking the Tsugaru Strait, a reminder of one of the few British influences in the opening of Hokkaido. For the colonial venture in the northern island, which required agricultural and engineering talents, the Meiji government chose to look away from Europe to the still anticolonial republic across the Pacific.

[3]

Here we must stop to meet two Americans who left a lasting imprint on Hokkaido. Their names are better known in Japan than in the United States. The more remarkable of them was *Kepuron Shogun*, as the Japanese called him, or General Capron. His military title was as deceptive as his drooping mustache that gave him a meek, even mournful, look. He was indeed a general who had commanded a brigade toward the close of the Civil War. By his own count he had fought in thirty-four engagements; by his own estimate he had ridden his horse 10,000 miles in Civil War campaigns.

But Horace Capron was not at all military, by training or inclination. He was an enlightened farmer from the Illinois prairies. In the 1840's he had bought 1,200 acres of semi-waste land near Laurel, Maryland, and transformed it into a showplace of modern technology applied to the soil. Newspapers and farm journals from Maine to Georgia described his intensive use of fertilizer, his success with crops that had not been grown in the Baltimore-Washington area before. President Andrew Johnson appointed him Commissioner (that is, Secretary) of the Department of Agriculture in 1867. Capron quickly proved himself a capable public servant.

In 1871, when the reforming Meiji government had been ruling Japan for three years, Kuroda, the young director of the Colonial Office, called on Capron in Washington. One of his purposes in coming to the United States had been to find a highly qualified American who could develop the farms, fisheries, mines, and communications of Hokkaido. President Grant himself suggested his Commissioner of Agriculture.

The Commissioner was willing—at a price. Why should he uproot himself and travel to far Japan, at sixty-seven, unless he were assured of money, comforts, and perquisites? His contract promised him a salary of $10,000 in gold, an amount comparable in those days to $50,000 today, plus "a furnished house, servants, guards, and attendants," and, of course, all expenses. In asking for a princely scale of living, Capron outclassed some European colonial governors of the nineteenth century and set the pace for the chiefs of American aid missions in the twentieth. In insisting on the outward attributes of prestige, presumably to impress the Japanese with his importance, he was both an apt pupil of Commodore Perry and a model for General MacArthur.

Capron spent more than three years in Japan; a few of his technical assistants stayed longer. At the height of the early efforts "to reclaim and people the island" forty-five Americans were at work among the seventy-two foreign technicians in Hokkaido. Capron's own three years were a time of checkered failures and successes. The General himself had personal quirks that made him unpopular. Although he could mix a pleasantly lethal cocktail, and could be charming when he chose, many of his helpers found him stuffy. In the American military tradition, he insisted on amassing costly equipment before pushing ahead with his program. He imported self-binding reapers, then the newest wonders of the American plains, and machines that could thresh a thousand bushels of grain a day, although

Hokkaido needed nothing so elaborate. Perhaps subconsciously, he assumed that all would be well if the Japanese could only learn to live like Americans: if they substituted wheat and meat for rice in their diet, if they built their homes of brick instead of wood, if they adapted to a cold climate as did the farmers in his own Illinois.

Yet in spite of disaffected helpers, ill-trained interpreters, and incompetent bureaucrats, the General earned the dollars he cost his Japanese employers. Some of his advisers left legacies that endure. His animal husbandryman, Edwin Dun, imported horses for breeding, and founded Hokkaido's livestock industry. One of his engineers, Joseph U. Crawford, surveyed and directed the building of the first railroad from Sapporo to Otaru, the forerunner of the 2,400 miles of track that were to reach to the farthest corners of the island. His geologist, Benjamin S. Lyman, began the systematic and effective mining of coal; his secretary, Stewart Eldridge, pioneered in teaching medicine and hospital management.

Capron himself proved to be a man of many talents. As a practical farmer, he introduced the wheat, oats, and potatoes still grown in Hokkaido today. As an engineer, he helped to lay out the checkerboard pattern of the new city of Sapporo and of the rich farming plain on which it stands. As a seasoned public servant, he was able to answer unending Japanese requests for information about American tax collection, law enforcement, city government, and public education. Above all, this "fine, dignified old gentleman," as one of his staff described him, brought a youthful optimism to the work of opening an unexploited land. He peppered his diary and his official reports with protests against those who saw Hokkaido as unfit for settlement. Repeatedly Capron argued that Hokkaido's climate was less severe than that of New England or the corn belt.

"This is a splendid island," he noted in his diary on October 8, 1872; "the real value of it is not well understood or appreciated. Its mineral resources are great, its fisheries unlimited, its timber abundant and superior in quality, its agricultural capacity great."

Others in his mission were less sanguine. Dun, a landowner's son from Ohio, concluded: "At least 90% of the island is unfit for cultivation of any kind. . . . There are less than 2 million acres capable of cultivation in the entire island." [2] This judgment proved almost uncanny in its accuracy. For in the 1960's, almost ninety years after Dun first appraised the island, only about 9 per cent of Hokkaido lay under cultivation.

But if Capron was extravagant in his forecasts of Hokkaido's future, was he more mistaken than those who saw no future for it at all? When Capron had finished his work, his employers knew at least what they had in Hokkaido: coal to meet the needs of future generations, farmland to give livelihood to new settlers, fisheries richer than those of Newfoundland, timber more splendid than in any other Japanese islands, an imperial nest egg there for the hatching whenever the Japanese were ready to apply the requisite effort. The old farmer-general had earned at least a part of the tribute which the American Minister, John A. Bingham, wrote him in 1876: ". . . your work was honestly done, and wisely done, and in every way well done."

[4]

Beside the busy highway that leads south from Sapporo, the observant traveler will notice a stone pedestal with three English words carved into it: "Boys, Be Ambitious." The figure that stood on the pedestal was pulled down during the Pacific War and melted, presumably, for shells to fire at Americans. But the inscription stayed as a re-

[2] Dun thought well enough of Hokkaido to marry a local girl. He stayed long after Capron, and in 1896 President Cleveland appointed him American Minister to Japan.

minder of the second American who left a lasting imprint on Hokkaido.

His connection with Japan, like Capron's, goes back to the early 1870's, when inquisitive agents of the Meiji regime were scouring the West for new ideas and techniques. In America they discovered the new land grant colleges, and admired their courses in practical agriculture. If such training had helped the Americans to tame the prairies, why should it not also help to build Japan's island colony? The government responded quickly to the appeals of its scouts. In 1872 it decided to set up an agricultural college on Hokkaido.

At first only a few dozen students attended classes housed in temporary buildings in Tokyo. In 1875 the fledgling farm school moved to the new colonial capital of Sapporo. By this time the Japanese were looking for an American who could give the new college a good start. Their search took them to Massachusetts Agricultural College, now the State university at Amherst, and to its President, Dr. William Smith Clark. Clark accepted their invitation to head the Hokkaido school for a year. By 1876 he was on the job in Sapporo, bubbling with energy and moral preachments.

Like Capron, he saw agriculture as the island's most valuable resource. He taught his students to grub in the soil with their hands, one of the hardest lessons for an educated Asian to learn. He made himself an evangelist for cool-weather Western crops, for commercial fertilizer, for sturdy barns and houses that would withstand the Hokkaido snows. Not content with preaching technology, Clark evangelized in other ways that were familiar in New England colleges of his day. At the opening exercises of the new college, he admonished his students:

"Let every one of you, young gentlemen, strive to prepare himself for the highest positions of labor and trust and subsequent honor in your native land, which greatly needs your most faithful and efficient service. Preserve your health, and control your appetites and passions, cultivate habits of obedience and diligence, acquire all possible knowledge and skill in the various sciences which you may have an opportunity to study. Thus you will prepare yourselves for important positions."

In his first annual report he noted that "every officer and student has promised not to indulge in the use of alcoholic drinks, opium or tobacco, and neither to gamble nor to be guilty of profane swearing while connected with the College."

Nor did he hesitate to save heathen souls. On his way to Hokkaido he argued hotly about the Bible with Kuroda, his traveling companion and escort. Every morning at the college he read a few verses from the Scriptures and expounded them to his students. Before leaving in April 1877, he drafted a "covenant of believers in Jesus," and every member of the first class at the college signed it. Later several of the students were baptized.

Looking back over almost a century, it is hard to understand how this New England preacher-professor was able to sway the young Hokkaido students of his time. If he had any respect for Japan's ancient culture, he did not show it. Like Capron, he did not doubt that what was good for America was right and good for Japan. He even forced a balanced American diet into the mouths of his students. Ironically, this civilian American was the first to introduce American-type cadet drill into Japanese higher education; other Japanese colleges then copied it from Sapporo, as Sapporo had copied it from New England.

Kuraku sensei—Professor Clark—became a legend in Hokkaido. As he started his long journey back to Amherst in the spring of 1877, all his students and teachers accompanied him on horseback for the first fifteen miles. They stopped for "a sad farewell lunch," as one of his students recalled years later. Clark asked the boys to drop him a few lines from time to time, so he could know how they were faring. Then he climbed onto his stallion, turned in his saddle, and shouted: "Boys, be ambitious!" With a prick of the spurs, the horse galloped off, and Clark was gone.

The agricultural college grew into a university, and still later into the Imperial University of Hokkaido. The original study of agriculture became encrusted by that of more conventional academic subjects. Other teachers, Japanese rather than American, deserve more credit than Clark for Japan's swift progress in technological training. Yet the practical flavor of Clark's teaching has survived. For decades the university at Sapporo remained outstanding for its research in agriculture. Among its graduates were Yamada, foremost authority on volcanic ash; Tokito on peat land; Ito on rice fungus; Shima on apples, so well known that he was called the Apple King; and, of course, the famous Inazo Nitobe, agriculturist, lawyer, teacher, and unofficial ambassador of Hokkaido to the outer world. After Japan acquired Formosa from China in 1895, it was graduates of Sapporo who developed new farming methods there, and laid the foundation for the skillful agriculture that was to excel anything on the Asian mainland.

A minor mystery of Clark's assignment to Hokkaido, and of Capron's, is worth exploring. Why did the Japanese turn first to the United States for help in developing Hokkaido? One would have expected the young reformers of the Meiji era to look elsewhere. In industry, technology, finance, and public administration, Britain led the world; in the arts, France; in military prowess, the new German Empire. The United States would seem to have offered few precedents to an imitative people striving for prestige and power.

Its representative democracy held no appeal to Japan, with a single line of emperors "unbroken for ages eternal."

The "United" States had just broken apart in the Civil War; they had been hammered together again at the price of unprecedented numbers of soldier dead. In the Washington of President Grant, as Henry Adams observed it, "the moral law had expired"; politicians, judges, bankers, businessmen, professional men, all were smirched "in one dirty cesspool of vulgar corruption." The Japanese emissaries of the early 1870's must have scented these evils.

Why, then, did they seek American guidance in opening their first colony? At least four reasons moved them. The first was political suspicion of Britain and Russia, and of European powers generally. The second was a business-minded outlook, a faith in merchants, bankers, and industrialists which post-Civil War America shared with the Meiji regime. The third, of course, was the knowledge that New England and the northern Middle West had mastered a climate like Hokkaido's. And the fourth was large-scale mechanized agriculture, in which, above all, the United States offered precisely the skill and experience needed in Japan's northern island. The Meiji leaders did not let American influence implant itself too deeply; they resisted Capron's repeated efforts to bring foreign capital, and even foreign immigrants, into Hokkaido. When the Americans had taught their lessons and disclosed their technical secrets, they could go home, and Japanese would carry on.

This, in truth, is what happened in Hokkaido. Capron and Clark went home. Other foreign advisers carried on for a few years, but their appointments were not renewed. When the Colonial Office reached the end of its first ten-year term, the government dissolved it and parceled out its work among various ministries in Tokyo. Kuroda, the locomotive that had pulled Hokkaido forward, was derailed in a public scandal and temporarily discredited. He had approved a scheme to sell the Colonial Office's assets to a carefully selected group of citizens, at a price far below their worth.

A reminder of the typhoon that spread destruction in 1954 through Hokkaido. This column in the Daisetsuzan National Park bears the inscription: "To the souls of the trees that died."

I

The city of Sapporo is laid out "in gridiron pattern, at first sight more like Omaha than Osaka."

II

"A village of paintless wooden houses on a dreary coast." Habomai village, Hokkaido, the nearest to Soviet territory of any settlement in Japan.

White-helmeted loggers in the Hokkaido forests that hold a third of Japan's timber resources.

"A Hokkaido lake is made for boating near the shore but not for swimming." Lake Shikotsu, in the Shikotsu-Toya National Park.

"Once the Ainu spread over most of what is now Japan. . ." A chieftain of this "departing race" lives in one of the last remaining Ainu villages, near Asahigawa.

"*La Union*'s regular mission . . . was to hunt pirates and smugglers on the Sulu Sea." The Philippine gunboat that ferried the authors to North Borneo.

A *vinta* of the kind used by Moro smugglers and pirates on the Sulu Sea: "a long canoe equipped with sail and bamboo outriggers."

La Union's three-inch gun broods over a *vinta* and Moro village on the Sulu Sea.

VI

"Jolo's long wooden pier. . . . As *La Union* sidles up to it . . . one almost expects a cry of 'Cheese it—the cops!' and a general scramble for safety."

In North Borneo "the land holds up a shining morning face." The mountain is Kinabalu, 13,455 feet, highest point in the Malay Archipelago.

A Chinese farmer tends his vines outside Sandakan, North Borneo. "Literate, enterprising, and free from discrimination, these Overseas Chinese have a better lot than their brethren anywhere else in Asia, and they know it."

The farmer's sturdy grandchildren will go to a North Borneo school "founded, staffed, and largely financed by the Chinese community for its own children."

[5]

With the extinction of the Colonial Office, the impulse "to reclaim and people" Hokkaido lost its force. Strategically Hokkaido no longer mattered. The chief motive of the Meiji leaders in opening the island had been, as we have seen, fear of Russia. Now the fear subsided. A treaty in 1875 delimited the northern frontier at last, giving southern Sakhalin to Russia and the northern Kuriles to Japan. No longer would Hokkaido have to be watched, guided, and subsidized to keep it out of Russian hands. Japan soon looked elsewhere for new resources: first to Formosa, then to Korea and Manchuria. The battleground of the bloody war with Russia in 1904–5 was not Hokkaido but Manchuria. Military unease about Hokkaido relaxed still further when Japan regained the southern half of Sakhalin in the treaty of peace. The international boundary moved north; Hokkaido became incidental in Japan's march toward world power.

Slowly, fitfully, the pattern of the present-day island emerged. Railroads pushed outward from the capital, opening forests and coal mines to loggers and diggers. Now "the northern gate of the Empire" was useful chiefly as a source of timber, coal, and fish for the rest of Japan. Settlers of two kinds moved northward to try their luck with virgin land. The first group were unemployed *samurai*, the fighting men of the old feudal regime; their transfer was subsidized, and they were given fertile land, often in the Ishikari Valley. The second group consisted largely of landless peasants from the inhospitable north of Honshu; they received poor land and found the struggle hard. By immigration and natural increase, the population of Hokkaido grew, though there was never any considerable overflow from the crowded south. When the Colonial Office was dissolved in 1882, Hokkaido had about 250,000 people. By the end of the Emperor Meiji's reign in 1912, the figure had risen to more than 1,600,000; when the next Emperor, Taisho, died in 1926 it had passed 2,400,000. If Tokyo had heeded Kuroda and Capron, if it had promoted crops and industries suited to the northland, the population would have risen faster still.

To show the government's lack of consistent planning and purpose, one example will serve. The immigrant farmers understood rice culture and little else. Naturally they planted rice. Instead of retraining them to diversify with cold-weather crops and dairying, the government made the mistake of offering two inducements: it pegged the price of rice, and it encouraged the Hokkaido experiment station to develop a new strain of rice that would ripen in a hundred days, approximately the length of the island's growing season. It was a technical achievement of brilliance, but a long-term disservice. For it hung an albatross around the necks of Hokkaido's farmers: a rice economy, sure to inflict crop failures, poverty, and even famine whenever freezing weather arrived too soon.

In the 1930's the government retarded Hokkaido's development in another way, this time for military reasons. The militarists who had seized power in Tokyo had only one interest in Hokkaido: to extract from it whatever they could—coal and timber in particular—to feed the Imperial war machine. They chose to make Manchuria rather than Hokkaido the seedbed of new industries and new techniques. Not being an important industrial target, Hokkaido suffered less from World War II than the rest of Japan. Its cities escaped bombing raids; the port of Otaru suffered nothing worse than a strafing, and the steel center of Muroran a naval shelling. Although its physical plant remained virtually intact, the island faced the postwar era with built-in handicaps from the past.

The Present-Day Hokkaidoans

We have seen how Hokkaido's remoteness, its wildness, and its cold repelled most Japanese. It would be strange if those who braved these hazards, and their descendants, had not made of themselves a distinctive people and for themselves a characteristic way of life. To assess the qualities of this borderland life, let us turn first to the man who overcame Hokkaido's physical obstacles: the prosperous farmer.

In the fertile Ishikari Valley, north of Sapporo, it is not uncommon to find a farm of twenty-five acres, which is double the Hokkaido average and twelve times that of the Honshu "mainland." Here stands the characteristic Hokkaido homestead, a two-story farmhouse with shining glass windows and metal peaked roof, and close beside it the green barn and silo. The Hokkaido farm family prefers an isolated, independent homestead to the crowded village life of southern Japan. The owner of one such homestead received American visitors with the courtesy, but not the reserve, of many southern Japanese. His broad, seamed face lit up when he discovered their interest in his work and his family history. In grimy working clothes, he was obviously no "gentleman farmer," no squire supervising hired help. His father had come to the valley as a pioneer, emigrating from ancient tradition-bound Kyoto.

"When I was a boy," he recalled, "all that you see here was dense forest. The clearing of the land was my father's work and mine."

Twenty of his twenty-five acres he had planted in forage crops, the rest (except for a small plot of rice for the family) in seed of sugar beet, feed beet, and spinach, his three cash crops. This farmer owned eleven cows (the average on a Hokkaido farm is two and a half) and enough machines to stock a showroom. In a matter-of-fact way, the old man pointed out an electric water pump, an electric threshing machine, and a gasoline-driven tractor. His living room, matted and unfurnished in Japanese style, was lighted with fluorescent tubes and equipped with television. In the adjoining kitchen, he casually motioned to an electric washing machine, an electric iron and mixer. The farmer's obvious pride seemed to spring less from these household gadgets, which were his wife's concern, than from the achievement of having carved a good living out of wilderness in two generations. One cannot understand the quality of this settlers' society without remembering that every member of it, whether farmer, fisherman, logger, or businessman, knows the meaning of struggle, either his own or that of a recent forebear.

A neighboring homestead belonged to the rare farmer who himself had pioneered and survived the struggle. A penniless refugee from Manchuria, he had shipped to Hokkaido soon after the 1945 surrender. On 2,500 acres of reclaimed marshland, the Japanese government had settled a hundred refugee families. Each received a twenty-five-acre plot for a nominal sum equal to five dollars. This refugee, who had been a petty bureaucrat, found frontier farming a desperate bootstrap operation.

Over fifteen years he had managed to acquire eight cows, two horses, and 200 chickens. Like his neighbor, he had concentrated on forage crops, along with some potatoes and soybeans, plus enough rice to feed his family. Inexperienced and with relatively poor land, he and his family had known hunger in the early years. They had subsisted mainly on potatoes through seasons of frost, flood, and crop failure. Little by little they had built the necessary barn and silo and finally the new farmhouse, modest but spick-and-span. The living room boasted wallpaper and a radio. Along the hard climb to what was obviously a better-than-tolerable life, these newcomers had found the self-reliance and self-respect which are hallmarks of borderland people.

Such farmers are, of course, among the lucky ones. Their river valley is the most fertile region of Hokkaido. Even the refugee from Manchuria, on his reclaimed marshland, is more fortunate than the thousands who scrabble for a living on upland fields among the mountains. These are the luckless ones. To understand their losing battles one should visit a community such as the lumber town of Kamikawa, on the fringe of the Daisetsuzan National Park. Here at the very heart of the island, in the shadow of its highest mountains, farmer-settlers have tried for almost eighty years to wrest a living from an environment too harsh for farming. One wonders why successive governments ever encouraged them to try. Poor soil, Siberian cold, inadequate capital or credit for draft animals—these are among the handicaps that face a Kamikawa farmer. Few in this area manage to live on the meager return from their crops. How could anyone so ill equipped hope to win so uneven a contest? In a year when sun and rain bless Hokkaido in just the right proportions, a farmer around Kamikawa harvests only twenty bushels of rice per acre. But when winter strikes in the third week of September, as it did in 1956, his yield drops to two bushels. Many Kamikawa farmers, and thousands of others throughout Hokkaido, kept alive in that fearful winter only with the help of rice rushed from abroad, including 776 tons contributed by church organizations in the United States.

Cold and bleak, a northern Ontario town set down on the edge of Asia, Kamikawa nevertheless lacks the drabness one could expect. The explanation is that this region offers part-time jobs for those who cannot live by farming alone. A government forestry research center on the edge of town gives some employment. An electric power station, with a new dam to store and harness the headwaters of the Ishikari River, provides other opportunities. The hot-spring resort hotels near the park boundary need maintenance workers as well as servants. And the white-helmeted loggers one encounters in the forests cutting trees with power saws, and sliding them over the snow with the help of horses and tractors—such men include farmers who have found salvation in supplementary work for Hokkaido's booming lumber industry.

There is another reason why Kamikawa farmers need not be hopeless or helpless. Even here, their children have something better to look forward to. The school building in this town of about 4,000 is more than a credit to the community. It also suggests why the younger generation are not content to plow the same furrows as their fathers and grandfathers. When Kamikawa children grow up, they are attracted to the fast-growing city of Asahigawa, only thirty miles away. Inevitably farmers will quit the sub-standard land in the mountains, or their children will leave the land untenanted in the long run. At the start of the 1960's the central government in Tokyo had pledged itself to get a third of all Japan's farmers off the land and into industry within the decade. In Hokkaido the movement had already begun, as it began long ago in New England, northern Scotland, Italian Piedmont, and other marginal farming regions where the hurdles proved too high.

[2]

If the young people who leave upland farms are looking for a soft life, they do not find it in Asahigawa, Hokkaido's coldest city. Here snow falls, on the average, for 131 days; by February, almost three feet of it blanket the ground. Yet Asahigawa people have learned how to master their antagonist. On one stretch of the main street, sidewalks are roofed to guard shoppers against snow and summer sun. Double glass windows in houses, Russian stoves in the corners of many rooms, woodpiles in the yard, snow shovels and rubber boots behind the door—these show that a southern Japanese can adapt to Hokkaido with no more pain than a Sicilian to Massachusetts. Because the heating of homes is a special problem, Hokkaido companies must give each employee an annual bonus of $41 to help pay for firewood and charcoal, which costs an average family $64 per year. Only in extreme cold spells must schools close because of the difficulty of heating the classrooms.

In spite of the climate, Asahigawa has burst from a frontier village into a hustling city of 200,000 within fifty years. In ten years alone, from 1950 to 1960, its population increased by 60,000 as workers streamed into its industries: cotton goods, *sake*, timber, and, above all, wood pulp. Industry, as we have said, is, and will continue to be, the salvation of farmers who have found mountain cultivation too much for them. This is where their children find work and a way of life more rewarding than the family farm. Asahigawa is by no means an intellectual desert. A public library and cultural center in its municipal park, bookshops as crowded as any in Japan, television aerials growing like forest saplings from the roofs of workers' houses—such amenities lighten the rigors of Japan's far north.

If the city becomes too small for the talents of its sons and daughters, they often move on, some to Hokkaido University and the wider opportunities of Sapporo, others even to Tokyo. The story is just as familiar in the West. Who has not discovered in London those other ambitious northerners, the Scots, holding positions of prestige and power? For the same reasons, ambitious Hokkaido men— following Clark's advice—have moved south and have climbed to the top of the Japanese ladder in business, the professions, and the public service. From Asahigawa, for example, came the Managing Director of Radio N H K, Japan's government-chartered broadcasting corporation; from Otaru, the President of the Japan Highway Corporation. The nationwide confederation of trade unions, *Sohyo,* chose a Hokkaido man as its executive secretary; the na-

tional teachers' union did likewise. Men are not the only
northern stars on the national stage. Hokkaido's most attractive export is an adored film actress from Otaru.

[3]

Along with Hokkaidoans' sturdiness of spirit, one finds an
individualism which is a characteristic of borderlands. The
northern islanders have responded to the challenge of
their new surroundings in the manner of most frontiers-
men or their descendants. Nor is their carelessness of
tradition a monopoly of youth, a mere extension of the
ferment afflicting the first defeated postwar generation in
Japanese history. In Hokkaido it is the older generation
that has the audacity to be different from its own age group
elsewhere in Japan. One cannot prove it statistically, but
one senses that conformity is not one of the islanders' major
worries. Transplanted traditions have not flourished in this
northern soil. Clan and neighborhood loyalties are less
tenacious than in the south.

"We don't care about hierarchy and social distinctions,"
said a professor in the west-coast port of Otaru. A student
who had just visited his ancestral home on the island of
Shikoku for the first time said: "I was appalled by the south
where everyone seems to know his place and stays in it. We
Hokkaidoans are different, thank goodness." A municipal
official in Hakodate, asked why his father had come to
Hokkaido, said: "For more land and a freer life—and he
found both." Although Japan below the strait may still
mean "home," as England or Scotland mean "home" to a
New Zealander, the Hokkaidoan believes his island to be
more free, more spacious, more open to opportunity than
what his forefathers left behind.

With physical and social elbow room, these northern
Japanese are not afraid to loosen some of the embedded
customs. Among the many individualists we came to know
was a family from a remote northern town. Like many

college-bred youngsters in Japan, the daughter was mildly rebellious and proud of being "different," which in her vocabulary stood for "Hokkaidoan." Her marriage had been on a traditional theme, but with free variations. In the established manner, the parents of the young man had approached her parents through a professional go-between. Once this hurdle had been conventionally cleared, and photographs exchanged, it was arranged that the boy and girl should meet casually, as if by chance. "It was exciting, and I didn't object because I kept the veto power," she said. "My father and mother told me that if I didn't like the young man, that was the end of it. I'm not a piece of merchandise to be put up for sale."

Another target of Hokkaido sophisticates is the institution of mixed bathing in the nude. Modern young women denounce it as uncultured. One of the hallmarks of culture, on the other hand, is familiarity with classical Western music. Students in Sapporo flock to the coffee houses to spend hours hearing recordings of Bach, Beethoven, and Stravinsky. In summer, Hokkaido's capital offers a pastime such as one might expect to find in Vienna: a hundred music lovers squatting on the grass in the public park during a concert of stereophonic recordings.

When it comes to politics, independent-minded Hokkaidoans will take their cue from Tokyo—when it suits their mood and their purposes. The national commotion of 1960 over the security treaty with the United States brought students of Hokkaido University into the streets to snake-dance. With them danced fifteen of their professors "to protest against the tyranny of the majority," as one of them explained. To this concept of tyranny, Hokkaidoans young and old are even more sensitive than their countrymen to the south. They show it partly in the strength of their Socialist allegiance.

A few statistics will point up the contrast. In the 1958 elections for the lower house of the national parliament, the Socialist parties accounted for 32.9 per cent of the whole national vote; in Hokkaido they polled 46.9 per cent. Two years later, the Socialist parties raised their share of the nation's popular vote to 36.3 per cent; they rolled up 47.8 per cent of the Hokkaido vote. This time only three prefectures in Japan gave Socialists and Communists combined a greater proportion of their vote than did Hokkaido, and these three were urban, industrialized districts. The Communist vote in Hokkaido has been insignificant—only 1.9 per cent in 1960 compared to not quite 3 per cent in Japan as a whole.

When they elect a provincial Governor, more Hokkaidoans vote Socialist than in national elections. In 1955, for example, they installed a Socialist by a landslide vote of 64 per cent, and this, be it remembered, at a time when the conservative Liberal Democratic Party dominated the national government and the nation.

What is the explanation? Does it mean that Hokkaido is independent-minded or that it is Marxist? True, labor in the Hokkaido coalfields and the steel mills votes as stanchly Socialist as in the mining valleys of Wales. But another force, more powerful than ideology, probably accounts for the dissent. This is an unsleeping awareness by Hokkaido people of their local and special interests, a conviction among masses of voters that their island must protest "agin the government" in Tokyo to make it heed their complaints and meet their needs. Two kinds of leadership have done much to generate local concern in recent years.

One is an extraordinary newspaper, *Hokkaido Shimbun*, owned by Hokkaido capital, edited in Sapporo, and printed in three other cities as well. Morning and evening together, it claims a circulation of 820,000, which means one copy for virtually every island family. Its circulation in Hokkaido exceeds that of all its competitors combined, including the island sales of the Tokyo dailies with their giant resources of professional, mechanical, and managerial skill. On the average, it devotes a full page to international news every morning and a page and a half every evening. Not content to compete in the minor leagues of provincial newspapers, it maintains full-time foreign correspondents in London and Washington.

But its pre-eminence lies chiefly in the zeal with which it crusades for Hokkaido causes: a deeper harbor for coal and newsprint carriers at Tomakomai; faster paving of Hokkaido's dirt roads; or that deathless dream of Hokkaido boosters, a tunnel under the Tsugaru Strait to the main island of Honshu. Naturally such a force has fed and, in turn, thrived on anti-government, pro-Socialist, and anti-American sentiment. Naturally, too, such dissent has helped to make the island a political maverick among the provinces.

So also has the leadership of a politician named Toshi-fumi Tanaka. For twelve years, from 1947 to 1959, this roughhewn figure personified his borderland, embodied its spirit, dramatized its strivings, and nursed its interests.

Tanaka was a minor civil servant in the Hokkaido Forestry Department when he announced, in 1947, that he would run for Governor. In those days of American occupation, power stemmed not from the elected Governor but from the American military commander. The Governor, as his agent, could only carry out the reforms which the Americans were trying to inject into the Japanese bloodstream. Socialist party leaders quickly sensed the vote-getting capacities of this newcomer to politics: a tall, rugged man of thirty-two, with a broad face, bright eyes, a ready grin, a shock of thick black hair, and a voice that might move multitudes. They promptly adopted him as their official candidate. He won easily, to become the youngest provincial head in Japan, one of four Socialists among the forty-six governors in the nation.

Did his socialism mean that he would nationalize industry? Would he, like his party colleagues in Tokyo, busy himself with agitation to ban the Bomb, to rid Japan of American bases and make it neutralist in the cold war? Tanaka's goals were more provincial and practical than these. After a triumphant re-election in 1951 he set out to reduce the island's swollen bureaucracy, enforce the new education and labor laws, and put more money and effort into social welfare. As a Socialist he was no more doctrinaire than Herbert Morrison in London or Ernst Reuter in Berlin. Growing impatient with the follies of the left-wingers in Tokyo, he seceded from the party and won again in 1955 as an independent, polling almost twice as many votes as his conservative opponent.

This moderate progressive had answered to Hokkaido's wishes. Except among miners and college students, a Marxist theoretician would not have appealed to the islanders. They wanted someone who would speak up for them in Tokyo and work for them at home. The strain of doing both for twelve years forced him to retire on doctor's orders, exhausted and half blind.

The lessons of Tanaka's long tenure were not lost upon the leaders of the conservative government in Tokyo. They knew they must find a candidate conscious of Hokkaido's special needs, a man of action, equally—if possible—a charmer who could galvanize the voters. Their choice fell upon Kingo Machimura, a member of one of Hokkaido's "first families," a well-to-do dairy farmer, a four-term member of the lower house in the national parliament. Machimura had momentarily barged into history after the Japanese surrender in 1945. As police superintendent of Tokyo, he was credited with foiling a last-ditch plot by army fanatics to seize the Imperial Palace and continue the war. This was six days after Japan's formal acceptance of defeat and the Emperor's recorded appeal for "enduring the unendurable and suffering what is insufferable." In Hokkaido, Machimura's reputation was enhanced by the gossip that he personally safeguarded the recording of the Emperor's speech which the army hotheads had tried to seize.[3]

Talking smoothly and coolly in his office in the red-brick headquarters of the prefectural government, Machimura took pains to stress his loyalty to the ruling party in Tokyo. He had no patience with the idea that Hokkaido needed an independent champion to speak up for its interests. "The government in Tokyo is well aware of Hokkaido's needs," he said. "It is doing everything it can to meet them." Conceivably this Organization Man can do more for the island, in a shorter time, than the Socialist Tanaka could do. As a member of the ruling team, he might channel governmental and private capital into Hokkaido on a grand scale, as Tanaka could not. If he succeeds, he will make obsolete the old argument about the island's development. Should the central government regard Hokkaido as just another prefecture? Or should Tokyo give it special treatment in view of its climate, its economic potential, and its frontier position? Official Japanese have never agreed. Each man's answer has depended on what he thinks Hokkaido is worth to the country.

Red Ink and Black

When the occupation authorities decided against preferential help for Hokkaido, they had ample reason. At that moment, Japan lay prostrate, most of the country in greater need of relief and rehabilitation than Hokkaido. By 1950, the policy had changed. The national parliament passed a Hokkaido development law and set up a Hokkaido Development Agency in the Prime Minister's office. In 1951 this agency brought forth a five-year island development plan to cost about $1,250,000,000, of which two fifths would come

[3] The role of the police is substantiated in the firsthand account by Toshikazu Kasé: *Journey to the Missouri* (New Haven: Yale University Press; 1959), p. 263. But Kasé does not credit Machimura with having saved the Emperor's recording: pp. 258–62.

from the central government, a tiny fraction from the Hokkaido provincial government, and the remainder—more than half—from private capital.

But the timing was unhappy. The Korean War was in full swing, bringing a hothouse prosperity at the beginning and something approaching a collapse of prices and profits at the end. The plan achieved a few good results, notably in harnessing the island's water power and coal to lift its kilowatt capacity by 50 per cent. But the plan failed to meet half of its goals. The central government decided that it could not afford its share of the cost, and private investors, by and large, shrugged their shoulders.

A second plan, from 1958 through 1962, set an even more ambitious investment goal of $1,950,000,000, to be shared equally by government and private enterprise. Concentrating chiefly on dairy farming and manufacturing, the authors of the plan hoped to lift the island's per capita income 7.1 per cent each year, and to boost production 60 per cent above 1955. After approving these new goals, the Cabinet again failed to provide for financing them. Again the government appeared schizophrenic in its attitude toward Hokkaido. In theory, the island's special handicaps merited a show of special concern. In practice, it merited not much more than a show. The truth was that it could not exert enough political pressure to squeeze the money it needed out of Tokyo.

[1]

Nor did Hokkaido offer enough economic inducement to dazzle the private investor. Where, indeed, could the investor hope to reap quick and lush profits? Let us run down the list of the island's resources.

Timber? It is, as we have seen, not only wasted but also a wasting asset. Reforestation lags behind destruction, even in the national parks. So insatiable is the demand for wood pulp and other forest products that the government again permits large-scale logging within the parks, not only to thin the existing growth but also to make money for the island. In 1957, for example, timber and wood products provided more than half of all Hokkaido's exports, a total of $21,651,000 to thirty countries. The most valuable single export is plywood; the most profitable is the plywood made from the straight and slender *sen* tree, a product that manages to leap American tariff walls because of its light color and delicate grain. Understandably, the Japanese put profits for the present ahead of conservation for the future.

The profit motive explains; it cannot excuse. Hokkaido is risking the erosion and floods that inevitably follow unwise lumbering. To conserve the dwindling quantity of large logs, Hokkaido's Forest Products Research Institute is experimenting with new uses for small twisted trees and mill waste. Chipboard and crystalline glucose are among the wood products the Institute believes have a commercial future. But current ingenuity cannot atone for past profligacy. Hokkaido has the good fortune still to possess a third of Japan's timber resources. A concerted effort to reforest and more disciplined conservation can save this treasure. Meanwhile, the Japanese are supplementing Hokkaido's forests with lumber imported from the vast Siberian supplies in the Amur River region—half a million tons in 1960 alone. Hokkaido processes much of the Russian timber and pays for it with manufactured goods. A Japanese ship sails up the Amur River each month during the unfrozen summer, to collect a cargo for Hokkaido mills.

Do other resources offer more return in the long run? Coal, for example? Hokkaido possesses a third of the nation's reserves. Its industries, old and new, benefit from the nearness of ample high-grade coal. The rest of Japan is bound to turn soon and increasingly to Hokkaido as the other main coalfields, in Kyushu, become exhausted. But Hokkaido coal has no better chance than any other of surviving the eventual shift to oil and atomic energy for power.

In Hokkaido as in South Wales, the outlook is made more somber by the demands of the miners' unions. Granted that men who work underground are usually justified in seeking more pay and better working conditions. If their demands are satisfied, the price of Hokkaido coal rises; if they are rejected, the industry is in for labor troubles that likewise hurt the economy of the island. Hokkaidoans know that the serious strikes of the 1950's in their coalfields and paper mills did as much as snow and ice to chill the climate for investment.

Let us continue the balance sheet of resources with fisheries. Here nature and politics have combined to reduce the annual harvest. The fish have moved northward not just from Hokkaido but from warming coastal waters all around Japan. The main victim is the independent fisherman, the three out of four whose boats are not motorized and who cannot venture far afield. At the same time the big companies which send their fleets into the northern Pacific are bringing back a smaller catch each season, under the quota agreements with the Soviet Union.

The last on our list is the most controversial of Hokkaido resources, agriculture. In this field, the Japanese have behaved like parents who do not know what to do with a gifted child. They have pushed the child into the traditional family business, rice growing, when its natural bent and equipment point toward dairying and stock farming. Hokkaido is ideal dairy country, but the Japanese know next to nothing about dairying. Most forage crops are strange to them; clover and alfalfa are foreign names. So the southern farmer who migrated to Hokkaido was encouraged to practice the rice culture he knew. It was as if Italian farmers had migrated in force to Wisconsin to plant rice as they do in the Po Valley. Both of the island's five-year development plans have persisted in this folly, with new investment to reclaim new land for new and larger areas of rice farming.

Dairy development is admittedly more difficult. It requires not only retraining the farmer but giving him the technical services and the capital to put his new knowledge to use. More difficult still, it requires a new outlook. Horace Capron saw Hokkaido becoming the stock and dairy farm of Japan. But those who succeeded him discarded the vision and the opportunity. Instead of eight or ten cows on a farm, the minimum for commercial dairying, the Hokkaido farmer owns two or three on the average—"pseudo-dairy farming," one expert calls it. When farmers argue that a glut of milk and butter drives prices down, the expert scoffs. "There is no overproduction, only underconsumption," he answers. He believes that Hokkaido's second chance to follow its true bent is at hand, and he has figures to back the contention. They show a revolution in Japanese eating habits: the average Japanese increased his annual consumption of milk from 6.8 pounds before the war to 43.6 pounds in 1959, of meat from 4 pounds in 1936 to almost 10 pounds in 1959. At the same time he cut his prewar eating of rice from 290 to 252 pounds. To prove the thesis of underconsumption of dairy products, the expert points to Japan at the bottom of the list of milk consumers among the industrialized nations. Using Canada's consumption at 100, the comparative figures in 1957 were: New Zealand 126, the United States 95—and Japan 3.25. Clearly a potential dairyland like Hokkaido has its future cut out for it.

Many progressive-minded Hokkaidoans insist that their island can and must follow its natural bent, and not only in dairying and cattle raising. They are eager to see it also develop its own industrial pattern. By this they mean that Hokkaido should process new products from its own forests, mines, and farms; it should also attract new industries like chemicals and plastics, which require high mechanization and little man power. Thus the island would shift its economic relationship to the rest of the country. It has been essentially a colonial relationship for a hundred years. Raw materials account for three fourths of the value of what Hokkaido ships south; finished products account for three fourths of its imports from other parts of Japan.

Must Hokkaido always be a dependency? Must it go on forever shipping raw materials and letting others do its manufacturing? Or can it develop new skills and specialties of its own? Undoubtedly it can—if the islanders make better use of what they have. For here is a borderland with wide-awake leaders, trained managers, literate workers and farmers. It holds enough resources in and under its soil, and in its waters, to give it a modest well-being like that, say, of Finland. In its first century, as we have seen, it faced the handicaps of climate, distance, and disrepute. At the start of its second century, it has begun to surmount them. One has only to watch the spurt of building in Sapporo and Asahigawa, the springing up of medium-sized factories along newly paved roads, to feel that the old era may be ending and a brighter one at hand. Of all the borderlands we shall examine, none stands as good a chance as Hokkaido of pulling itself up from the status of poor relation to that of partner.

2

Islands on the Sulu Sea

FROM MINDANAO TO
NORTH BORNEO

*Man, biologically considered, and whatever else he
may be in the bargain, is simply the most formidable
of all the beasts of prey, and, indeed, the only one
that preys systematically on its own species.*
—WILLIAM JAMES

WHETHER there is a ratio between the bounty of nature
and the meanness of man we do not pretend to know. But
it is clear as a tropical noonday that where men have not
had to fight the elements they have fought each other instead. This is one of the first truths to emerge from a more
than casual look at the necklace of tropical islands that half
encircles Southeast Asia.[1] Here the growing season is
twelve months long. Man can satisfy his basic needs for
food and shelter without hard labor. Perhaps that is why
he came to the Indies in successive waves of conquest, and
perhaps that is what got him into so much mischief. Descendants of early settlers show Negroid or Mongoloid

[1] These islands, numbering more than 10,000, were known to early
European explorers as the *Indies*. Modern geographers call them the *Malay Archipelago*, which includes Indonesia, the Philippines, and Borneo.

traits. They fled into the island interiors as waves of brown-skinned Malays arrived from neighboring islands and from Southeast Asia. A steady stream of traders and settlers trickled across from China. All paid heavily for the privileges of warmth, sun, and rain. They paid in violence.

Before Europeans fell upon them, Asians preyed on one another. Head-hunting tribes feuded as a way of life. Sultans and rajas toppled each other in close succession. The seas, the coasts, and the jungles echoed to violence. Even against their common European foe, the islanders could not form a common defense. In the end, most of the *Indians*, as their conquerors called them in the early days, lost heart and became subjects and servants of Portugal, Spain, the Netherlands, Great Britain, or the United States.

In bending the natives to their will, the empire builders occasionally struck granite. That is, they came up against people they could not pacify, people who simply would not bend. These were not just good fighters; their strength consisted also in never knowing when they were beaten. It was a further advantage, in holding out, to be a borderland people, too remote and not so troublesome as to be worth sustained attention from the ruling center. In the Malay Archipelago we find such a people on the islands of the Sulu Sea. For more than 400 years these seafaring Malays refused in turn to be conquered and converted by Spain, to be "civilized" by the United States, and to be ruled by their brother Malays of the Philippine Republic. In the process, they made their homeland of more than 2,000 coral atolls and volcanic isles, as well as their tropical sea, an unhealthy place for intruders. Where no natural frontier exists, they raised a human wall. Although Spain tried to push southward through the Indies, and although the Dutch and English occasionally penetrated northward to Luzon, the Sulu islanders held them apart.

In time, the wall became a political boundary, the only important one left in the Indies. It is this boundary and its adjoining borderlands, Mindanao and North Borneo, that concern us here. Mindanao, the second largest and potentially the richest of the Philippines, bears the imprint of three colonial philosophies. First an outpost of Spain, then a special ward of the United States, it remains essentially a dependency of Manila. Borneo fell under the rule of the Netherlands and Britain, who divided its vast area amicably and proceeded to neglect their respective slices. When history delivered the Indies back into Asian hands after World War II, it left the northern third of Borneo, with characteristic untidiness, in the hands of imperial Britain. The Colony of North Borneo, a lonely outpost of London, still holds one end of the broken lifeline of empire and still trails Victorian petticoats beneath its modern dress. The two borderlands, Mindanao and North Borneo, have necessarily grown apart. They face in different directions, operate on different wave lengths. So effective is the frontier between them that they might almost be on opposite coasts of the Pacific.

Crossing the Sulu Sea

To understand a frontier one should cross it, if possible. But to cross the Sulu Sea is more easily resolved than done. It is a small body of water compared with the South China Sea to the west of it, the Celebes Sea to the south, and the vast Pacific stretching eastward. It is a reasonably well-behaved body of water; tropical typhoons pass it by, and largely for this reason men have made good use of it for trade, conquest, and piracy. The legitimate traveler, trader, explorer, or botanist on peaceful missions always faced certain risks in getting across. But in recent times the highway has been firmly closed to him. The Sulu Sea is simply not for crossing. This island-studded puddle refuses to conform in a world that everyone knows is shrinking.

The passage from Mindanao to North Borneo should be

a routine matter. Mindanao's southernmost arm stretches like a crab's claw into the Sulu Sea. On its tip perches the seaport of Zamboanga. Two hundred miles across the sea, the seaport of Sandakan provides a busy back door, a sort of tradesman's entrance to North Borneo. Both towns have up-to-date airports, but no plane service links them. Both have harbors, but no scheduled passenger ships ply between them. At the Philippine Embassy in Washington, an official well acquainted with the area discussed the problem of crossing the Sulu Sea. He said there were occasional passenger ships, but these would not be "suitable" for American travelers. Why? They were usually chartered by Moslem pilgrims, and were always overcrowded. Sometimes they capsized and sank without trace. As for making the brief journey by freighter, this would be "extremely unsuitable." Cargo ships might well be manned by pirates or smugglers, in which event the Philippine Navy must give chase and shoot them up in line of duty. At this point, the conversation lapsed into perplexed silence. Then the official said: "It is just possible that the Philippine Navy might ferry you across, but you will have to ask about that in Manila." It was this suggestion that eventually led us to Zamboanga, 450 miles south of Manila, on the Sulu Sea.

Zamboanga is a name that Americans of two generations, separated by almost half a century, have reason to remember. One generation took it over peacefully from the Spaniards in 1899; another won it back from the Japanese in 1945. Between these two operations, many outside influences shaped the city: American soldiers and administrators; American saloons and schools; merchants and planters from Switzerland, Australia, China, and Britain. (Somehow, also, the city's name became attached to a popular American song, the burden of which was that "the monkeys have no tails in Zamboanga.") But if any influence predominates, it is the durable stamp of Spain. To realize this, one should take a short walk down Spanish Street,

from the City Hall through a grove of towering acacias, out
to a point of land surrounded on three sides by the sea.
Here the abandoned Spanish fortress of Nuestra Señora del
Pilar broods over the tranquil scene. On its wall of forbidding stone, a bronze tablet records Zamboanga's violent
past in capsule form:

> Fort Pilar: Founded as southern outpost of the
> Spanish domain under the supervision of Melchior
> de Vera 1635; attacked by the Dutch 1646; de-
> serted when troops were concentrated in Manila
> to drive away Chinese pirates 1663; reconstructed
> by the Society of Jesus 1666; rebuilt under the
> management of Juan Secarra 1719; stormed by
> Dalase King of Bulig with 3000 Moros [2] 1720; can-
> nonaded by the British 1798; witnessed the mutiny
> of 70 prisoners 1872; abandoned by the Spaniards
> 1898; occupied by the Americans under General
> J. C. Bates 1899; seized by the Japanese 1942;
> taken over by the Republic of the Philippines
> 4 July 1946.

Under the wall of the fortress, which the Spaniards saw
fit to dedicate to the sorrowful Virgin, Zamboangans have
built a shrine. Toward evening, as the sun, a red ball, drops
into the sea, they stroll out to the fort to light a candle to
the Lady patroness. It is an appropriate gesture. The
shrine, like the fort, is an outpost. Here ends the empire of
Christianity; just out to sea begins the empire of Islam.
Here also ends the undisputed authority of the government
of the Philippine Republic.

But Zamboanga is in no sense a ghost town. It has a
provincial character of its own, and a spirit about which
Manila knows little and cares less. The man Zamboangans

[2] The Spaniards called the Moslem Malays of the Sulu Sea *Moros*,
probably a variation of *Maurus* which was the name of the Moslem natives
they had known in Mauretania in northwest Africa.

elected as their Mayor embodies this spirit to a remarkable degree. He is Cesar Climaco, an accomplished young politician of the Fiorello La Guardia school. His passion for civic uplift can be seen all over the town: in traffic lights, in public gardens, in street signs exhorting the citizens to "Keep your city clean—put rubbish here," in the newly built market, and finally in the Mayor's pet project, a children's amusement park. Mayor Climaco's perquisites of office include a sleek American sedan. He holds this in reserve for visiting dignitaries and prefers to drive his own jeep around town, waving gaily to his fellow Zamboangans. From his exposed desk on the broad veranda of the City Hall go defiant telegrams to Manila, which the Mayor accuses—not without cause—of ignoring his city's existence.

A five-minute walk down Madrid Street from the City Hall leads to another hallmark of Zamboanga's character: the hotel of Antonio Bayot. Behind the traditional high walls of a Spanish home, a collection of frame houses rambles along the sea front. Recently, on his seventieth birthday, Mr. Bayot assembled his large clan and about 500 of the town's notables to celebrate. The party was an animated portrait of the city's elite: professional men and women, wealthy planters and their wives from the nearby island of Basilan, prosperous Chinese merchants, and an occasional European cleric in white cassock. It was an elite with sophistication and local pride. A mark of its sophistication was that Mayor Climaco's political opponents were neither in prison nor leading a terrorist band in the jungle; they were his amiable fellow guests at the party. One learns in Asia to appreciate such things in a capital, to marvel at them in a borderland.

At Zamboanga the Philippine Navy takes charge of the journey. It ties up at the end of the long municipal pier in the form of *La Union*, a 200-ton subchaser type. Built during World War II for the United States Navy, she measures 130 feet in length, mounts a three-inch gun and two fifty-caliber machine guns. *La Union*'s regular mission, said her young commander, Lieutenant Simeon Alejandro, was to hunt pirates and smugglers on the Sulu Sea. Her special and immediate mission now is to ferry two strangers safely wherever they want to go—within reason. Thus at six o'clock one warm, sunny morning, the ship weighs anchor. Like the background music in an old-fashioned silent film, the Sulu Sea begins to act up. Dark, menacing clouds hang low in the sky. The tail of a typhoon passing farther north lashes the waters. *La Union* wallows bravely south and east, past a string of small islands.

After about six hours of tossing, the ship heads into the protected harbor of Jolo. A fleet of small boats has taken refuge there, and *La Union*'s three-inch gun covers them. Jolo's long wooden pier is evidently the late-afternoon gathering place of the men of the town. As *La Union* sidles up to it, the animated company of about thirty freezes into immobility, as if posing for a still picture, eyes riveted on the deck. One of the ship's crew tosses a rope onto the pier; nobody jumps to catch it. Nobody moves a muscle. The rope slips into the water. Again it is tossed ashore. A sailor leaps from ship to pier and ties up. Another slides into place the narrow board that serves as a gangplank. The captain walks across it; his passengers follow under the cold, hard stares of the citizens of Jolo. Clearly the Philippine Navy is not welcome in this part of the Republic. One almost expects a cry of "Cheese it—the cops!" and a general scramble for safety.

The city of Jolo is the capital of the 2,000-island province of Sulu. Colloquially known as Moroland, it crowds as much of the wonder and beauty of nature into a small space as any part of the Indies. On the island of Jolo, which is not much larger than Greater New York, explorers have found an awesome volcanic crater as well as forested foothills and fertile rice fields. But all this is denied to the outsider. The Moro has padlocked Jolo against the world. Nowhere on his own water and earth are life and property secure. A rough estimate recently put the number of outlaws roaming the islands at more than 1,200. Because of them, no family can feel safe fishing from its boat, farming in its field, or sleeping in its home. Because of outlaws, peaceful persons go armed as well. This they can do, for the American forces carelessly left behind more than 10,000 rifles after liberating the Sulu Sea from the Japanese.

In the crowded market place of the town, scrawny boys sling mudballs and then dodge behind wagons. A teen-age youth darts alongside and grabs the stranger by the arm. "Rolex? Rolex?" he whispers. Swiss watches, cigarettes, cosmetics, and a profusion of other luxury items fill the rickety stalls.

As darkness falls, the Filipino gunboat captain asks his passengers to board *La Union*. He posts an armed sailor to stand watch through the night. Heat, flies, and unfamiliar sounds combine to drive away sleep. More disturbing is the question: what afflicts Jolo? One expects to find poverty and neglect in any Asian city. All too soon, the Westerner loses his first sense of shock. It is not Jolo's misery that causes the flesh to creep. The place has a furtive quality. It smells of fear.

Here a stranger's diagnosis can go astray. The Western scale of values tends to connect human dignity with civic concern. Clean streets, tidy gardens, a law-abiding citizenry —these are thought to manifest a people's pride and self-respect, and often they do. Zamboanga, for example, expresses these values, but Zamboanga has absorbed massive doses of Western cultures. In Jolo, it is necessary to reverse this reasoning. The Moro seems to equate personal dignity with defiance of non-Moslem law and authority. His pride and self-respect swell in direct proportion to his prowess as a fighter. To refuse to co-operate with Manila and its agents becomes a virtue. The elected Mayor, an intelligent Moslem, wishes he could stop the violence. In his City Hall, a frame building in need of plaster and paint, he beseeches the United States to clean up Jolo. How? By buying the 10,000 illegally held weapons at $100 apiece. Across town, spacious barracks house the representatives of the armed forces of the Philippines. Manila has sent well-trained officers to pacify Sulu Province. They exhibit photographs of the dead bandits their men have trapped and shot. But they do not pretend to be making much headway or to know the answer. At another headquarters, that of the Roman Catholic mission, a powerfully built man claims to be one of the few who can walk unarmed and safely in the countryside of Jolo. The Most Reverend Francis J. McSorley, Prefect Apostolic of Sulu, believes that his cassock is his shield, and thus far he has been right. He would like to send some of his Oblate Fathers into rural Jolo to teach the farmers to grow better crops. He, as well as the Mayor, would like to see the long-proposed fish cannery built, as a sensible way of putting Moros peacefully to work. Perhaps most important of all, in the Bishop's opinion, is to teach respect for law in the schools which his mission conducts on six of the 457 islands of his diocese. "If in the next ten years we can get that idea across to our children," he says, "then we'll have accomplished something worth while for these people."

This was Jolo on the eve of the two great fires of October 19 and 21, 1960. Within forty-eight hours the flames wiped out three fourths of the town. When they finally died down, some 20,000 were homeless. Like Jolo's other services, its fire-fighting equipment was found utterly inadequate, and its brigades disorganized. The Mayor decreed a curfew. The Minister of Defense flew down from Manila to investigate. Suspicion fell on two Chinese merchants whose stocks had been well insured.

.   .   .

Following the Sulu Island chain, *La Union* churned south and west. The sea remained in a wicked mood until, just before sunrise, the gunboat sighted the last of the Philippines: a cluster of coral strands called the Turtle Islands. As the ship anchored off Taganak, the largest of the group, the sea changed abruptly from boiling pea soup into blue plate glass. The crew dropped an aluminum dinghy alongside. Two sailors armed with rifles, and a third carrying a walkie-talkie, rowed their passengers toward Taganak's gleaming beach. The Navy was taking no chances. Even a seemingly innocent sand spit, fringed with palms, might harbor outlaws. On that morning, Taganak belonged to its rightful owners, its 117 fishermen and their families. This atoll and its neighbors enjoy a special treasure and distinction. Giant turtles, eight to ten feet wide, use the warm sands as a hatchery. After dark they crawl out of the sea, dig great holes in the sand, lay their eggs, often more than a hundred at a time, cover them up, and waddle back into the water. Each turtle's path through the sand might have been made by a small tractor. According to those who have been lucky enough to catch a lady in the act of egg-laying, her concentration on the job is so intense that one can sit astride her great shell without distracting her. In the morning, islanders dig up the eggs, which resemble soggy ping-pong balls and have a strong fishy smell. Moros find them both tasty and marketable.

La Union's crossing had almost ended. There was no doubt: the border was real and man-made. On the horizon Borneo floated serenely under a dazzling sky. True to the literal Malay translation of its name, it was indeed a land below the wind.

Britain: To Pacify and Trade. 1881–

A burly Briton wearing white shorts, sport shirt, and golf stockings strode onto the newly built wooden dock at

Sandakan. The Resident had come to welcome strangers from across the Sulu Sea to British soil. This was the soil of Queen Elizabeth's youngest colony. On the Resident's broad shoulders lay the task of administering the largest of its four provincial parts. From him the chain of command ran directly to the Governor in Jesselton, 140 jungle miles to the west, thence to Whitehall and Buckingham Palace. But from the Governor upward the chain was long and slack. North Borneo is not just half a world away from London in miles; it is a world away from London's thoughts. The reason has nothing to do with the colony's size, which is about that of Scotland. Rather it is that the territory has lain, like some Victorian curio, half forgotten in a corner of the Empire's attic. For sixty-five years, under five sovereigns, it gathered dust as the property of a British-owned, London-directed, private Chartered Company. Not until 1946, after a cruel Japanese occupation, did the private preserve become a public ward of the Crown, a proper colony.

What a moment to be born a colony! North Borneo fell out of Mother England's attic and into her official lap at the very moment when other colonies were proclaiming themselves nations and, in some instances, even cutting the family ties. How would the imperial mother decide to raise this belated addition to the family? Would she experiment with modern ideas? Were the old-fangled ways now discredited? If the moment had not been so anguished, such questions might have simmered in Westminster. They might even have moved the government to appoint a Royal Commission to look into the whole business of colony-raising. But London had more immediate worries, among them the devastation of England itself. North Borneo was of small concern, if North Borneo was considered at all. Deposited on the doorstep of the Colonial Office, it set up a feeble cry for help. Allied bombs aimed at the Japanese had efficiently flattened most of what the Chartered Company had wrought in its sixty years of stewardship: a few small towns, docks, workshops, and plantations. Out of the rubble limped hundreds of near skeletons, the European survivors of Japanese prisons. As for those North Borneans whose home was the rubble itself, their needs were total: food, clothing, shelter, and a measure of public order in which to rebuild their simple lives.

A brigade of seasoned colonial officers stood ready to take charge and in so doing to write another chapter of imperial history. Some of the best in the service were about to be uprooted from India, Burma, Ceylon, and Malaya. Men serving in the Malay Peninsula could bring a special competence to the new colony just across the South China Sea: a knowledge of the culture and language of many of its people. Together with a few stalwart survivors of Chartered-Company rule, they were to shape and manage Britain's latest and probably its last new colonial venture.

The slate could hardly have been cleaner. In theory at least, the masters of the new colony could write any prescription they chose. No European rivals hovered over the Indies, as in the old days of empire building. Spain had left behind only an unsavory aroma. France and the Netherlands had received eviction notices. The United States was fulfilling its promise to step out of the Philippines and out of its unbecoming colonial role. Nobody challenged the birth of a new colony in the area. Yet a challenge was there, not European but Asian. It came from all sides, from the dissolving of old empires, from the hardening of new nationalisms, and finally from the chaos that followed the exit of colonial rule.

North Borneo lay and still lies in the eye of a political hurricane. Here there is no chaos, but peace and order; no national spirit, only faint stirrings of political awakening. A frontier in Frederick Jackson Turner's sense, North Borneo is "the outer edge of the wave—the meeting point between savagery and civilization." The land is hardly exploited and not even fully explored. Its people, only about 425,000 and thinly scattered, are not averse to being lightly governed and "brought along." The task would have delighted Raffles if he could have put his genius to work on it. For in this colony the time is early morning. The land holds up a shining morning face soaked by sun, doused by rain, almost untouched by man. Though the colony sits only four degrees from the equator, its air has a freshness rare in the tropics. The temperature seldom exceeds ninety degrees on the hottest days, and seldom falls below seventy on the coolest. It is a climate hospitable not only to man, but also to jungle, which clothes four fifths of the colony's surface. The jungle is in perpetual motion, spreading and growing. Wherever man scratches the surface, nature rushes in to cover the wound.

How does one pacify, govern, and develop a country that is four fifths jungle? In this element the European is a fish on a sandbank. He slogs down a jungle trail sucked by mud, drenched by cloudburst, assaulted by leeches, and periodically hit on the head by branches. In the same situation the North Bornean is happily at home. A six-year-old sets out at dawn to walk five miles to school—if he is so inordinately lucky as to have one within reach. He trots through the trailless wild, stops to kill a snake with his knife, and cooks it for breakfast over a fire he builds on the damp ground.

The European can move in small boats on North Borneo's rivers. He cuts jeep and pony trails through the forest, knowing they may be washed out and overgrown in short order. Never in all his eighty years of occupancy of the territory has he driven a road across it from east to west. Before the day of air travel, officers of the Chartered Company had to circumnavigate their property in ships, dodging rocks, reefs, and pirates, as if one had to sail around the northern tip of Scotland to reach Aberdeen from Glasgow. By 1962 the colony had eight airfields. In Sandakan, his headquarters on the Sulu Sea, the Resident can board a plane and report to the Governor in Jesselton on the South China Sea in a little more than an hour. Beneath the wings of his plane the forest rolls out an endless carpet of dark green. Approaching the west coast, the plane rises to 8,000 feet to cross the Crocker Range, and passengers focus their cameras on Mount Kinabalu. This is the cloud-capped crag of 13,455 feet, the highest point in the whole Malay Archipelago. Like Kanchenjunga, Ararat, and other borderland peaks the reader will encounter in these pages, Kinabalu evokes emotions in the people of the area. For the tribal folk who live within sight of it, the peak connotes the haunt of spirits and the gateway to heaven. For Australian survivors of the Japanese, its name spells horror. It was their Bataan, the setting of a death march in 1945 from which only six out of 1,406 prisoners returned.

Although the airplane is useful to the colony's brass, it is not a practical tool in the daily work of policing and ad-ministering. The men who do such jobs must literally cover the ground. And this means covering the jungle. The Chartered Company made one early gesture in the direction of jungle transport. It began in 1896 to build a 116-mile narrow-gauge railway along the coast and into the interior. The project was almost as ambitious in its Borneo context as tunneling the English Channel. Some of the Company's directors in London could not imagine anything more fool-ish or extravagant. They had a point. The railroad cost the Company £800,000 and took ten years to build. But it be-came an essential lifeline and by 1924 was paying divi-dends. Not a single locomotive, bridge, or mile of track survived the war intact. Yet by 1958 the railway was once more a going concern, with fifteen locomotives traveling nearly 10,000,000 passenger miles and carrying 51,000 tons of freight in that year. Even with this sturdy vein, the colony's circulation system remains feeble. Its lifeblood trickles mainly through tiny capillaries of jeep and pony trails. The country cries out for arteries: all-weather roads, of which it had in 1958 less than 300 miles, including those in the towns. How else to chart its forest wealth, or cultivate its upland valleys that are waiting for cash crops? How else to reach and develop its richest untapped resource, the people themselves?

[1]

About 2,000 Westerners and Eurasians sit on the point of North Borneo's broad-based human pyramid. The Chartered Company did not attract many colonists to its property, nor did it lure wildcat speculators in search of gold and diamonds. For reasons hard to explain, the Company was content to feed modestly on rubber (a smidgeon compared with Malaya's), on speculative tobacco, on copra, hemp, and timber. As a result, North Borneo enterprises, all of them private, needed the services of only a few hundred British managers and businessmen, plus the unskilled labor of a few thousand natives. Outside this narrow circle, the vast majority of North Borneans went about their own business of hunting, farming, and fishing, little affected by the enterprises or even the presence of the Europeans on the lofty point of the pyramid.

Who are these North Borneans? The tribes living deep in the interior are Dusuns,[3] Muruts, and other pagans who fled inland when waves of Malays landed from Southeast Asia and neighboring islands. Christianity made converts among the pagans. Among the Malays, the Moslem religion took hold and survived. A third contingent, small but important, had been sailing across from China long before the first Europeans came. The Company was able to subdue the ill-organized assortment with never more than 500 trained police and a score of British in command. It was a triumph of persistence and courage. There remains no

---

[3] *Dusuns* prefer to be known as *Kedazans*, but they have not yet succeeded in popularizing that name. To avoid confusion, we shall stick to the familiar name of *Dusuns*.

vestige of rebellion and little crime. North Borneans are as secure as any Asians and more law-abiding than most. A foreigner may not be welcome, but he is not likely to be knifed in the jungle or felled by a poison dart.

Among the tribes, the short, smooth-skinned, brown Dusuns are the most settled and easiest to "bring along." There are Dusun clerks in government offices, Dusun drivers, schoolteachers, and farmers. One finds Dusuns working in the rice fields and rubber groves that flank the railway for its first fifty-six miles south of Jesselton. Then the line turns abruptly inland, and for the next forty miles it cuts through a natural incision in the jungle, the Padas River gorge. The Padas is known as a haunt of crocodiles, which can be spotted sunning their scales on a mudbank. Occasionally a Padas crocodile catches a child or an old woman and enjoys a feast. Wild pigs scuttle along the right of way; wild geese squat placidly on the tracks and bring the train to a halt. In this upland hunting country live the Muruts, a tribe that appears to be evaporating, the victim of malaria, tuberculosis, and perhaps also a home-brewed rice wine. The last of the North Borneans reluctantly to renounce head-hunting, the Murut still carries at his waist a dagger hung with human hair and over his shoulders a long, slender blowpipe. Although firearms must be licensed in the colony, there are no restrictions on blowpipes or on the poison-tipped darts that can kill a man in ten minutes. This equipment is taken for granted as necessary for hunting animals. The assumption has held true for several decades except during the four years of Japanese presence. Like other tribesmen who would rather hunt than farm, Muruts—when they do farm—practice slash-and-burn cultivation, to grow dry rice and millet for food.

While the Muruts are fading into the jungle or filtering down to the coast, the colony's seafaring people seem to be multiplying. The largest group is the Bajaus, the Moslem sea gypsies of Malay origin. From prosperous piracy, the

Chartered Company forced them into fishing and, in recent years, stock raising. Wherever one comes upon a village built over the water, each house a box on stilts with a small boat moored to it, this is likely to be a community of Bajaus or a related band of former pirates.

Over the Dusun, Murut, Bajau, and smaller tribal groups, the colonial authorities wield a mild and paternal scepter. They sum up the job in seven words: keep them quiet and bring them along. This policy fits three out of four North Bornean subjects of the Queen. The fourth belongs in a different category. He is Chinese and he does not need to be brought along. Indeed, he is coming along all too fast.

The town of Sandakan, raised from the ashes of war, suggests perhaps as well as anything what the Chinese means to North Borneo. The colony's metropolis of 15,000 people sprawls along a strip of the west coast and then climbs a steep hillside. A new courthouse, modern and white, stands halfway up the hill. Its architect is Parker Kwan, a Chinese. In the nearby post office, equally modern, a clerk who weighs and stamps letters is a Chinese. On the town's spacious playing field a cricket game is in progress. It might be a Saturday afternoon at Eton, except that the players, in spotless white, are all Chinese. They are students at the large high school, part of the remarkable education system founded, staffed, and largely financed by the Chinese community for its own children. Inside a new recreation club, British and Chinese members cluster around the bar over gimlets and beer. The club's president is a wealthy Chinese. Their number and influence grow. Literate, enterprising, and free from discrimination, these Overseas Chinese have a better lot than their brethren anywhere else in Asia, and they know it. They are, of course, products of the great Chinese emigration to Southeast Asia which has gone on for centuries. It spurted in the nineteenth and early twentieth centuries as the call went out for coolie labor from the Dutch Indies, French Indochina, British Malaya, and the American Philippines. Colonial masters found the Chinese indispensable, not just for the rough work of plantations, roads, and mills, but also as minor officials and links with the indigenous peoples. The word filtered back to overcrowded southern China: there was work, opportunity, even land; and thousands streamed into the colonies as indentured labor. When the struggle was too hard, they died of tropical diseases or somehow worked their way back home. But many stayed to prosper and multiply as merchants, farmers, or a combination of the two. Gradually a middle class of Chinese emerged, of shopkeepers, rice millers, rubber brokers, and moneylenders. Little by little they came to control the finances and essential services from cities to jungle villages throughout Southeast Asia.

The North Borneo authorities are not unmindful of the speed with which the Chinese are multiplying in their own colony. Without sizable immigration, the community doubled its numbers between 1931 and 1958, when the total reached 102,000. The rate of growth has been more than twice that of the native community. That the Chinese were still only a fourth of the population was small comfort. In skill and power, the distance between them and the rest was widening. Fifty or even twenty-five years ago, the non-Chinese majority in North Borneo might have had a chance someday to inherit their country. If the Company had "brought them along" faster, they could, perhaps, have competed with the Chinese minority. But the Chinese were allowed a head start, and they made the most of it. Why should a commercial enterprise, even one chartered by the Crown, be expected to act with political foresight and social vision? In fairness to the Company, one should remember that colonial governments were not conspicuously wiser. Not a single one in Southeast Asia envisioned or met the problem of Chinese economic and intellectual dominance.

In recent years the British in Borneo have begun to control the Chinese schools; they are also severely limiting Chinese immigration. Artisans can come into the colony only on a temporary basis, under contract. A few selected farmers are welcome as permanent settlers because they are pioneers. None, of course, may enter from Communist China itself. North Borneo Chinese are the first to oppose the opening of the gates to even a few Chinese immigrants. The last thing they want is sudden change. The worst thing that could happen to them would be an invasion of unskilled labor to develop the colony. On this subject there is a large degree of consensus. Almost everybody has an interest in keeping things pretty much as they are. More than anyone, the British provide the reasons why North Borneo has changed so little, why it is still early morning on the colony's clock.

[2]

How does it happen that the clock has ticked so slowly? To find the answer, it is worth looking briefly at North Borneo's sixty-five years as the property of a private company.

The early European explorers and colonizers did not seriously bid for North Borneo. Its two native Moslem rulers, the Sultans of Brunei and Sulu, claimed the land between them, though neither controlled it. Not until the 1860's did an oddly assorted band of Chinese and American adventurers reach for the plum. Their leader, Claude Lee Moses, was reported to have deserted from the United States Navy. He "bought" but never paid for a large tract of what the Sultan of Brunei claimed. On it Moses put out a shingle "American Consulate," and offered to protect American settlers in return for a cut of their profits. A small Chinese-American settlement lasted for about a year. Then the bubble burst for lack of money and official American backing. In 1875 there arrived on the scene a slightly less shifty and shifting band of British. Their temporary leader, an Austrian, Baron

Overbeck, from Hong Kong, ran guns to the Sultan of Sulu
and wangled from that trustful ruler his claim to Borneo.
The Baron called the deal "cession" and promised the Sultan an annual "rent" of 5,000 Straits dollars. At the same
time, the Baron offered the Sultan of Brunei a flat 15,000
Straits dollars for the land on which Moses had defaulted.
In the manner of the period, the adventurers set up "con-
sulates" and "residencies" on their real estate, and hoisted
the Union Jack.

The gamble survived because a respectable London businessman decided to put capital into it. He was Alfred Dent,
who formed a Company and, over the protests of the British
Colonial Office, persuaded the Foreign Office to grant it a
royal charter. Helping Dent to extend British power was
none other than the Liberal government of William Ewart
Gladstone, the professed anticolonialist, the enemy of the
Forward Policy of expansion on Britain's Indian frontier.
The device of a Chartered Company suited the Liberals'
purpose. It was a quasi-private venture, from which the
government could dissociate itself. The Company was
pledged to abolish slavery but otherwise respect the local
culture, giving the enterprise a moral tone. The thing would
not cost the British taxpayer a penny; the stockholders, all
Britons, might in fact turn an honest pound. Without imperial stigma, an imperial purpose was served, namely to secure a new link in the lifeline of Empire.

The men who conquer and rule others, as distinct from
the historians, usually discover a moral rationale for their
careers. For North Borneo, one moralist was Sir West Ridgeway, a lusterless but tireless imperial servant. After duty in
Persia, Afghanistan, Ceylon, and South Africa, Ridgeway
retired with many letters after his name, to become in 1910
President of the British North Borneo Company. In that capacity he explained, quite simply, how the Company came
to be. "This corner of Borneo," wrote Sir West, "—most important from its strategic position, commanding the routes

between China and Europe on the one hand, and China and Australia on the other—was in danger of being acquired by a Foreign Power, when at the eleventh hour a small body of English gentlemen stepped in and purchased it from the native rulers." Which was the power more "foreign" to Borneo than his own? Who were the "gentlemen"? Sir West did not say. Nor did he bother to mention the slight misunderstanding over the meaning of "purchase." The Sultan of Sulu maintained, as his heirs still do, that his claim was leased, not sold. As evidence, the Sultan cited the annual "rent." Out of such mishaps are empires built.

The North Borneo Company prospered, though modestly, for it never dug deep into the hidden riches of the jungle. Not wishing to engage directly in development or trade, it sold concessions to planters, timber companies, and the trading firm of Harrisons and Crosfield (Borneo) Ltd., which, being both canny and first on the scene, did not do too badly. The firm's man on the spot likes to tell the story of the visit of one of the directors from London, who remarked that pirates seemed to have diminished along the Borneo coast. "Yes, sir," said the local Resident who was guiding him. "They cleared out soon after Harrisons and Crosfield appeared on the scene."

As the Chartered Company developed its property indirectly, so did it govern. Being weak and relatively poor, it had no choice but to lean on native chieftains as instruments of rule. It was a holding operation, run on a shoestring by a skeleton staff of experts in gradualism. No hustler needed to apply. It took twenty-one years to clean up the most blatant forms of slavery. Although the period was one of major discoveries about tropical diseases, the new knowledge trickled like molasses to North Borneo. Both malaria and beriberi greeted the Japanese in chronic form when they came as conquerors in 1942 to end the Chartered Company's rule. In its last twenty years, however, the Company did try to curb smallpox and yaws. And it allowed the Rockefeller Foundation to come and show how hook-worm could be wiped out. Gradually health measures came to be recognized as not only humanitarian but profitable.

The same could not be said of education. That, in the Company's view, was a private matter. The Chinese community took care of its own children. A few native children squeezed into missionary schools. To expose the masses to education was considered extravagant nonsense. Moreover, it was dangerous. Besides, there was no demand for it. In the 1930's, a progressive Governor named Douglas J. Jardine tried to break down the walls of lethargy. By this time, there was no question about a demand. Native chieftains had besought the Governor to give their children schooling in their own languages. (The Malay language seemed and still seems to the British the practical alternative to the multiplicity of native tongues.) By 1941 there were twenty-eight government-supported primary schools serving 1,663 native children, and every school had a long waiting list. The Japanese stamped out this flicker of learning. Such was the Company property dropped at the end of World War II on the British Colonial Office doorstep.

[3]

In the second half of the twentieth century there are not many places left on the earth where one can still study the early phases of colonialism. One such place is North Borneo, which is re-enacting the pantomime in its essentials. The chief actor is, of course, the Governor, a constant reminder of the protection and majesty of the Crown. The Governor relies on his Secretariat to administer the colony. The pantomime requires him to have two councils, one "executive" and one "legislative." These simulate respectively a cabinet and a parliament. The more adventurous of these bodies is the Legislative Council, or "Legco" in the idiom of colonialism. To this nursery school of self-government, the Governor appoints nine "official" members from his own staff and ten "unofficial" or nominated members from any source. Since 1955 the Governor has permitted local organizations to submit a panel of names from which he selects some of the Unofficials. They include prominent Chinese and Moslem Malay leaders, an Anglo-Dusun newspaper editor, and one or two of the pagan chieftains. While the Unofficials hold a nominal majority, the Governor has taken care to number among them three prominent members of the British community, including the chief representative of Harrisons and Crosfield. He thus assures himself of a British majority of the Council, one that can be relied upon to support his measures. Someday this precaution may come in handy. The Legco has so far done its duty and raised its right hand collectively for every important government motion.

The semiannual meeting of the Legco opens with a pageant. The North Borneo Police and its brass band, splendid in red fezzes and white breeches, assemble for review on the Governor's badminton court. His Excellency, half smothered under a white-plumed helmet, walks stiffly between the police lines and takes the salute. The band plays *God Save the Queen.* In the modest council chamber adjoining Government House, "H.E." takes his place on a dais. The Legco has already assembled around a long table below. At the far end of the hall sit two rows of English ladies, formal in hats and white gloves. H.E. reads his budget message, much of which suggests the annual report of Harrisons and Crosfield's Chairman of the Board. The "debate" that follows may spark a question from an unofficial member. Often this question reveals how poor is his comprehension of the measure and its background. Why should he understand it? He has had no part in preparing it, no experience in the daily administration of the colony. Toward the end of the two-day session, Unofficials may offer criticism and suggestions. The Governor encourages them, as a good teacher encourages a shy pupil. The Legco, one feels, is well produced, but a mere puppet show, a game of playing Parliament. It puts a tiny elite through the gestures of power without responsibility. Below this layer, few get the training needed to manage self-government when it arrives. The same game used to be played in other non-self-governing colonies in more leisurely days. In North Borneo, "the dogmas of the quiet past" still rule.

Like many small capitals, Jesselton magnifies its own importance in the colonial structure. Modern and pleasant, but not plush, the town and its people are far removed from the jungle and its people. Closer to the realities of North Bornean life are the colony's eleven district officers, the men at the end of the line. For the district officer is the driving wheel of the old-fashioned engine of colonial government. Take him away and the contraption would rattle and wheeze but get nowhere.

The range of his duties is awesome. Over a wilderness bigger than many American counties, he is supposed to preside like a Pooh Bah: registrar of births and deaths, certifier of land transactions, budget officer of every township, maintenance officer for the pony trails, solemnizer of marriages where he is asked to be, dispenser of justice in lesser cases, the eyes and ears of the colonial government, and the Queen's man on the spot in crises great or small. When we stayed with a young district officer and his wife in their bungalow deep in the interior, the crisis happened to be a flood. It had engulfed villages and made hundreds of families homeless. The "D.O." was organizing relief, bombarding Jesselton with reports and appeals for help. He was using the local school to house the homeless, and his wife was working around the clock to see that food, clothes, and medicine reached the victims. To the "D.O." the unexpected is routine. A flood, a plague, an insect pest, however hard to reach across swampland or forest, these are simply among the hazards of the job. It is not a life for sissies, snobs, or fools.

In the days of the Chartered Company, a district officer needed only to be a gentleman of good character, meaning the product of a British public school. This standard no longer applies. Virtually every district officer recruited since 1946 for the new colony has come equipped with a university degree. In addition he must undergo a year of postgraduate training at Oxford or Cambridge, plus three months of language study at the University of London's School of Oriental and African Studies. The district officers are, in short, a brand-new crop; often they are adventurous in thought as well as temperament. Their advent has produced stirrings of change. It is partly to their credit that the colony has undertaken six experiments in local self-government. The first was launched in 1951 with the district of Kota Belud, a farm market town in the foothills of the Crocker Range about fifty miles up the coast from Jesselton. A center of rich farmland, Kota Belud comes to life on market day. Dusun and Bajau families ride their buffaloes to market, tether them in a shady grove, pay a parking fee, and plunge into the Bornean equivalent of an Iowa state fair. The market is one responsibility of Kota Belud's mixed native and Chinese local authority. In addition, the authority can raise and spend revenue and regulate agriculture, irrigation, buildings, and public health, all of course under the careful tutelage of the district officer.

How Jesselton views the process was explained in 1958 by the Governor: "We here in North Borneo are seeking to preface the accepted forms of democracy by its day-to-day practice, in the deliberate hope that the emergence of a normal democratic constitution will be a natural growth, the various stages of which will attract little more attention than does the spectacle of a boy growing out of his pants."

This reflects the belief that only extreme gradualism can save North Borneo from racial strife. A pervasive fear of such strife prompted the Governor to report to the Legislative Council in these terms: "We have the problem of two racial societies, widely different in background, culture, and standards. Their ability to live together so amicably is a matter almost for wonder. But let us not delude ourselves. The possibilities of conflict are always there; unless we move cautiously they will be realized here as they have been realized in so many other countries. . . . And I do most solemnly advise that nothing in the nature of the electoral process should be introduced until our native peoples are strong enough to play their full part."

The advice was sound, but sadly out of date. Time of itself does not cause a boy to grow out of his pants. He must be well nourished as well, and in colonial terms this means educated to play his part in his world. Hardly three years after the Governor made his plea, North Borneo's first political party appeared. The founder was the young Anglo-Dusun newspaper editor and member of the Council, Donald Stephens. His party, he said, would be constructed on strictly interracial lines. In 1962, the colony expected to begin to elect some of the members of its local authorities.

The race was gathering speed: between education for political responsibility and politics itself, between the tortoise and the hare.

[4]

One of the first things to be inscribed on the new colony's slate was a concern for schooling. The responsibility which the Company had shunned the colony accepted. The goal of universal education, which the Japanese accepted for Hokkaido in 1872 and the United States for the Philippines in 1900, North Borneo accepted in 1946. This is how the colonial government listed its priorities: "firstly, rehabilitation and reconstruction; secondly, economic development; thirdly, the extension of social services; fourthly, the association of the local population in the work of government."

Splendid, but where was education? It was hiding in "social services." When, the uninitiated might ask, will governments think of education as an investment in human resources and bracket it with "economic development"? The colony's postwar economy shot ahead. By 1958 its exports outvalued the best prewar year six and a half times. Let us see what happened to education. In its first year, 1946, the devastated colony put just over 10,000 of its children into school. Three fourths of these attended Chinese and mission schools, or what could be salvaged of them. The government was able to provide teaching for 2,706 children, most of them native. This meant that one child out of twelve in the colony got to school that year, which considering the chaos of the time was a respectable effort. Twelve years later the restored colony reported a total of 40,000 children in school. Who was getting the teaching? Considerably more than half of this total, or 23,439, were Chinese, although Chinese represented less than a quarter of the colony's population. Moreover, the rate at which the government was expanding its public schools offered little hope to the native children who were not yet served. The Governor forecast in 1958 that between 2,000 and 3,000 new places could be provided in the years just ahead. At that rate, how long would it be before the native peoples could "play their full part"?

The prospects looked no less pinched when it came to the scope of education. The colony had high schools to accommodate only 3,000 children—again mostly Chinese; it had one trade school with fifty-six students, and not a single agricultural school. Except in the field of teacher training, a youth had to go abroad for higher education. And to accomplish this he had either to belong to a well-to-do family or win one of the 110 scholarships on which North Borneans in 1958 were studying overseas.

The colony's officials, to their credit, do not fall back on the old excuse that tribal people have no interest in schools. North Borneo echoes to the same popular clamor for education that can be heard throughout Asia. Villagers have not waited for bureaucracy to move. More than 125 North Bornean communities have gone to work and built schools for their children, hoping the government would send them teachers—not Oxford graduates or even the few score trained in the colony's fine new teacher-training school, Kent College. The Dusuns and Bajaus would gladly settle for sturdy sixth graders to drill the three R's into their young. What, then, are the limiting factors? Officials rightly answer "everything": roads, buildings, equipment, teachers, administrators, and teaching tools; and the overriding limitation: lack of money. Then they repeat the universal plaint of those who administer colonies: "We are poor; we support ourselves; to provide schools for all, even elementary schools, is quite beyond our means." In the main, British colonies have supported themselves without help from British taxpayers at home. After the war, Parliament passed a series of colonial development and welfare acts. Under these new programs North Borneo received a small grant for development purposes, such as new crops and public works. In 1958, for the first time, 2,000,000 Malayan dollars of this money ($666,000) was diverted to the building of schools.

Is the colony really poor? And if so, why? To measure wealth in colonial terms one must consider the motives of colony-seekers. The earliest urge seems to have been to find gold or its equivalent and take it home. The idea of staying to enjoy one's riches on the spot came later, as did the impulse to seize a strategic spot ahead of a rival power. Thus what one could take home by dint of trade, robbery, extraction from the soil, or a combination of all three, became an important measurement of a colony's value. By this standard North Borneo can be rated modestly useful. We say "modestly" because it lacks, so far, the most glittering and fluid of assets, the modern form of gold: namely, oil. The colony's main wealth is in its massive stands of virgin forests. Only partially mapped, and hardly cut, the jungle stands a fair chance of survival. The authorities proclaim an impeccable conservation policy. If only they can muster the money, the men, and the backbone to fulfill it, timber alone could keep North Borneo out of debt for many a year. Timber, rubber, and copra account for more than three fourths of the value of what the colony sells abroad.

Two of the other forest products deserve mention, not for their value but because they have for generations added to North Borneo's renown. Long before English gentlemen rushed in to save the territory from a "foreign power," Chinese had taken an interest in the territory for other reasons. One was their passion for a soup made from birds' nests. On an island in Sandakan bay, vast limestone caves shelter myriads of swallowlike birds called swifts. Out of their saliva, a sticky white substance, the swifts make nests. And out of their nests the Chinese have, from time unmeasured, made a soup which some gourmets permit themselves to call "great."

Mangrove swamps along the east coast yield another strange substance. In a shed on the Sandakan waterfront one can watch the processing of mangrove bark into cutch, an extract used to dye khaki cloth and to tan leather. The bark bubbles in giant vats and dries to the consistency of brown sawdust. Then it is stuffed into bags and shipped mostly to the United States. Cutch is one of the few raw materials processed from start to finish in the colony. For North Borneo's is a typical colonial economy. It sends its resources abroad, either raw or partly processed and therefore cheap; it imports mainly what has been processed and is therefore expensive. From the outflow of raw materials and the influx of manufactured goods the colonial government derives most of its revenue in the form of customs duties. The export of cheap raw materials keeps the colony's revenue low and limits what it can spend for roads, schools, and other development. Here we have the chief explanation for colonial "poverty."

There is another reason. Colonies start "poor" because
they part with their resources raw, keeping their government revenues low. Colonies remain poor because they also
part with most of the profits from their resources. Instead
of being plowed back into the colonies, the profits go to
stockholders in London. The dividends that dribbled from
North Borneo could not have kept many stately homes of
England in repair. But what a different kind of property the
Crown would hold today if more of the profits had been
plowed back into North Borneo over the past seventy years,
to be reinvested in mills and canneries, water power and
roads, and the training of North Borneans! Even after fifteen years of good intentions, its people remain the colony's
most wasted asset. Its export industries put to use less than
one out of six of the so-called "gainfully employed."

There is a fixed belief among Britons in the colony that
only substantial injections of outside capital can break the
circle of colonial poverty. Capital, however useful, may not
suffice. The governments of the new nations are pumping
impressive proportions of their regular budgets into the
building of new school systems. Cambodia, for example,
which does not roll in wealth, has been putting 20 per cent
of its revenue into education. New African countries are
also thinking in bold terms. They are beginning to treat education as a gainful economic investment, not a welfare item.
North Borneo has not yet freed itself from the old groove.
Even as the Governor vowed his concern for schooling, he
was presenting a budget that gave education hardly more
than 6 per cent of the year's ordinary expenditures. That
was the year, however, in which for the first time the government diverted to education 2,000,000 Malayan dollars
from its Colonial Development Fund, making the total just
over 7 per cent of the combined budgets. To catch up with
the new nations of Asia and Africa, the youngest colony
would have to think and act anew, a doubtful prospect.

Stability and gradualness are not just colonial treasures.

They are values of British life that have held the Empire and now the Commonwealth on a steady course. They have kept North Borneo safe for the moment from the hurricane that swirls around it.

What could be the political future of such bits and pieces of Empire as North Borneo and its British neighbors, Sarawak and the protectorate of Brunei? Is it to be independence for each to pursue its own course, naked to the hurricane? If so, what are the chances of their survival, first against Indonesian nationalism, eventually against Communist China? When, in 1958, the Governor of North Borneo put out feelers toward a closer association among the three Borneo fragments of Empire, he was quickly rebuffed. Little Brunei, rich in oil, refused even to talk about it. By the end of 1961, however, another and bolder idea had reached the talking stage. An old word, *Malaysia,* has been given a new meaning by the Tengku Abdul Rahman, the elected Prime Minister of independent Malaya. The idea is to federate five former and remaining pieces of Empire into a single independent state, *Malaysia.* Independent Malaya, with about 7,000,000 people, would naturally dominate the federation. Singapore, a self-governing but not yet independent city-state, would add 1,600,000, while the three dependencies, North Borneo, Sarawak, and Brunei, would more than double the land area but contribute less than 1,250,000 people. The motivation was, of course, to prevent Singapore, four fifths Chinese and leftish in politics, from cutting adrift, and to rope it loosely but safely to dependable Malaya, its commercial hinterland and natural complement. The addition of the three Borneo dependencies would keep the over-all population balance of the new Malaysia non-Chinese, as its name implies. At the rate the Chinese were multiplying, however, it was doubtful how long the balance would last. Proponents of the scheme talked about getting it under way by 1963. But it presented many problems, one of which no one seemed able to unravel.

What about the right of self-determination? The citizens of
Singapore and the independent Malayans had reached a
level of political sophistication at which they could be asked
to vote on their future. But the Bornean Dusuns, Dyaks,
Muruts, and Bajaus were not ready even to take over their
own governments. Would the British decide to put them as
puppets through the motions of a plebiscite, knowing how
unequipped they were in the simplest knowledge and practice of politics? This dilemma itself is perhaps the most revealing commentary on the British stewardship of North
Borneo over more than eighty years.

Direct comparisons between colonial systems can only be
misleading. Every nation proceeds to rule another from its
own cultural base. Thus the British fashioned their system
out of their traditional values. Let us see how the Spanish
and American systems put their respective imprints on the
other side of the Sulu borderland.

Spain: To Plunder and Convert. 1565–1898

Spain was the first European power seriously to covet the
Philippines and to collide with the wall of Sulu islanders.
Fifty years after Magellan first staked out the claim for
King Charles, the Spaniards had the conquest and conversion of the northern islands well enough in hand to turn
southward. Their purpose was twofold. First they wanted
to lay hands on the trading metropolis of the area. From
Jolo, the islanders had sailed their ships to China and Japan
to fetch silks, silver, amber, and porcelain; to the northern
Philippines for gold dust, dyes, saltpeter, and slaves; to the
southern Indies for spices, rubies, copper, brass, cannons,
and gunpowder. Second, the Spaniards wanted to put a
stop to the raids of Sulu pirates up and down the coasts of
the Philippines. They never succeeded in either of their
purposes. During all its 333 years in the Philippines, Spain
was able to keep a garrison in Jolo for only thirty-two years

and a governor in the Sulu islands for only twenty-two years. History offers few examples of so dismal a failure of superior power and organization over so long a time. The experience suggests two possible explanations: one the nature of the Spanish attack, another the character of the resistance.

If the Spaniards had learned anything from their long and bloody encounter with Moslems in the Mediterranean, they did not apply it to the Philippines. In the first wave of every attack on the Sulu islanders, it was the warrior priests of Rome, sword in one hand, Cross in the other, who led the Spanish troops. Records of the time tell of the honors that Spain heaped on her fighting Fathers for bravery in battle. Could anything have stiffened Moro resistance more effectively than the sight of the Cross in the enemy's hand? In contrast, Islam had come to them peacefully, offering knowledge and prestige. The Mohammedan missionary had been a learned man. He arrived as an immigrant, backed by no church, no army, no organization. An educated man, he would attach himself to the local chieftain, perhaps marry his daughter and inherit his title. Thus, in 1450, Abu Bakr became the first Sultan of Sulu. And thus a descendant of the Prophet himself planted the faith on neighboring Mindanao.

About the character of the Malay there is a good deal of conflicting opinion. One need only take down Volume XIV of the 1945 *Encyclopaedia Britannica* to read: "The Malays are indolent, pleasure-loving, improvident. . . . They are addicted to gambling, and formerly were much given to fighting, but their courage on the whole is not high if judged by European standards. The sexual morality of the Malay is very lax. . . ." Thus the oracle spoke until 1959, when the outraged Malays of the newly independent Federation of Malaya protested. The author, Sir Hugh Clifford, G.C.M.G., G.B.E., F.R.G.S., had served as High Commissioner for the Malay States and as British Agent for Bor-

neo. At the other end of the critical spectrum, we find the
romantics. The first American Episcopal Bishop in the Philippines summed up the typical Moro as "a fanatic in religion, a pirate by choice, and a gentleman by instinct." An
American general who had the job of subduing them
judged them "the fiercest, proudest, and most powerful people in the Philippine Islands." Still another admiring American pronounced them "the best professional pirates in the
world."

[1]

What, exactly, is a professional pirate? There is no easy
answer. More sea robbers should settle down to give their
point of view in memoirs. For the most part, they have left
it to Conrad, Masefield, Stevenson, and a library of lesser
craftsmen to sing their world-wide sagas. An articulate pirate is said to have protested to Alexander the Great that
"because I pillage with one little ship I am called a pirate;
because you do it with a great navy you are called an emperor." Who, then, shall cast the first cutlass? From the
fourth century B.C., this has been a fair question. The
Dutch East India Company and other great trading firms
armed their ships with cannon and muskets to defend
themselves, as they put it, against rivals as well as pirates.
Sir Francis Drake loaded his *Golden Hind* with jewels and
specie for his Queen. Most of it he took from the ships of
Spain with which England was technically at peace.

To the Malays of the Sulu Sea, piracy was a profession
and a way of life. A young Moro would follow his father into
the fleet much as Junior follows Dad to Annapolis or West
Point. Or he might branch out and go into business for himself as a privateer. In that event, he would seek the approval of the Sultan, in return for one quarter of his booty.
The pirate fleet served as the Sultan's navy; he had no
other. It furnished him with status, money, slaves, and
wives.

The ships of the fleet were generally of two kinds. The *garay* was a narrow sailboat, about seventy feet long with room for up to fifty oarsmen. Superbly trained, the oarsmen were able to move against the wind and outmaneuver an enemy. The smaller *vinta* was a long canoe equipped with sail and bamboo outriggers. The *garay* mounted small brass cannon called *lantakas*, which the Moros obtained from the Chinese, along with many other things. A Sulu pirate wielded two personal weapons: an iron-tipped bamboo spear which he hurled with accuracy, and the deadly *kris* or wavy-edged sword for the final assault. His standard armor was a coat of carabao horn, cut into plates and held together with brass wire.

Without discrimination, the raiders preyed on one another, as well as on Chinese junks and European galleons and frigates. Wherever the returns seemed promising, they chased, boarded, killed, and looted, taking home the cargo and enslaving women and children they found aboard. When European ships arrived on the scene in the sixteenth century, the rewards multiplied. Thus the harassed Spaniards estimated that in 1645 more than 10,000 Christian slaves were held captive in Mindanao alone, while the harems of the Sulu islands were overflowing with women of every nationality in the area. Malay records, if they could be found, would probably rate this a boom year.

Not until the middle of the nineteenth century did piracy lose its attraction as a profitable profession and a good way of life. Then, in 1848, the arrival of steamships drove the "best people" out of the profession. Steam shifted the odds too heavily against the sail of the *garay* and the *vinta*. Whether the credit should go to the Spanish Navy or the British is a matter of dispute. Both claimed it. In any event, it took only a few steamboats to convince the Sulus that piracy was no longer the profession of a gentleman.

From that time on, the occupation degenerated. As gentlemen bowed out, riffraff, brigands, and outlaws took over to plague the gentlemen, as well as the British, Dutch, Spanish, and later the American conquerors. General Leonard Wood, the first American Governor of the Moro Province, had the satisfaction of capturing a whole pirate fleet in 1903, soon after he took office. "The days pass quickly and happily in this sort of work," he noted in his diary. The most notorious of all Sulu bandits eluded both British and Americans for three years until his capture in 1910. He was called Jikiri, and he had an unpleasant habit of cutting off the ears and fingers of his prisoners.

Malay piracy may have had its back broken by the steamship, but its arms flail destructively to this day. Not even the best effort of the police of British North Borneo and the Filipino Navy in collaboration have succeeded in ridding the Sulu Sea or its shores of holdup men. It is not uncommon to find an item such as the following in a Philippine newspaper: "Five Muslim fishermen were massacred by pirates in Bato-Bato, Sulu on September 15, after which the bodies were divested of everything of value. The pirates then gathered all the fish in the victims' fishing boat and escaped." Or the pirates catch up with the smugglers: "Off Tawitawi Island a *kumpit* [launch] with an illegal cargo of 250 cases of cigarettes was held up and robbed last night. . . ." Occasionally, an innocent-looking launch slips quietly up a river in North Borneo; its crew descends on a village shop, usually Chinese-owned, loots it, and kills the owner and his family. The colony's report for 1958 deals with the whole subject in three succinct sentences: "During July a party of armed men from the Philippines raided Bombay Burmah Trading Corporation Limited's timber camp at Kalabakan. There were no casualties but money and property were stolen. General piracy activity was reported off Kunak, Lahad Datu, in August."

The man who probably knew as much as anyone about modern pirates and their ways was Colonel A. R. "Dusty" Millar, a veteran of Canada's North-West Mounted Police.

Millar held the title of Acting Deputy Commissioner of North Borneo Police. He was actually the colony's anti-piracy director, and he worked in close harmony with the Royal Navy and Air Force in Singapore, as well as with Filipino authorities. On December 9, 1958, a dismal, cloudy day rare in North Borneo, we boarded a Malayan Airways Dakota in Jesselton, bound for Kuching in neighboring Sarawak, and found Colonel Millar a fellow passenger. He was on his way to Labuan and thence by Royal Air Force plane to Singapore, where he was scheduled to deliver a lecture to the Royal Air Force on antipiracy techniques. Under the Colonel's arm was a brown leather brief case bulging with exhibits and notes for his lecture. For about an hour he ranged conversationally over the subject of pirates. Out of his brief case he pulled a picture of three recently captured specimens. They were qualified to pose for the FBI's ten most wanted men. To clinch the analogy, they wore blue jeans, T-shirts, and baseball caps.

When our Dakota touched down at Labuan, Colonel Millar gathered up his brief case and mackintosh, stepped off the plane, boarded an RAF Shackleton flying boat that was waiting to fly him to Singapore—and was never seen again. The Shackleton disappeared without trace in the South China Sea. To piece together the record out of many assorted clues tells little about the fate of Colonel Millar. The last word from the Shackleton came at 12:30 p.m. At that time the flying boat signaled Singapore from over Sin Cowe reef, about a hundred miles west of the Philippines, an area still marked on maps as "unsurveyed" and "dangerous." The plane reported that it had spotted twelve or thirteen men on a coral reef, that it had directed a native fishing boat to the reef, and that the boat was about to pick up the stranded men. After that, silence.

A routine signal should have been received at 13:00 o'clock. None came. Then Singapore set in motion the biggest search in the history of its Far Eastern operations.

Nineteen British planes, one American, and one Philippine, plus merchant ships and the available British Navy, scoured the whole area. Three days later, a Shackleton based on North Borneo radioed back a clue. Flying near Sin Cowe reef, it sighted the letters "B-205," the identification of the missing plane, cut out of the grass on a lonely atoll. The New Zealand frigate *Rotoiti* hastened to the atoll and put a landing party ashore. Near the "B-205" markings they found a fresh grave, and in it the body of Flight Sergeant Dancy, a member of the missing crew. Someone had fashioned a rude cross of wooden planks over the grave. A landing party from the British aircraft carrier *Albion* then went ashore on the nearest inhabited island. They found a fisherman who said he had seen the Shackleton crash into the sea. He said he had recovered one body, had buried it, had memorized the plane's markings (though he did not read English), and had cut them as a signal in the grass. The nationality of the fisherman, or of the atoll, could not be learned, but he seemed to be Chinese. This explanation of Colonel Millar's disappearance in "dangerous" and "unsurveyed" waters satisfied no one. The native fishing boat, about which the Shackleton had radioed Singapore, could not be found, nor the men it had presumably rescued. Had the boat shot down Millar's plane? The possibility could not be dismissed, though evidence there was none.

Not even the demotion of piracy from a profession to a mere gainful occupation brought the Moros to heel. They never recognized the authority of Spain, never submitted to its rule. The net result of Spain's presence in the Sulu Sea over more than 300 years can be summed up quickly. It was to inflame the Moro against the white man and the Cross of Christ. This the Americans found out when they took the Philippines from Spain and embarked confidently on their first colonial venture.

The United States: To "Civilize." 1898–1946

On May 6, 1898, Americans awoke to find themselves in strange company. They had crashed the imperialists' club. The morning papers shouted that Admiral George Dewey had sailed the Pacific Fleet into Manila Bay and had sunk ten Spanish warships. Dewey was waiting for reinforcements to land and take over.

The news from Manila was the first sensation of the ten-day-old war with Spain, a war to liberate Cuba from Spanish tyranny. Instead, the American Navy had liberated 7,000 distant islands that nobody knew much about. What was Uncle Sam going to do with them? Clearly, some other power would nab them if the American fleet pulled out. Did the United States have the right to abandon 6,000,000 souls to another tyranny after freeing them from Spanish rule? Could the American Republic, under the Constitution, become an empire?

To occupy a continent, thinly held by a few Indians, Spaniards, and Frenchmen, did not disturb the conscience of Anglo-Saxon colonials; but to take over 7,000 islands and 6,000,000 brown men halfway around the world was a different matter. It was to trouble Americans deeply for many years.

President William McKinley wrestled with the American conscience. As he later confessed, he "walked the floor of the White House night after night" and "prayed Almighty God for light and guidance more than one night," and one night late, he said:

> "It came to me this way—I don't know how it was but it came: (1) that we could not give them [the Philippines] back to Spain—that it would be cowardly and dishonorable; (2) that we could not turn them over to France or Germany—our com-

mercial rivals in the Orient—that would be bad business and discreditable; (3) that we could not leave them to themselves—they were unfit for self-government—and they would soon have anarchy and misrule over there worse than Spain's was; and (4) that there was nothing left for us to do but to take them all, and to educate the Filipinos, and uplift and civilize and Christianize them, and by God's grace to do the very best we could by them, as our fellow-men for whom Christ died, and then I went to bed, and went to sleep and slept soundly. . . ." [4]

So the United States "bought" the Philippines from Spain, for $20,000,000, under a treaty signed at Paris. Then the rationalizing began. President McKinley said America's mission in those islands was "one of beneficent assimilation." General E. S. Otis, the first military Governor of the islands, said the purpose was to "give the blessings of peace and individual freedom to the Phillippine people." The Senate resolved not "to permanently annex" the islands, but to prepare the people for local self-government and "in due time to make such disposition as will best promote the interests of the United States citizens and the inhabitants of the islands."

Blessings of peace or any other kind had to wait. The United States found itself obliged to crush a full-fledged independence movement. (Americans called it insurrection.) Apparently thousands of Filipinos, including some highly educated and responsible leaders, had mistakenly thought the American forces were about to liberate them, not just from Spain but from all foreign rule. Convincing the rebels that they were wrong took three years and cost thousands of lives, both American and Filipino. Another five years were

[4] Charles S. Olcott: *The Life of William McKinley* (Boston: Houghton Mifflin Co.; 1916), Vol. II, pp. 108–11.

needed to root out the bands of insurrectionists who had fled to the forests. More than 120,000 American soldiers were involved in all, as many as 70,000 at one time. There were acts of cruelty on both sides and, as a result, a good deal of lasting bitterness. The conquerors had to station 639 garrisons to hold the northern islands and to prepare them, one by one, for civil administration.

The battle in the north was a mere skirmish compared with the ordeal of conquering the southern islands. How could Spain, which had never subdued the Moros, sell them to another power? To the credit of the conquerors, they at least tried peacefully to stake out their shaky claim. They dispatched General John C. Bates to make the best possible deal with the Sultan of Sulu. Bates persuaded the Sultan to sign an agreement. He could not have foreseen how the terms would look to the people at home. The Sultan agreed to "acknowledge" American authority and to let the Stars and Stripes fly over all his islands, which must have delighted the Daughters of the American Revolution of that day. Everyone agreed to suppress piracy except the pirates themselves. The Sultan's "government" would deal with crimes among his own people according to their own law and custom. Crimes involving other peoples would be handled by American authorities. Slaves owned by Moros were entitled to buy their freedom at the market rate. And finally, the United States would pay the Sultan and his chieftains "monthly salaries." Moros had had another word for past payments from British and Spanish authorities. They had called these payments "tribute." The Sultan's stipend was $250 Mexican a month, those of his chieftains from $75 to $60. Signed in Sulu and English texts at Jolo on August 20, 1899, the Bates Agreement was not considered a treaty needing ratification by the Senate. But news of it drifted across the Pacific to that body. By the following January the dome of the Capitol began to tremble.

This, it should be remembered, was the start of an election year. The American people were getting ready to entrust President McKinley with a second term, and one issue was to dominate an otherwise dull campaign: was expansion noble or wicked?

Theodore Roosevelt, McKinley's running mate, carried the banner of nobility across the country. He had favored the war with Spain: it would, he wrote, be fine practice for the United States Navy. "The guns of our war-ships have awakened us to the knowledge of new duties. . . . Our flag is a proud flag and it stands for liberty and civilization. . . ." Such were the happy results of the war, and they made campaign material.

William Jennings Bryan, the Democratic candidate for President, blasted away at the wickedness of Republican motives. "Imperialism," he said, "would be profitable to the army contractors; it would be profitable to the shipowners, who would carry live soldiers to the Philippines and bring dead soldiers back." The campaign did not help an electorate already divided and confused. For many, it was a moment of pride and joy at having beaten a much smaller, weaker power. For a few, it was a time of pain and disgust. In taking the Philippines, wrote Professor William James, the Republicans would commit the United States "to puke up its ancient soul, and the only things that gave it eminence among other nations, in five minutes without a wink of squeamishness."

The Senate debate exploded on January 10. That was the day a young Republican from Indiana delivered his maiden speech. Thirty-seven-year-old Albert J. Beveridge enlisted the Almighty on the side of the Americans in the Philippines: "We will not renounce our part in the mission of the race, trustee, under God, of the civilization of the world." Not all Republicans went along with Beveridge. A distinguished member of the party, Senator George F. Hoar, a pillar of the Anti-Imperialist League of Boston, rode into the fray brandishing the New England conscience. He found an uncongenial ally in the Senator from South Dakota, a Democrat. On January 17, the Honorable Richard F. Pettigrew delivered one of a series of orations, attacking Republican policy in general and the Bates Agreement in particular.

"It has developed," he told the Senate, "that we have bought six million Christian people who are members of the Catholic Church, occupying the northern islands of the Philippine Archipelago; that we have purchased from one to two hundred thousand Mohammedan slaveholders, polygamists, who live by prosecuting the slave trade against the native population of the southern islands of the group; that we have agreed to maintain this condition of affairs; and the [Bates] treaty is so arranged that it goes into force without the legislative bodies of this government having anything to say about it. . . .

"Who," asked Pettigrew rhetorically, "insisted that our flag should fly above a harem and a slave market? . . . Are we going to rely on the doctrine that we are going to bless those people with our civilization against their will, and that God has ordered us to do a great work? That is the English doctrine, the doctrine which has justified the plunder of every colony she has conquered on earth."

The Bates Agreement was a political bobble; moreover, it never worked. The Moros went about their usual business of slave-raiding and piracy. The Sultan had neither the moral nor the physical force to keep his people in order. His American masters, especially General Leonard Wood, the military Governor of the Moro Province, had contempt for him. "A little oriental," Wood wrote to President Theodore Roosevelt in 1903, "with half a dozen wives and no children; a state of affairs I am sure you thoroughly disapprove." And Wood's aide, Captain Frank R. McCoy, reported home that after a trip to Singapore the Sultan "wears golf stockings and a tweed suit, a black turban; instead of the pair of green breeches, purple jacket, pearls as buttons for which he has long been famous."

In September 1903, Wood's legislative council made it a crime to buy, sell, or own slaves. Six months later Wood told the Sultan that the Bates Agreement was no more, but that the United States would go on paying monthly "salaries" to him and his chieftains.

Sometimes Uncle Sam in imperial dress looked almost as silly as the Sultan in tweeds. The anomaly tickled the fancy of one of the great humorists of that day. George Ade wrote a musical satire, *The Sultan of Sulu*, which opened at Wallach's Theater in New York on December 29, 1902. Frank Moulan played the Sultan, supported by a chorus of six pretty young wives, and a seventh who of course was a hag. Enter the American conquerors in starched white uniforms to "liberate," "assimilate," and "civilize." They bring along six adorable schoolmarms from Boston to "educate" the natives. The Sultan learns that the Constitution and cocktails follow the flag. He allows an unlimited number of cocktails to "trickle down the corridors of my inmost being." But he gags on the Constitution, which forces him to divorce his six pretty wives and to pay each of them half his income in alimony. The last act brings a figurative Lone Ranger to the rescue in the form—of all things—of the United States Supreme Court. The Court rules, as in fact it had done in the Insular cases of 1901, that the Constitution does not follow the flag; or, as Ade puts it, that "the Constitution follows the flag on Mondays, Wednesdays, and Fridays only." The clear interpretation of this decision was that the Sultan could keep his wives and his cocktails too.

Any satirist who builds his last-act climax around a Supreme Court decision and sets it to popular music must be a fair judge of the sophistication of his audiences. Broadway loved *The Sultan of Sulu*, all the more since Ade had taken care to lard the book with hit songs such as *Lulu, You're My Sulu Lulu Loo.*

[I]

The forty-three-year struggle to "civilize" the people of the Sulu Sea was not a George Ade comic opera but a long-drawn-out drama of misunderstanding, of the Eugene O'Neill genre.

From the start, Americans treated "The Moro Problem" as a special problem, which indeed it was. The first Philippine Commission set up a Bureau of Non-Christian Tribes, under which the Moros came for administrative purposes. By act of Congress, all island peoples were divided into two main categories: 6,000,000 or so who were Christian and "civilized"; the other 500,000 or so who were non-Christian and "wild." These were the official terms used in the first American census of 1903, which reported that two fifths of the "wild" people were Mohammedans, "well known in the island as Moros." Bracketing the Moros with pagans and calling them "wild" may have served an administrative purpose. But it was not calculated to endear the white man to the Moro, who knew himself to be superior to all infidels, Filipino and American alike.

The islands of the Sulu Sea became the Moro Province, largest of all the forty provinces of the colony. Into it went more than half of Mindanao and every island south and west of it, to within sight of Borneo. In it lived almost half a million people who had no intention of submitting to foreign rule. The ordeal of taming and ruling them taught their masters a good many hard lessons. One lesson was in jungle warfare: a jungle unhealthy with snakes, malarial mosquitoes, and ambushes; a warfare in which the enemy was either invisible or at your throat with a wavy-edged knife. The raw American was getting training for Guadalcanal and New Guinea; unfortunately it was his grandsons who had to relearn the business forty years later. Sometimes the Moros barricaded themselves in *cottas,* the square hilltop forts mounted with brass swivel cannons. Americans

would storm the forts only to find the defenders dead inside to the last man and woman. Not infrequently a single
Malay, seized by a suicidal frenzy, stabbed every infidel
within his reach before being killed. Whether the *Juramen-
tado,* as he is called, acted out of religious or patriotic
frenzy or madness has never been decided.

Moro fanatics kept their province under strict military
rule for fifteen years. To subdue them, the United States
Army sent some of its best soldiers. Their officers included
Leonard Wood, Tasker Bliss, and John J. Pershing. It was
Pershing who mopped up the last resistance, collected
7,000 firearms from the rebels, and handed control to the
first civilian Governor, Frank Watson Carpenter. With the
end of military rule in 1914, Moro Province became the Department of Mindanao and Sulu, and the work of "civiliz-
ing" began in earnest. Military government would have
lasted even longer if the Americans had carried with them
only their rifles. Like the Spaniards, they brought their
faith, but it was the faith of the New World, born of America's colonial experience and history. Chief among its tenets
was freedom of worship, embodied in the First Amendment
to the Constitution. Britain and the Netherlands practiced
the same tolerance, but the Moros had known only Spain
and its soldier priests. Americans were a novel enemy, waving a flag, not a Cross. The effect on the Moros was pro-
found. Equally strange was the Americans' talk about making good citizens, and their apparent belief that the way to
make them was through education. No other colonial power
preached education so fervently and practiced it so widely
as did the United States in the Philippines.

From the beginning the Army did double duty. Between
jungle campaigns and police patrol, the soldier became a
teacher. An elderly Filipino remembers learning English
from "a soldier who used to come to the classroom wet with
perspiration from military drill." George Ade's chorus of
Boston schoolmarms was taken from real life. The year

1901 brought 765 American teachers to the Philippines, most of them on the Army transport *Thomas*. The Thomasites, as these stalwarts came to be called, scattered to all corners of the new colony, sometimes where American garrisons could protect them, sometimes where they were entirely on their own. They knew as little about the tropics as about the people they had come to teach, but they coped. Without intending or wanting to, they worked themselves out of jobs by training Filipinos. In 1903, there were 691 American to 2,496 Filipino teachers; twenty years later the figures were respectively 322 and 26,014. The new republic in 1950 had only eight American and 85,396 Filipino teachers. By 1962, thanks to the Peace Corps, the process had been reversed, with more than 600 Americans again teaching in the Thomasites' footsteps.

In education as in other fields, Moro Province under American rule lagged far behind the colony's general average. Yet it moved, largely because Governor Leonard Wood chose a remarkable man as its superintendent of schools. He was Najeeb M. Saleeby, an American of Syrian origin. Although a Christian, Dr. Saleeby was an Arabic scholar and a meticulous chronicler of Moro history, law, and culture. Whoever would gain some understanding of these voiceless people must study the all too slender works of the Syrian-American doctor. He was their voice, too, in pleading for education in the vernacular as well as in English. Manila had decreed that English was to be the language of instruction. Dr. Saleeby got permission to prepare the first Sulu reader in the Moro dialects. It appeared in 1905 to revolutionize teaching in the religious schools which for centuries had taught the Koran in Arabic to Moro boys. To his phonetic primer and reader, Dr. Saleeby added three chapters: one on the importance of education, one a brief history of the Sulu people, and one on the government of the Moro Province.

In trying to conserve Moro culture, the good doctor was

swimming against the current. American ideas and institutions were flooding the colony. So were eager, well-meaning Americans. Considering the trend, the wonder is that Leonard Wood picked Dr. Saleeby as superintendent, listened to him on educational matters, and perceived his unique value to the American authorities. In political matters, Dr. Saleeby had little influence. He preached the wisdom of indirect rule, through the *dato* or chieftain, who was "God's viceregent on earth." The *dato*, he argued, "was the first Moro to put on shoes, buy American candy, and sit in a chair." And he concluded that "it is an inefficient teacher who does the student's work and it is an unsuccessful Governor who cannot leave for the *dato* the latter's own duties and work." Saleeby lost this particular battle, but he won many others.

[2]

Progressive ideas had a chance in the new Department of Mindanao and Sulu under its first civilian Governor, Frank Carpenter. Indeed, Governor Carpenter's first report to Congress in 1914 reads like a model five-year plan that could well be submitted to the Congress of the Philippines in 1964. Land ownership for every farmer, with a clear title to his land; federal aid for schools, roads, and harbors; adult education in public health, sanitation, and child care —for these the Governor asked $500,000 a year for five years. In addition, he proposed to resettle 75,000 farm families on new land with agricultural loans over five years. Finally, Governor Carpenter was determined to begin to teach the people of Mindanao and Sulu popular government. The law setting up the new department had authorized elections to provincial boards. Carpenter set out "to encourage the organization of two opposing political parties in each locality where elections are authorized." Looking ahead, Carpenter decided that it would be prudent to persuade the Sultan of Sulu to give up remaining claims to sovereignty, and this was done in an agreement signed on March 22, 1915. The Sultan was without legal heirs, but he did have a highly intelligent niece, and this young girl Carpenter undertook to educate. Thus, in 1914, he arranged for the Princess Putli Tarhata to live in Manila and receive special public school training. In due course, the Princess went on to the University of Illinois, from which she graduated with distinction in 1925. Her late uncle was the twenty-fifth and last Sultan of Sulu. The Princess lives in Jolo, inheriting some of his prestige if not his title. It is tactless to ask this charming and sophisticated woman about her uncle's claims to his former domain in North Borneo. The Princess declares with spirit that the Sultan owned all of North Borneo, that her uncle never ceded this territory but only rented it to the British, and that the "rent" still paid to her is pitifully small and insufficient for her to live, much less to travel.

Carpenter's drive to educate Malays and to ease them into local self-government distressed the British just across the Sulu Sea. (The British came around to Carpenter's ideas forty years later.) Indeed, they found the whole American performance disquieting. Americans, they felt, did not understand the native peoples as they, the British, did. The native was not yet ready to learn self-government; he was not interested in education. To talk as if he were was to show one's ignorance. Americans were amateurs who ought to be asking advice instead of giving it.

Amateurs they certainly were. The first Philippine Commission began work with five distinguished members, two of them judges. Only one of the five, a professor of zoology named Dean C. Worcester, had ever been in the Philippines before. Not having a colonial service on which to draw, the United States ran the colony with amateurs. It lavished money on public schools and public health. American novices, moreover, had the insolence to talk condescendingly to British veterans. In 1904 General Wood wrote to his friend J. St. Loe Strachey, Editor of *The Spectator:*

> You are quite content to maintain rajahs and sultans and other species of royalty, but we, with our plain ideas of doing things, find these gentlemen outside our scheme of Government. Our policy is to develop individualism among these people and, little by little, teach them to stand upon their own feet independent of petty chieftains.

Years later, William Howard Taft looked back in mellow reminiscence to those ebullient days when he was head of the first Philippine Commission. "The English student of colonial government," he said, "is fixed in his view that we have pursued a wrong course in the Philippine Islands by conferring upon the people much more popular control than was wise and by attempting to give them an education, which instead of tending to improve matters will tend to create popular agitation and discontent and constant conspiracy and plotting against the government." [5] Taft felt that American rule, attacked for opposite reasons by British imperialists and American anti-imperialists, had come close to achieving a golden mean.

The Philippine Republic: To Absorb and Develop. 1946–

July 1946 made history on both sides of the Sulu Sea. North Borneo became a proper British colony on the fifteenth; on the fourth, Mindanao and the Sulu islands emerged from colonial rule as parts of the new Republic of the Philippines. Sulu Province, with its approximately 325,-000 Moros, greeted the glorious moment in sullen silence.

[5] William Howard Taft: *Addresses*, Vol. I, pp. 201–2.

Except for the occasional crack of a rifle, one of the 10,000 left behind by the United States Army, the hush persists over the islands. Their people have not so much defied the authority of Manila as they have disregarded it. A single reliable statistic, where statistics are apt to be as unsafe as drinking water, explains what is happening. Between 1955 and 1960, registered imports into the Sulu Province shrank by 93 per cent; their value dropped from 3,757,000 to 246,-000 pesos (a peso was then worth fifty cents in American currency). This means that the bulk of the watches, cigarettes, and other luxury items on sale in Jolo, not to mention those transshipped, had entered illegally. They had been smuggled. From the free ports of Hong Kong and Singapore, via North Borneo where the trade is legal, to the coves of the Sulu islands where cargoes are dumped after dark, the contraband flows. Some items are subject to embargo, others to tariffs. They pour in free, despite the efforts of *La Union* and other subchasers. Meanwhile, hardly anyone profits, legally or illegally, from the natural riches of the Sulu Sea. Pearl oysters, sponges, and fish have procreated undisturbed for twenty years. To capitalize on this marine population explosion means risking one's life while pirates roam the sea. A few Moros are willing to take the risk and they bring in a small catch. Of the islands' field crops, only corn and tobacco have increased much above the wartime subsistence level. Logging is almost at a standstill. Paralysis like that of a general strike grips the seas and the countryside. Are the Moros simply being themselves? Must they remain unreconciled, impervious, in order to keep their identity in a Christian republic?

On neighboring Mindanao these questions are being tested. Rich, spacious, and relatively empty, Mindanao has experienced something like an Oklahoma land rush since the start of Philippine independence. Beginning with less than 3,000,000 people in its eleven provinces, the island has taken in more than 1,483,000 new settlers, most of them Christian, from the islands to the north. The newcomers combined with the natural increase to double Mindanao's population in little more than twelve years. A government resettlement program accounted for less than 100,000 of the migrants. The rest came on their own, not knowing where they were headed or what they would find. Almost half of them gravitated to the two largest provinces of Davao and Cotabato. Still they come and there is plenty of room. Even with its population doubled, Mindanao still had only 21 per cent of the Republic's people on 37 per cent of the Republic's land area.

The influx has brought Christian and Moslem face to face on a broad front. The immigrant squats on the best unoccupied land he can find. While good land is plentiful in the river valleys, it usually belongs to the Moslem community. The Moslems may have no piece of paper to prove it, but they know the land is theirs; it always has been. Thus the confrontation is not only between Moslem and Christian but also between the traditional and the new. Dr. Saleeby, it will be remembered, urged American authorities to work through the chieftain or *dato*. Well, the *dato* survives, "a combination landlord, political leader, jurist, religious functionary, and nobleman." The *dato* system functions on one level, the superior authority of Manila on another.

The *dato* system, in so far as it survives, serves the Moslem as a shelter against the blast of change. The Moro farmer looks to his *dato* as a constituent to his political boss, for protection and favors. Like the Mormon in Utah, he pays his tithe in the form of 10 per cent of his crop to his leader. Next to clan loyalty, and no less strong, comes family loyalty. The average size of the combined farm family varies between twenty and thirty. There is no objection to plural marriage, if one can afford it. A prosperous abaca planter, for example, has ten wives and fifteen children. Moro farm people marry early, divorce easily. When it comes to education, the Moro farmer is reluctant to send his sons outside the *dato* system, or to school his daughters at all. Mindanao's schools reflect this attitude. The children in its public schools are predominantly Christian, with the addition of a few sons and daughters of wealthy Moslems. Most Moslem boys, and a few girls, receive a smattering of learning over three to six years in religious schools maintained by the Moslem community with the help of missionary teachers from Egypt. Thus it is not surprising that Moro techniques of farming and standards of living lag behind those of the Christian community. On a Moro farm one is even less likely to find electricity, a tractor, a newspaper, a radio, a contour-plowed field, a compost pit, or a bag of fertilizer than among Chinese or Christian farmers. (In these respects, the pagan tribal people lag far behind the Moslems, it should be remembered.)

Even in the painful process of change, Mindanaoans have advantages over other borderlanders. Their internal differences are not of race or even primarily of religion. The Chinese in their midst do not threaten them either with numbers or with power, as in North Borneo. No predatory neighbor looms over their border, as in Hokkaido. They live with breathing space in a storehouse of natural wealth. Let us tick off some of the elements of this wealth: harnessable rivers, exploitable minerals, cuttable timber, tillable topsoil, and trainable people. In theory, Mindanao could be as electrified as Switzerland, at a fraction of the cost. Lake Lanao, a natural reservoir, could alone yield 750,000 kilowatts. Its waters already produce 50,000 kilowatts at Maria Cristina, but even this is not all sold. Who can afford electricity? Not one person in a hundred, not one town in four, not island industry, which employs only 15,000 out of nearly 6,000,000 people. In theory, Mindanao's mineral wealth could be worth more than $6,000,000,000. It includes gold, silver, iron, coal, and a mountain of iron-nickel-cobalt ore that presents difficult smelting problems.

Majestic forests cover more than half of the island's surface, a prime asset if they can be cut and conserved. The
same can be said for the island's topsoil, which an early
explorer found "deep and black and extraordinarily fat and
fruitful." It grows rice, rubber, cocoa, coffee, abaca—
almost any crop—until the soil is swept into the sea. From a
plane one can watch the silver ribbons of rivers turn dark
brown as they receive the precious topsoil and carry it far
out to sea. It is a sight to make a soil conservationist weep.

We come to the fifth element: Mindanao's people. In
theory, they could compete with any in the Far East. Like
the Formosans, they could grow two or three crops on a
single field. Like the Japanese, they could learn to process
iron, lumber, food crops, and fish, and thus lift their
economic lives out of a colonial strait jacket. In June 1961
the Philippine Congress passed an act setting up a Mindanao Development Authority. It was during a national
election campaign, and the government of President Garcia
was giving belated thought to the provinces. After Garcia's
defeat, the new government of President Diosdado Maca-
pagal took office in 1962. The new Vice President, Em-
manuel Palaez, was a Mindanao man. Perhaps the borderland had gained a voice that would be heeded in Manila.

To call North Borneo and Mindanao "lands of the future"
implies no undue optimism. It is simply a way of saying
that these borderlands have in dead storage, as it were,
resources both material and human for the twenty-first
century. It is not to say that their resources will be used
wisely or at all. What is to prevent their being eroded,
gouged out, and squandered in the manner of the past?
An overworked Spanish proverb warns that "he who would
bring home the wealth of the Indies, must carry the wealth
of the Indies with him." On this principle, knowledge and
capital have been infused into the Indies and wealth has
been taken out of them without any comparable enrich-
ment of the islands and their peoples. In this manner the

rulers of the forthcoming *Malaysia* could develop their Bornean provinces and the northern Filipinos could drain Mindanao's wealth and make good use of it. But the old principle is obsolete. It never presupposed that the borderlanders might become conscious of their own needs. As they grow articulate, and as they generate political pressure, a new principle may somehow be worked out. Under it, he who would bring home the wealth of the Indies must somehow leave enough of it behind to enrich the lives and expand the capacities of the borderland peoples themselves.

3

Burma's Borderland

HOME OF THE SHANS AND KACHINS

I had not expected that the work of building up a nation would be so difficult. I had thought that everything could be accomplished at the stroke of a pen when one became a wielder of power.
> —U Nu, to the students of the
> University of Rangoon, 1953

IN THE predawn darkness of January 4, 1948, Burma proclaimed its freedom from British rule. Astrologers had chosen 4:20 a.m. as the moment for the ceremony. Official guests from abroad found it hard to show their joy at such an hour. Dutifully they assembled outside the parliament building in Rangoon and watched through sleepy eyes.

The Union Jack came down; a new flag rose in its place. It was red except for an oblong corner of blue. One white star on the blue stood for the new Union of Burma, five smaller stars around it for the five major peoples that would form the Union. It was Burma's way of announcing that it would make *e pluribus unum:* out of many, one.

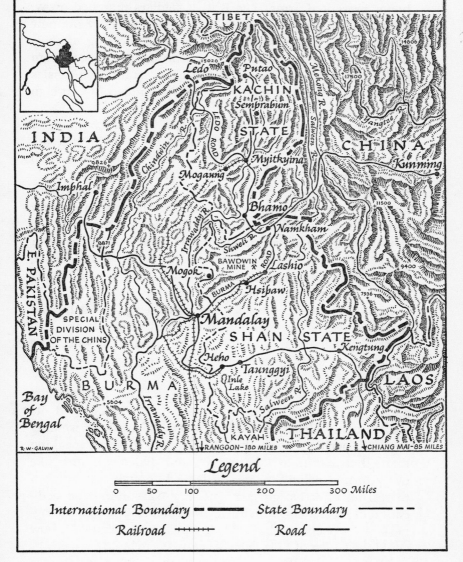

NORTH BURMA
The Shan and Kachin States

TIBET

INDIA

CHINA

15020
Ledo
Putao
KACHIN
Semprabum
STATE
Myitkyina
Mogaung
9826
Imphal
Bhamo
Namkham
9871
Mogok
BAWDWIN MINE
Lashio
Hsipaw
BURMA ROAD
Mandalay
SHAN STATE
Kengtung
SPECIAL DIVISION OF THE CHINS
Heho
Taunggyi
Inle Lake
LAOS
E. PAKISTAN
BURMA
Bay of Bengal
5604
KAYAH
THAILAND
RANGOON-180 MILES
CHIANG MAI-85 MILES

Kunming
14606
17500
11500
9400
7936

Mekong R.
Salween R.
Yangtze R.
Chindwin
LEDO ROAD
Irrawaddy R.
Shweli R.
Salween R.
Irrawaddy R.

R.W. GALVIN

Legend

0   50   100   200   300 *Miles*

International Boundary ————   State Boundary — — —
Railroad ++++++   Road ————

A salvo of guns split the air, fired from the British cruiser *Birmingham* in the river. A Burmese guard of honor presented arms. The British soldiers marched away, their band playing *Auld Lang Syne*. The leaders of the new government trooped indoors for the first meeting of their independent parliament. At last Burma was a sovereign nation; it could issue stamps and coins, station embassies abroad, and assume all the other attributes of sovereign power.

But it takes time to build a nation. The proclaiming of independence is only the first step on a painful road. Examples spring to mind from every continent: from America, where "a more perfect Union" is still in the making; from Europe, where the old kingdoms of northern and southern Italy are not yet congenial in spirit a century after unification; from Africa, where half a dozen new nations threaten to fall apart. From Asia come other examples: the island chain that calls itself the Republic of Indonesia, or—as good an illustration as any—that mixture of many peoples known as the Union of Burma.

Prime Minister U Nu acknowledged in 1953 that he had not expected nation-building to be so difficult. He was addressing students at the University of Rangoon who were impatient at their government's slow progress. Why was it so slow? The Prime Minister could have cited at least three reasons. First, the new Union had to start life in the midst of war wreckage, its land scorched, its towns bombed, its society demoralized. Second, it faced the work of welding together perhaps 125 ethnic and tribal groups, speaking more than a hundred languages and dialects. Third, like every former colony in Asia, it lacked enough trained men to run an effective government. Even assuming the dedication of its leaders, which was undeniable, and the willingness of its people to be welded, which was debatable, how could the Union of Burma have been easy to build?

That some of Burma's people were wary of union was

not strange. Never had all of them been joined; each had some reason for distrusting another. What troubled the minor groups especially was the lopsidedness of the new Union, the dominance of one member because of overwhelming numbers. This group was the Burmans, four fifths of the country's total population of about 20,000,000.[1]

The Burmans speak one language, Burmese; they follow one religion, Buddhism; they look back on centuries of precolonial history under the rule of Burman kings. Their territory, Burma proper, stretches almost a thousand miles from the Malay Peninsula in the south to the Tibetan frontier on the north. This is the heart of modern Burma.

Other peoples, less numerous, live in a semicircle of hills that frame the Burman homeland. On the east and the north, the three most important non-Burman groups are the Karens, Shans, and Kachins; on the northwest a fourth, the Chins, farm the slopes of their almost inaccessible hills. It was these four and an assortment of minor peoples that made a union necessary for Burma. Not all of them were reconciled to citizenship in the new nation, and a few of them bitterly resisted absorption. Their resistance helped to make nation-building in Burma an ordeal.

The most formidable rebellion among the outlying peoples came from Karens in the east. They fought from 1948 to 1955 for an independent "Karen Country," while Burma proper was torn by civil war among rival factions. As late as 1960, 3,000 Karen insurgents had not yet surrendered. The Kachins, too, produced a freebooter whose followers robbed, killed, and terrorized soon after independence. As for the Shans, unrest among them was so persistent that at times the central government in Rangoon had to concentrate two thirds of its army in the eastern Shan country

---

[1] Official usage in Burma (and the United States) calls this major group *Burman;* majority and minority peoples together are *Burmese* just as English, Scots, and Welsh are *British*. In British usage, *Burman* and *Burmese* are reversed.

in virtual occupation. The first seven years of independence brought the outlying areas little peace or safety.

Were the architects of the new Burma to blame? Perhaps, in retrospect, they were. They had too little experience in governing, and too much confidence in their capacity to govern. As political idealists brought up in the Buddhist way, they hoped that generosity toward the minority groups could pull the new Union together. With fairness as well as shrewdness, they offered to set up borderland states in which the hesitant joiners could manage their own affairs with a large measure of autonomy. Three such states were created at the Union's birth, a fourth soon afterward; and in recent years local politicians have agitated for the creation of two more.

Because their populations were intermingled, the state boundaries had to be set on administrative rather than ethnic lines. In the Shan State, about the size of Great Britain, less than half of the 2,000,000 people are Shans. The majority consists of Chinese and Indian traders in the towns, Kachin and other tribesmen in the hills. In the neighboring Kachin State, about the size of Denmark, the pepper-and-salt mixture of Kachins and Shans makes it impossible to guess their respective numbers or more than guess the over-all population, probably between 300,000 and 400,000. Together, the Shan and Kachin States blend into a well-stirred stew of peoples, languages, and loyalties.

Remote from the center of political and economic power in Rangoon, both are relatively empty lands. For 950 miles they share a common frontier with China, whose nearness they have dreaded whenever their neighbor was unified and strong. Their schooling, health, and general well-being got little attention from their own rulers or from the colonial regime.

By one of the mockeries that is common to former colonial borderlands, the anti-imperialist Burmans now appear to the minority peoples in the guise of imperial masters.

Now it is not the British but the Burmans who often seem to be alien intruders. Now it is in Burma's interest, as it was in Britain's, to win and keep the allegiance of the Shans and Kachins and of other reluctant groups. Now Burma must shoulder the burden of defending them and merging them into a true and enduring union. The Shan and Kachin States, in short, illustrate many of the problems of modern Asian borderlands. Let us see how these problems arose and how the Burmans have been coping with them in the two States, beginning with the Shan.

"A Cleaner, Greener Land"

To step from a plane at Heho airstrip in the south of the Shan State, only 400 miles from the steam bath of Rangoon, is to whiff oxygen at the end of a stifling day. Most of the Shan State forms a plateau, higher and healthier than the Irrawaddy Valley to the west or the jungles along the State's eastern rim. Here is "a cleaner, greener land" that Kipling never saw.

The green of the Shan State cannot be real; it must have been laid on with paint. In the south, the valleys of farmlands merge into ridges of blue, and the ridges into valleys beyond. Rain trees shaped like giant umbrellas are a child's crayon masterpiece. The roofs of Buddhist temples, in the Chinese style of three or five layers, float with the lightness of horizontal blossoms on a dogwood tree. The houses of woven palm might sail away at any moment on a puff of breeze. In the north of the State, the vegetation thins and the scene shifts to rolling range. At last the hills drop away into the Shweli Valley on the edge of China. The Shweli River, tender as the Thames above Marlow, winds between fields of rice. Like Alan Paton's valley in South Africa, this one is "beautiful beyond the singing of it."

The people move through their countryside with a
peculiar grace. Theirs is the smooth and small-boned charm
of most Southeast Asians. A Shan girl covers her head
with a turban of white bath toweling; a careless thing, it
frames her face with as much art as if she had spent an
hour in draping it. A Shan farmer wears a conical straw
hat to shield himself from the sun. In the village bazaars,
men and women alike carry shoulder bags woven in poster-
paint colors. Somehow these people fit their landscape to
perfection, whether tilling their fields, weaving their cloth,
selling their produce, or saying their prayers.

It is their good fortune to have lived for centuries in
river valleys or in the flatlands of the Shan plateau. The
cycle of their year brings them ample monsoon rains followed by sun, producing more than enough rice and supporting more than enough draft animals for their needs.
Their surplus they sell to hill people who cannot feed
themselves. Therefore climate and setting combine to give
them in abundance what most Asians lack: enough food,
water, warmth, and fertile land. Therefore, too, they have
been able to live a continuous settled life in their villages
and towns.

In this settled society, the Shan farmer has not radically
changed his ways for centuries. Why should he? His soil
needs no chemical fertilizer. His farm covers only two and
a half acres, on the average, but in the good earth of the
Shan State it is enough. Half of it he sows with rice, the
other half with soybeans, potatoes, peanuts, or garden vegetables as cash crops. The State owns all the land; the farmer
is supposed to pay a crop tax, but not an oppressive one—
if he bothers to pay. By any rural standards in Asia his
house is ample. Poor though the Shan may be by that
most misleading of all statistical measurements, his annual
cash income, he is nonetheless a man with many blessings.

If a revolution of rising expectations has hit him, the
Shan gives little evidence of it except in two insistent

desires. The first is education. Like most other people, he wants better opportunities for his children; so he sends them gladly to the government school, if one is available. The second desire is health. He does not want his children to die young, so he co-operates gratefully when a health officer comes to inoculate them or spray his house against malaria. His apparently cloudless life has been shadowed by the usual tropical killers: malaria, dysentery, cholera, typhus, leprosy. Now that malaria is being controlled, the most dangerous of his enemies has become tuberculosis, a leftover of wartime, when tens of thousands of Shans hid in the woods, living the lives of animals to escape the Japanese.

With all their stability, the Shans' family system is not as rigid as that of the Indians or Chinese. It adapts to circumstances. If the house is large, young married couples live with the husband's parents; if not, they set up housekeeping for themselves. Although modern cravings seem to have passed him by, the Shan is no paragon of thrift; he is a born gambler, and his cash has a way of vanishing at the time of the autumn festival. Yet the center of his social life is still the local pagoda or monastery rather than the cinema. A suspenseful moment in a Shan village is the drawing of lots to decide which family will feed and entertain the Buddhist monks. A joyful social occasion is the coming of friends to celebrate the monks' visit. Merit, satisfaction, prestige, all come from a donation, however small, to a monastery.

Of the forces that keep the Shans rooted to their way of life, the most compelling is Buddhism. It acts as a magnet to draw in each new generation and to pull back any who may stray. Among Shans, as among Burmans, Buddhism is nearly universal. The last reliable census, taken in 1931, reported that 99.35 per cent of the Shans were Buddhists, outdoing even the Burmans in their allegiance. Shan Buddhists, like their kinsmen in Thailand and Laos and their

Burman neighbors, follow the Hinayana or southern variety, as distinct from the Mahayana of Japan or the tantric Buddhism of Tibet. Devout Shan parents send their sons to the monastery for a short time at various ages. First, as small boys they go overnight to be initiated, have their heads shaved, and don a miniature monk's robe of yellow homespun. This ceremony is preceded by a lavish feast for family and friends. In his teens, the boy returns to the monastery periodically, to spend a few months serving the monks and learning the austere precepts of the Lord Buddha. Service in the monastery brings together Shan boys from all kinds of backgrounds and gives them a common memory which they carry through their lives.

In a Shan boy's early youth, Buddhism has another chance to exert an even stronger pull. The monastic school, separate from the monastery but staffed by monks, used to be the only place where a Shan family could send its sons for free instruction. The two alternatives, Christian mission schools and the few British colonial government schools, were concentrated in Burma proper, and most of them charged tuition. Independent Burma produced a bold new plan for free public education, but the Shan and other border states are inevitably the last to benefit. Although the government in Rangoon frowns on the monastic schools, it has lacked funds and teachers to make free education universal, even for the lowest elementary grades.

Monks, therefore, continue to teach in the Shan State. Many of them are ignorant; their teaching of modern knowledge hardly deserves the name. Daw Mi Mi Khaing, principal of a British-supported college in Taunggyi, wrote of an uncle who was a university student in 1922 when she was a child. He told her that the world was round, but that the monks said: "This is not true and most older people don't believe it." Much has changed since then, but the best one can say for the monastery school is that it fills a vacuum by giving Shan boys the rudiments of reading and writing in their own language, and simple arithmetic. To this extent, a Shan boy is literate. To this extent, he is better armed for modern living than, say, a boy in an Indian village where there is no religious or public school.

[1]

By all outward signs, the Shans lead a serene life. But except for about fifty years of the imposed *Pax Britannica,* they have known little security from rebels and outlaws. When in 1954 we first jeeped through the northern part of the Shan State, we were warned to leave money and valuables in Rangoon. The countryside was infested with armed bands who robbed and killed road travelers, held up railroad trains, and ambushed the police.

"You'd be foolish to go outside Rangoon," a Scottish bank manager told us. An American, trying to be helpful in a more practical way, said: "If they hold you up, just hand over your wallet quickly and don't argue." On the road to Lashio, the approach to the old Burma Road, trees and bushes had been cut back for twenty yards on either side to make surprise attack more difficult.

Security improved after 1955. But as recently as 1960 the Governor of the Shan State thought it prudent as well as courteous to have us escorted to Taunggyi, his capital, by a jeepload of armed police. An Austrian attached to a United Nations team had been shot in this area not long before while walking in the hills in search of botanical specimens. Other acts of banditry or rebellion (the words often mean the same) had set official nerves on edge. The road that ribbons through the valley toward Taunggyi was flanked with units of the Burmese Army. As though this were a maneuver area, their barracks dotted the 5,200-foot ridge where, in the 1890's, the British planted their headquarters.

Why did the Union government think it necessary to concentrate so much of its armed strength in the Shan State?

Though it is hard to connect rebellion with this land of tinkling temple bells, rebellion there is. A substantial minority of the million or so Shan people is bent on seceding from the Union of Burma; a few thousand are attempting it by force of arms.

A young Shan intellectual talked frankly of this aim in a closed room in Taunggyi. He first shut the door and window to make sure that he would not be overheard. For in Burma as elsewhere, the police have ears open for treason.

"We Shans want to be independent," he began. For emphasis he added: "Independent, like Laos." At that time, outside attack was dissolving Laos into chaos, but the young Shan seemed unaware of the irony. He went on to recall that a few Shan students from the University of Rangoon had gone underground in 1958 and had crossed the border into Thailand. There, he said, they recruited a Shan Liberation Army which staged a rebellion.

The truth about this uprising was as hard to pin down as the rebel fighters themselves. The young secessionist in Taunggyi placed insurgent strength at about 8,000; careful estimates in Rangoon put it at 2,000. The rebels hoped to win support from the spirit of nationalism among the Shan people, from grievances among the former feudal landlords, and from the remnant of Chiang Kai-shek's defeated Chinese Nationalist armies still encamped near the Thailand-Burma frontier. Arms smuggled from Thailand were their weapons. Hit-and-run skirmishes were their tactics. Rebel groups exchanged volleys with Army units around Kengtung, then disappeared into the bush to reappear when the troops had gone. The uprising was more than ordinary banditry, but there was no pitched battle, and no villages changed hands. In 1961 about a thousand Shan rebels were believed to be at large inside Burma, half of them hiding near the Thai boundary, the other half in the northwest of the State.

Historically the Shans have some basis for regarding

themselves as a separate people, distinct from the Burmans. Their language resembles that of Thailand; their name for themselves is *Tai*. They are indisputably one branch of the Thai people, which has other branches in Laos and parts of Yunnan. The Shans are believed to have migrated southward from eastern Tibet as part of the age-old movement of tribes from the cold heart of Asia. But this, like the traditions of most ancient migrations, cannot be proven. Whatever their origins, the Shans had spread by the fourteenth century over what is now northern Burma and into Assam and Thailand. The memory of ancient glories stirs Shans to this day. It gives them an excuse to fly a Shan flag and to sing a Shan national anthem. Here is a free translation:

> *All the people in the Shan State are of*
> *fine and noble race.*
> *The flag with the moon in the middle—*
> *We can see this moon from everywhere.*
> *Let us all have respect for each other,*
> *Let all the people be united,*
> *Let you and me agree with each other.*

Unhappily for the Shans, their ancestors did not remain united or "agree with each other." By the sixteenth century their territory had shrunk to northern Burma and had split into forty-four small states, each ruled by a feudal prince or sawbwa. In time the sawbwas came under the loose control of the Burman kings. But the Shans were never reconciled. As late as the last quarter of the nineteenth century, first in 1879 and again in 1885, they rose in revolt against King Thibaw, the last of the Burman monarchs who reigned at Mandalay.

When the British snuffed out Thibaw's kingdom in 1885, and packed him off to exile in India, they found themselves in charge of an imperial domain without a policy or purpose to guide them. In the words of one of their more candid proconsuls, Sir George Crosthwaite: ". . . the country was taken and its government destroyed before we had decided what we would do with it, or considered the effect on the people." The Shans, in particular, were a puzzle. Thirty-four sawbwas or rulers of lesser titles were still feudal masters of the assorted Shan States. One of them, at Keng-tung near the Thai border, ruled 12,000 square miles; another, twenty square miles. In his own territory, the sawbwa wielded life-or-death power over his people. His authority was not only mystic and semireligious; it was also political and economic. He owned all the land. He conscripted labor and took whatever goods or crops he wanted. Unless he lived outside his State and ruled it as an absentee, the sawbwa commanded the loyalty and support of his people. When they came into his presence, they pros-trated themselves before him as if he were as puissant as the Emperor of China.

The British might well have been tempted to forget the Shans and apply themselves to the conquest of the Bur-mans alone. But an expanding empire can always find good reasons for thrusting ahead, if only to keep other intruders out. The French in Indochina had been dickering with King Thibaw. Americans had been cutting into British trade with China through Shanghai and Canton. Would it not be wise for the British to occupy the lands of the Shans and Kachins as a form of commercial insurance? It was a British dream of those days to open a trade route from China's South to the Bay of Bengal, using Shan and Kachin territory for part of the way and the Irrawaddy River for the rest. Expeditions went out to survey possible road and rail routes into Yunnan. Only the vague hostility of China dissuaded these restless empire builders from pushing north. Lord Dufferin, the Viceroy in Calcutta, had to caution his officers in northern Burma; China was a powerful neighbor "who might greatly harass us if she or even her subordinate officials chose to worry us." Where the frontiers of Burma touched China, he said: "Feel your way, and when you come against anything hard, draw back."

Where Burma touched weaker neighbors, the British were less cautious. Even when they had swallowed most of the Shan States, they felt a compulsive appetite for more. The French and Thais alike were coveting the easternmost strip of Shan territory between the Salween and Mekong rivers, a wilderness of mountains and jungles. Could the British tolerate this threat to their position in India? Again, according to Sir George Crosthwaite: "It was decided to accept without flinching the full burden of responsibility which fell on us as standing in the King of Burma's place." Even in the halcyon days of Empire, it seemed, the British had to advance with stiff upper lip.

In dealing with the Shans, the British lacked the men and money to rule them directly. They therefore adopted the compromise which Lord Lugard and Sir Donald Cameron were to apply later in African colonies. They would persuade or compel each sawbwa to submit to the Queen and pay a yearly tribute; they would station a British officer in his capital to "guide" him. The sawbwa would have to obey British orders; the British would have the sole right to exploit natural resources and would be free from interference. Through this device, they seized the substance of power and left the sawbwas little more than the shadow.

Sometimes submission was easy to win, sometimes it called for derring-do. Often the British achieved it by sheer bluff, as they did in 1890 at Kengtung. A detachment of British troops found itself surrounded by a far greater number of Shans. One muleteer of the British column had been shot and wounded, another killed; the commander, later Sir J. G. Scott, demanded the culprit dead or alive. Discovering that the guilty one was none other than the sawbwa himself, Scott insisted on 500 rupees for the wounded man and 1,500 for the grieving relatives. As he recalled the story:

We were 300 miles from any possibility of help.
We were 400 miles from the railway. We had not
even heliographic communication. The party [of
troops] was absurdly small and could be rushed by
numbers anywhere, especially if we were moving.
The only thing it seemed to me was to carry off the
situation with a high hand. Prestige was everything. The slightest hint of nervousness would be
fatal.

The bluff paid handsomely. When the sawbwa agreed
to pay, Scott marched his troops into the palace grounds
for a military show. Knowing that he had only a few
Britons in a crowd of thousands, Scott reminisced:

I went up on to the verandah, and sat beside the
Sawbwa, and my Pathan [orderly] stood straight
up behind me ready to put a bullet through the
chief's head at the first sign of treachery . . . All
the time I told the Sawbwa of cannon so big that
men could get inside them, cannon that could
throw shell incredible distances, shell that burst
and killed everybody over acres of ground.[2]

Once the British had tamed the Shans, they guided them
with loose imperial reins. In theory, each sawbwa still
ruled his State as before. The British were content to build
roads and railways, to set up circuit houses for their traveling officials, to establish charming hill-stations for their
families—and to appear to intrude upon the sawbwas as
little as possible. They kept the princelings happy by dispensing honors and titles among the more loyal, bringing
them to Calcutta or Delhi for durbars or to London for
coronations. Although the Shan rulers were not as free,
in theory or practice, as the princes of India, they prospered.

---

[2] J. G. Scott: *Scott of the Shan Hills: Orders and Impressions* (London:
John Murray; 1936), pp. 147–50.

And their people remained submissive until an ocean of woe rolled over Burma in the form of the Japanese invasion.

[2]

What the British had built, with all its flaws, was nevertheless the only institutional foundation on which Burma could rise to independence after the war.

Everything the British had controlled, east to the Mekong, north to the wild border of Yunnan and Tibet, west to India—all this the new Republic of the Union of Burma inherited. With this inheritance went little trained leadership in Burma proper, even less in outlying areas. Towns were devastated, communications paralyzed, governmental authority defied by insurrections. Nevertheless the leaders of the new Burma set out to create a union of many peoples who had never been truly united before.

Their first step on the eve of independence, in 1947, was to summon leaders of the Shans, Kachins, and other border peoples to a conference at Panglong, not far from Taunggyi. Here the Founding Fathers of Burma promised to set up autonomous Shan and Kachin States; here the most influential of the Shan sawbwas and the Kachin chiefs, or *duwas*, agreed to join a Burmese Union. The second step was to write a constitution that would carry out the promises. Drafted by British-trained Burmans, it proved to be too liberal, too permissive, to withstand the stresses of disunity in the first fourteen years of nationhood. Twice during those years a military regime headed by General Ne Win took power, with the announced aim of shoring up the national structure. The first time, in 1958, the General kept the parliamentary forms, and after two years returned Burma to civilian rule. The second time, in 1962, he suspended the constitution and ruled by fiat.

The constitution was a first attempt, and a brave one in spite of its defects. It provided a Union Parliament at Rangoon consisting of two houses: a Chamber of Deputies, the lower house, with 250 members of whom twenty-five would come from the Shan State; and a Chamber of Nationalities, the upper house, with 125 members of whom twenty-five would come from the Shan State. The new Kachin State, much smaller in population, received seven seats in the lower house and twelve in the upper. Burmans would dominate the lower house by reason of their population, but in the upper house, designed as a forum for the minority peoples, the Burmans would be heavily outnumbered. The constitution gave the Shan State and others (but not the Kachin) the right to secede at any time after ten years, subject to a plebiscite and other safeguards. January 1948 was the month the constitution came into effect; thus the Shans had the theoretical right after January 1958 to break away from the Union.

Paying further respect to the Shans, the constitution proclaimed a device unusual, if not unique, among modern governments: "All members of Parliament representing the Shan State shall constitute the Shan State Council." The Council would elect the Head of State from its own number. The Head of State would also serve as Minister for Shan Affairs in the central government. Perhaps this provision was more than a courtesy; by compelling the Shan leader to spend a part of every year in Rangoon, it gave the central government a chance to watch and probably control him. (Until 1867, the Tokugawa autocrats of Japan guaranteed themselves control by compelling each *daimyo*, or feudal chief, to spend time in the central capital, almost as a hostage.) The same arrangements applied to the three other States, Kachin, Karen, and Karenni (now called Kayah). Burma proper, large, populous, and dominant, needed no special safeguards. Certain powers such as control of police, schools, and public health were reserved to the States, but the Supreme Court of the Union could overrule acts of the State Councils at any time.

It was an ingenious system, as if the New York State delegation to Congress, or the New South Wales members of the Australian Federal Parliament, acted as a State legislature as well and elected the Governor from their own members. The Governor would thus wear four hats: one as chief executive of the State, one as a member of the State legislature, a third as a member of the national legislature, and a fourth as a member of the national cabinet.

Certainly this was not a federal system, as the drafters of the compromise were quick to concede. With American, Canadian, and Australian federal experience before them, Burma's Founding Fathers declined to copy any one pattern. They chose from many what would meet their special needs: a figurehead president from the Third and Fourth Republics of France; a cabinet system and legislative and judicial procedure from Britain; a supreme court, with powers of constitutional review, from the United States; national ownership of natural resources from Yugoslavia, another Marxist and multipeopled republic like their own. The Burmese were fearful of old-style capitalism and separatism. Their chief concern was to make Burma an effective nation. Their second was to attract the Shans, Kachins, and other non-Burman peoples into the Union on terms they could accept.

Why should the Shans have been unhappy with such a constitution? Sure of one member of the cabinet at all times, sure of a sizable bloc of their own "race" in Parliament, sure of their own State government and State civil service, they would never lack spokesmen or champions in a Burmese Union. The first President of independent Burma was a Shan prince, Sao Shwe Thaike; his role was merely ceremonial, yet he was evidence that his people had become respected partners in the Union. Nevertheless, many Shans have been dissatisfied. Leaders of the Shans and other minority peoples met in Taunggyi in 1961 and demanded the creation of a truly federal union, with

Burma proper relegated to the position of a constituent State like their own. Their speeches shocked Burmans by their bitterness. Their continuing demands gave General Ne Win one of several pretexts for taking over the central government in 1962 and suspending the constitution. We ourselves listened to a stream of complaints from moderate Shans in both the southern and northern parts of the State. They understood the need for union, yet felt ill treated in one way or another. Their grievances, taken together, make a formidable list. At least five of them are worth considering here.

Grievances of a Border People

The most deeply felt discontent springs from the presence of the Union of Burma Army in large numbers on Shan State soil. The Shans do not pretend to be a martial "race"; few of them volunteer for Army service. Inevitably, then, the soldiers stationed in the Shan State are largely Burman, with a sprinkling of Kachins and Chins. In Shan eyes, the Army is foreign.

If these units were the best behaved in the world, they would still be unwanted. They happen to wear broad-brimmed hats something like those of old-time Boy Scouts. But there the resemblance ends. The troops in the Shan State are high spirited and not always disciplined. In strange surroundings, far from their women at home, they find Shan girls attractive and Shan girls willing. One hears many rumors of rape, and more solidly based reports of intermarriage. To Shans this is an affront and a peril.

"It's genocide, that's what it is!" one Shan patriot protested. "It's a deliberate policy to get Burmans to marry Shan girls. Those fellows in Rangoon are trying to destroy the Shan race." The target of resentment is always "Rangoon," as it used to be "Delhi" or "London" in colonial days.

The second grievance of the Shans is cultural: the compulsory use of the Burmese language in all schools, from the third grade onward; the lack of higher education in the Shan language, and, indeed, the lack of a university in Shan territory. Not many Shans can afford to go to Rangoon or Mandalay universities in Burma proper; moreover, they fear discrimination and resent what looks to them like a deliberate smothering of Shan culture. It does not blunt the edge of these complaints to recall that both Shans and Burmans follow the teachings of the Lord Buddha, or that urbanized Shans now speak some Burmese without having been forced to. The Burman way of life may be close to that of the Shans, but its Burmanness rankles all the same.

Setting them apart from the Burmans was the Shans' ancient system of hereditary feudal rulers, or sawbwas. The recent liquidation of their powers gave Shan patriots a third grievance, in certain areas the bitterest of all. From the moment of independence, it was obvious that the sawbwas were incongruous in a democratic, Marxist-oriented welfare state. They also constituted rival centers of political and economic power, which stood in the way of the central government. Like India's maharajas, they would have to go. The government at Rangoon moved slowly and cautiously to strip them of their privileges. Under General Ne Win's first period of military rule in 1959, it felt strong enough to take away the last of their administrative, financial, and judicial prerogatives. Thenceforth these survivals of feudal days became private citizens or public servants, not masters.

Some of the sawbwas accepted the new era gracefully, and even welcomed it. The head of the Shan State in 1961, for example, Sao (Duke or Earl) Hkun Hkio (pronounced *koon cho*) had been a powerful sawbwa. Yet he strongly supported the Union and later the yielding of sawbwas' privileges. He became Foreign Minister as well as Minister for Shan Affairs in Rangoon. His moon-faced calm, his moderation and good sense, helped U Nu and the central government to keep the Shan State relatively stable. But his moderation did not save him from arrest and detention, along with less temperate Shan patriots, in 1962 when the Army seized power.

His rival for the leadership, Sao Hom Hpa, was more prickly for the Burmans to handle. As the sawbwa of the richest of the old Shan States, from Lashio north to China, he lived in tweedy comfort like an English squire. His daughter was married in 1954 with festivities as lavish in their setting as those of a royal wedding in England. Hom Hpa, like other sawbwas, proved his courage against Japanese invaders. He made secret contact with the famous Force 101, composed partly of cloak-and-dagger men from the United States Office of Strategic Services, and he formed a guerrilla band that became a torment to the Japanese in their last retreat. In 1949, he personally led the fight to recapture Lashio from the insurgents. Perhaps because he always disliked U Nu's welfare-state policies, he was one of the few Shan leaders left at liberty by Ne Win's second military regime.

Another influential leader is Sao Sai Long, the picturesque former chieftain of Kengtung, in the territory along the Yunnan, Laos, and Thailand frontiers. Attending school in Australia during the war, he picked up a down-under twang and some peppery Australian slang. He also acquired the nickname Shorty, by which he is affectionately known to his fellow sawbwas and to the English-speaking leaders in Rangoon. He is both anti-Communist and anti-Chinese, for his former State suffered more cruelly than any other from invasion by the ragtag of Chiang Kai-shek's army in 1951 and 1953. One cannot conceive of Kengtung without Shorty in some official or unofficial role. Yet he was clapped into detention by the Army regime in 1962, and perhaps with reason. For Shorty held a special grudge

"His Excellency [the Governor of North Borneo], half smothered under a white-plumed helmet, walks stiffly between the police lines and takes the salute."

The North Borneo Railway "cuts through a natural incision in the jungle, the Padas River gorge . . . a haunt of crocodiles."

"Kota Belud comes to life on market day." Dusun girls in North Borneo saunter through "the Bornean equivalent of an Iowa State fair."

OPPOSITE

Kachin girls love to put on their finery to pose for pictures at Bhamo, on the Irrawaddy. Dr. Gordon Seagrave trained girls like these as nurses in his hospital near the Burma-China frontier.

RIGHT

Dr. Gordon S. Seagrave, the "Burma Surgeon" whose "legacy goes far beyond mere healing."

BELOW

A leader of the Kachin National Congress at Bhamo, with his children. He is one of those educated Kachins who want a stronger state within the Union of Burma.

XIII

These women staked out deck space for three days
and nights on the Irrawaddy flatboat in Burma.
"Far from complaining, they faced the journey
with a gay and triumphant air."

Military police shared with the authors the sloping tin roof of an Irrawaddy River flatboat. "Between eating, sleeping, doing their laundry, and playing games, these young men guarded the ship from the rebels. . . ."

"The Shweli River, tender as the Thames above Marlow,"
marks the Burma-China border; the folded hills in the
distance are in Yunnan.

against Rangoon, stemming from the special interest of the territory he used to rule.

This grievance, the fourth on our list, is scented with the sickly sweetness of opium.

[1]

White opium poppies carpet parts of the northeastern Shan State, near the China and Laos frontiers. Nobody knows how many tribesmen of this area grow opium as a cash crop. Whatever the number, it is enough to have made the growers and dealers a political force and the crop a source of profit to others as well. The cultivation of opium is legal on tribal lands in the Shan State, though forbidden elsewhere in the Union. Its sale and purchase are likewise legal under license; in Lashio one sees a shop that advertises its license to sell.

Far more lucrative than the legal trade within the Shan State has been the smuggling of narcotics—not only of the home-grown supply but also of quantities grown by tribesmen within China. The Shan State has long been the most convenient corridor through which Chinese opium and its derivatives reach the outer world. The route leads first to Kengtung, thence over mountain trails to Thailand, and on to the opium dens and peddlers of Singapore and Hong Kong. In processed form, much of it reaches Europe, Canada, and the United States.

Officially the Burmese government frowns on this traffic. A Shan State regulation forbids anyone to bring opium within ten miles of any town except by special permit. But smugglers are clever and bold. In the summer of 1960, Chinese dealers in the Shan State were brazen enough to charter three DC-3's belonging to the government-owned Union of Burma Airways to carry valuable cargoes southward. Staying within the law, they brought the opium by mules over forest and mountain trails to the Lashio airport, which happens to be slightly more than ten miles from the town. The chartered planes flew it to Kengtung airport, again more than ten miles outside the municipal limits. The first of the three cargoes weighed 5,040 pounds, the second 5,300. For the triple shipment of about seven and a half tons, the growers were reported to have asked about $40,000 a ton and gladly accepted half that amount. The three cargoes could produce about 1,650 pounds of heroin, which, in the illicit world traffic, would of course bring far more than the original crop.

One must assume that the entire consignment got through to Thailand. The Thai government has been only intermittently able and willing to stop the traffic over the winding mountain trails from Kengtung into Thailand. For Burma, the plane shipments meant nothing worse than public embarrassment. *The Guardian* of Rangoon, with a courage characteristic of its editor, quickly exposed the story. It chided the central government for having let its own civilian aircraft be chartered for such shipments. Shorty, the sawbwa of Kengtung, reproached the editor for printing such news. He did not say it was untrue; he simply argued that publicity would incite the Burmese and Thai governments to crack down and thus deprive hundreds of opium growers in his State of their livelihood. The incident gave this former feudal ruler a chance to identify himself with his people and to register his distrust and dislike of any meddling by the Burmans in Rangoon.

The Shans have yet a fifth complaint which might better be described as a vague suspicion. Rightly or wrongly, many of them believed that "Rangoon" is taking too much from the Shan State's natural resources, leaving too little revenue for the Shans themselves.

[2]

In the old days, Shans held hereditary rights to the world's largest ruby mines at Mogok, 6,000 feet above the

Irrawaddy Valley. British promoters entered northern Burma with the glint of these rubies in their eyes. Their government took good care to include the Mogok area in Burma proper, rather than in the Shan States. To this day, Mogok remains outside Shan territory, although Shans live there and have worked around the mine for centuries. The mine area has been gerrymandered as if it were a Congressional district in New York City. The British company's revenue from the mine amounted to a paltry $70,000 a year at the turn of the century; by mid-century, under Burmese government ownership, the diggings showed signs of exhaustion and yielded trifling returns. Yet to the Shans, Mogok is their treasure snatched from them by foreigners. Who knows when another ruby might be dug up like the forty-two-carat gem unearthed in 1918? In its uncut state it fetched $134,400. Since the days of the Nibelungen, mines like Mogok have symbolized wealth and power.

The Shan State possesses other minerals: newly opened zinc mines in the south, and an estimated reserve of 30,000,000 tons of iron ore only seven miles from Taunggyi, the capital. Until these were discovered, probably the most spectacular natural resource in all Burma was the Bawdwin Mine, this one officially in Shan territory not far from the ruby diggings. So vast was its extent, so fabulous its store of metals, that the first Westerners who heard of it refused to believe the rumors. The story of its rediscovery and exploitation brings into Shan history the improbable intrusion of a young man who was to be President of the United States.

In 1904 a mining engineer named Herbert Hoover was a passenger on a steamer crossing from Penang to Colombo. At the age of thirty he was already a mature, skeptical, and prosperous engineer, with experience in remote parts of China and Australia behind him. On the ship he met a British contractor who had been building the railroad from

Mandalay to Lashio, eighty miles from the Chinese frontier.
The contractor told of colossal mine workings in the Shan
jungle, and described them as an abandoned lead and
copper mine. Understandably curious, Mr. Hoover's British
employers sent a young engineer to see what truth the
story might contain. He dispatched a cable estimating that
at least half a million tons of lead lay on the surface in
slag heaps. As Mr. Hoover confessed in his *Memoirs,*
written almost half a century later, he simply did not believe "that any such amounts of loose lead could exist in
the world." Still unconvinced, he assigned an older American engineer to check the story. The second report, in April
1905, was so staggering that Mr. Hoover made up his mind
to see this El Dorado for himself.

He took the train to the dusty town of Hsipaw, then the
capital of one of the northern Shan States, and stayed with
the local sawbwa at his modest palace. From Hsipaw, Mr.
Hoover and an American colleague rode horses through
the dripping jungle. The sense of amazement and wonder,
not conspicuous in Herbert Hoover, overcame him when he
saw the mine at last. He found hundreds of dumps and
tunnels and one open pit almost 1,000 feet long, 500 feet
wide, and 300 feet deep. Like the nineteenth-century
travelers who first gazed upon the Maya ruins, Mr. Hoover
wondered what manner of men had wrought these prodigies of labor, and when, and how. He soon had his answer.
The Chinese, he learned, had worked the mine intensively
for 450 years until about 1850; then the Moslem revolt in
Yunnan stopped the digging. The Chinese had dug for
silver, not lead. So remote was this treasure-trove that
they could not carry the lead away; they separated the
silver and left the lead ore, hundreds of thousands of tons
of it, on the surface.

Having rediscovered the mine, the company's next tasks
were to process the old slag for hungry markets and to
resume cutting the seams that had lain untouched for more

than fifty years. Mr. Hoover and his associates did both in the grand manner.

With persistence and drive, the President-to-be persuaded the sawbwa to recruit 20,000 workers to build a railroad spur to the mine. According to his own account, he arranged wage scales "above any standard the jungle had known—and the first money thousands had ever had." In the mine itself, his employers, the Burma Corporation, Ltd., drove a two-mile tunnel and started workings 700 feet beneath the old ones. There they opened "one of the largest and richest lead-zinc-silver ore bodies ever discovered," and proved the existence of more than 5,000,000 tons of ore above the tunnel. By 1908 the company had finished the railway spur, had built a smelter at Mandalay, and had begun producing salable metal at last.

The output from the mine was beyond belief. In its first thirty years under new management, this single plot of earth gave up more than 1,500,000 tons of lead, 135,000,-000 ounces of silver, and substantial amounts of zinc—all worth, according to Mr. Hoover, more than $350,000,-000. One reads in his *Memoirs* that the mine gave a "living," directly and indirectly, to 100,000 Shans, Chinese, and Indians. What the feudal rulers of Hsipaw received as their share of the slag, during almost two generations, one can only surmise.

By 1918 Mr. Hoover had sold his interests in Burma and stepped onto the world stage as director of war relief. Thus ended the American financial connection with the Shan country, remote in every way from American preoccupations of those days. The British went on working the fast-dwindling reserves until the eve of the Japanese invasion.

To an old-fashioned capitalist, the history of the mine since 1940 makes melancholy reading. First the retreating British wrecked the mine to keep its metals from stoking the Japanese war machine. The Japanese ordered the

Mitsui Company to restore it, but mighty effort brought
meager returns. When the Japanese fled southward on
their last retreat, they, too, blew up what they and their
prisoners of war had rebuilt with so much toil. The British
found the property wrecked. Survey teams estimated in
1947 that it would cost $9,000,000 to bring the mine and
the smelter back into production. Neither exhausted Britain nor newly independent Burma had such funds to invest.

The civil wars in Burma inflicted new destruction and
neglect upon the mine property. The Union government,
bleeding from insurrections, could spare little thought or
effort for the once-profitable mine far to the north in the
Shan State. In 1951 it did make a halfhearted attempt.
It compromised its Socialist theories to the extent of setting
up a "joint venture" to reopen the mine; the government
of Burma paid half the capital of a new company, equivalent to about $6,600,000, and British investors the other
half. Mining began again in the following year, and in
three more years the yield was up to 8,500 tons of ore a
day.

We have told the story of the Bawdwin Mine at length
because it explains some of the Shan grievances and at
the same time exposes some of the fallacies in their thinking about natural resources. No matter how vast or how
wisely managed, a mine does not last forever. The colossal
Mesabi mines in Minnesota, for example, seemed virtually
inexhaustible, yet their substance was shot away from tens
of thousands of guns in two world wars, and a substitute
source had to be found—in Labrador. The depletion of the
Bawdwin Mine had become apparent long before the Japanese invasion. Nonetheless, some Shans still think of it as
it was when Herbert Hoover's bedazzled eyes beheld it,
forgetting that there is little wealth left in it. In any event,
the central government contributes to the Shan State's
budget a far greater amount than its income from the mine.

[3]

Another kind of natural resource that has shrunk in the Shan State, and elsewhere in Burma, is the teak forest. To a foreigner who knows little else about the country, teak is a trademark of Burma almost as exotic as the golden Shwedagon Pagoda in Rangoon. The teak industry, like a zoo and a circus, has depended on the elephant. For centuries, elephants have been trained in Burma to butt their way into the roadless forests and to lift and roll the teak logs into a river, which carries them to sawmills and markets downstream. The late Burton Holmes seldom failed to include these elephants in his travel lectures on Southeast Asia; travel magazines offered them as staple food, and pictured them almost as often as the temple dancers of Bali. Burma used to have more than 6,000 trained elephants, each worth about $1,300 to its owner in the immediate prewar years. Invasion and war set most of them free to forage for themselves in the jungle. A hundred or so were put to work on the Ledo Road in the far northwest. Of the rest, only a small proportion was ever rounded up, and by 1960 all Burma had only about a thousand elephants that could be used in teak logging.

Three fourths of the world's teak grows in Burma, about one tenth of this in the Shan State, where it is more accessible than in the trackless forests of the northern hills. The British made this prized hardwood one of Burma's most profitable exports. In 1940 alone—by no means the best teak year—225,000 tons of it were shipped abroad, worth more than $9,000,000, to be used for ships, houses, and furniture. But the forests, like the mines, have fallen on evil days. At least 400 square miles of Burma's forests were destroyed and others damaged by violence or neglect during and after the Japanese invasion. So deep was the damage and so slow the recovery that by 1959, almost twenty years after the Japanese plague hit Burma, exports

of teakwood were still only about a third of what they had
been in the last prewar years.

Gradually, as the government mops up rebel bands and
makes forest areas again safe for lumbering, Burma may
recapture some of its income from timber. To make up for
the shortage of elephant power, the Union government and
the American aid mission have experimented with machinery to fell the teak trees and drag them right out of
the jungle as green teak. Denmark and other European
countries are using green teak for the tops of highly var-
nished tables. But some experts gaze on this new market
with something less than rapture. They would rather
export seasoned wood which does not warp. "Foreigners,"
said a forester in the Shan State, "will get a bad opinion
of Burmese teak. Selling it green will do us no good in the
long run."

Despite such new departures, Burma is unlikely ever to
reap its old-time foreign exchange from its trees. Reforestation, of which the British were proud in colonial days, has
all but stopped. The Burmese do not concede the need for
it in their hot, rainy climate. They prefer to trust to natural
regeneration. Too often the result is that the teak trees are
stunted by the unplanned new growth around them. This
is one of the reasons why Burma is not making the best
use of its forest treasures.

In the Shan State, at least, there are other reasons.
Many Shans have an abiding suspicion of outsiders, whether
Westerners or Burmans, who try to exploit their resources.
And they have been unwilling to do much exploiting them-
selves. When the British took lead and silver from the
Bawdwin Mine and rubies from Mogok, they had to import
Gurkhas and Chinese for the underground labor. Burmans
who take charge of ringing and felling teak trees are for-
eigners in Shan eyes. In short, Shans do not welcome foreign
enterprise that will bring employment and money to their
State.

An example was a recent proposal from Israel. Because Israel is too distant and too small to be dangerous, because it offers technical skills of a high order, and because its political philosophy is socialistic like Burma's, the two governments have struck up what can only be described as a continuing love affair. Yet when the Israelis offered to help put a million acres into wheat in the southern Shan State, with the blessing of Burma's central government, the Shan State Council vetoed the plan. Their reasons were two. They had not been consulted, and they felt such a large-scale foreign enterprise would interfere with Shan State rights.

In this, as in other efforts to use their resources, the Shans will not let themselves be hustled. They have little desire to dig like moles beneath the earth or to tend machinery like robots. Except for a minority, they are not aflame with craving for a steel mill as a status symbol, or for large-scale industry.

Such perversity does not mean that the Shans lack mechanical aptitude. On the contrary, many of them take to machinery with a resourcefulness that better-trained Western mechanics can envy. A Shan has to be resourceful. Except for bullock carts, almost everything on wheels in the Shan State is of war vintage. Buses are usually springless trucks with ramshackle bodies. Jeeps that must have seen service with Vinegar Joe Stilwell still clatter, seemingly immortal, over the Shan and Kachin State roads. When we jeeped from Mandalay through the northern Shan State to the Chinese frontier, our steering shaft split, our brakes gave out, our canvas top flew off more than once. Yet the Shan driver met every crisis with bits of wire and string. No, the Shans do not lack ingenuity. Where they fall short is in that stamina, attention span, or whatever else it takes to keep an enterprise afloat, particularly one that does not rank high in their estimation. Among many examples, we think of a food-canning scheme which a group of Shans undertook with enthusiasm when they saw an American woman at work in her own kitchen near Taunggyi. The Shans realized the worth of preserving their seasonal food surplus and asked the American to teach them. The idea blossomed into a school for canners and then into a small industry. But when the American left Burma several years later, the impetus went with her: the industry sickened and died.

Apart from a lack of doggedness, these people seem not to connect mechanization and industrialization with the good life. In their scale of values, such twentieth-century blessings hold a low place. The jargon of industrial development leaves them unmoved.

The Shans, by and large, do not want to change. They are what they are. Deep in their character lies a passiveness, a resolve to saunter through the twentieth century at their own cheerful pace.

The Kachins: Border Warriors

From its northernmost border State come two of Burma's greatest assets: the Irrawaddy River, the Union's lifeline, and the Kachins, the Union's best fighting men. The Kachins move southward like the river waters, erasing, as we have said, any ethnic frontier between their own and the adjoining Shan State. Through the ages they have steadily wandered from their tribal surroundings in the hills down to the fertile valleys and settled communities of the Shans. Sometimes a Kachin chieftain's daughter has married a Shan princeling. More often Kachins have had to do the menial jobs in order to attach themselves to Shan society.

With all their intermingling, the two peoples remain as different as hawks and pigeons. Kachins, in general, cherish a hereditary contempt for Shans, who betray an ancient fear of Kachins. When a Shan baby squalls, the mother is likely to shush him with: "Be quiet, or the Kachins will take you away!" It is one of the quirks of this borderland that two peoples so antagonistic and unlike should nevertheless, in Winston Churchill's phrase about two other peoples, remain "mixed up together in some of their affairs for mutual and general advantage."

So it happens that they loiter and chaffer together without any outward sign of enmity. In the town of Namkham, for example, men and women of a dozen mountain tribes crowd the outdoor market; their clothes are as dazzling as the fruits, vegetables, and spices on display. As the human river flows slowly between the stalls, a Kachin girl stands out clearly. If she is unmarried, she wears no turban over her boyish cropped hair; her workaday neck-to-knee garment, often of black and red, gives her the look of an Amazon. A Kachin man appears burly, broad-shouldered, snub-nosed. Kachins have little to sell on market days; they roam the hills and grow what they can on temporary clearings. The only way to irrigate such terrain for rice is to terrace it, as enterprising hill farmers have done for centuries in Japan, Formosa, the Philippines, and Nepal; but terracing requires back-breaking labor as well as skill, and comparatively few Kachins have tried it. Most of them practice slash-and-burn cultivation, the curse of highland Asia. They choose a likely tract, cut the bigger trees, and set fire to what remains of the jungle. Rain and wood ash make it possible to grow dry rice, millet, corn, or opium poppies— as long as fertility lasts. When the soil of a clearing is exhausted, usually in one year, the Kachin farmers abandon it and repeat the process elsewhere.

The slashers should let the burned plots lie fallow for several years. But land is not limitless, even in the Kachin hills; and too many farmers return to their old regrown clearing after only a year or two, to denude it and farm once more. The process not only exhausts the soil; it also brings erosion. Monsoon rains hit the naked hillsides, wash the topsoil away, and flood the Shan farmlands below.

The Kachins have never built a settled society like that of the Shans. They have no organized religion like the Buddhism of the Shans; most of them are animists, fearing and placating the spirits in nature or those of their ancestors. Perhaps one Kachin in ten is a convert to Baptist or Roman Catholic Christianity.

[1]

With no surplus of food and nothing much else to sell, Kachins took to preying on their neighbors or to hiring themselves as mercenaries in foreign armies. They had built up a solid reputation as hawks before the British conquered Burma. Geography favored them, for in their hills they sat astride the ancient main caravan route from China to the headwaters of the Irrawaddy. Mule caravans bound for Bhamo in past centuries brought Chinese silk, vermilion, quicksilver, and jade for the markets of Burma and beyond. It would have been strange and out of character if the Kachins had not extracted toll for the safe passage of every trader.

Dr. Gordon Seagrave has written that if the British had not arrived in strength, nothing would have stopped the Kachins, with their long knives, from cutting southward through all of Burma. Let a Kachin fortify himself with opium, let him make sure that his knife edge is keen, and he will cheerfully tackle a tiger. The British, who value brave fighting men, recruited Kachins into their forces in colonial Burma. American and British veterans of World War II remember them as superlative allies. Like the Gurkhas from Nepal, they were an unending terror to the Japanese, stealing up on them in the forest and pouncing without a sound. If American or British fighting men were wounded or lost, they had orders to get off the roads in the hope of finding a friendly Kachin in the jungle. The forti-

tude of these hillmen knew no limit. On the walls of the
British war cemetery outside Rangoon, among thousands
of names of British and Indians with no known graves,
are carved the names of many Kachins who fought the
invader to the end.

The martial prowess of these people is both an asset
and a potential danger to the Union of Burma. It reassures
the Burmese government to know that such unterrified
fighting men live along the Chinese border. It stiffens the
Burmese Army to have Kachins among its enlisted men
and sometimes among its officers. But if this fighting spirit
were ever turned against Burma, the Union would find
itself in even deeper trouble. Understandably, Burman
leaders pay something close to deference to the Kachins—
when deference is needed.

On a journey to Peking in 1956 to negotiate a settlement
of the long-disputed frontier, U Nu took a group of Kachin
leaders with him. The Chinese held out for three villages
which, they claimed, were rightfully theirs. U Nu studied
the record; he had decided that this small Chinese claim
was "reasonable." The Kachins flatly refused. Chou En-lai
fixed them with his glittering eye; they outstared him.
They would not budge.

"I made a final appeal to the Kachin leaders," U Nu later
told his Parliament, "pleading with them to agree in principle . . . but the head of the Kachin State said that he
did not have the authority to give his agreement, and that
he needed to consult his colleagues in Burma before taking
any decision."

Perhaps U Nu was not as artless as he seemed; he seldom
is. Perhaps he knew in advance that the Kachins would
resist and thus help him gain time. It took three years of
imploring and cajoling before the Burmese, through U
Nu's successor Ne Win, could induce the stubborn Kachins
to give up a square inch of their soil. Even then they
remained unreconciled. When the border settlement came

before the Kachin legislature for approval, the State leader and two of his closest colleagues stalked out of the room in protest.

This was one of many signs of a new Kachin national consciousness. Kachins educated in mission schools have moved in recent years to Bhamo and Myitkyina, the largest towns of the State, where they promote Kachin interests through State and national politics. Theirs is not a separatist movement like that of the Shans; the Kachin State cannot legally secede from the Union, nor has it the resources to live on its own. An American mining survey, commissioned by the Union government, found nothing of value except gold-bearing gravels in two small areas. What the Kachin leaders want is a stronger State within the Union and more Union benefits for their people. It says much for the supposedly crude and uncultured Kachins that education ranks highest among their priorities. When the wartime British Governor of Burma, Sir Reginald Dorman-Smith, returned to Myitkyina in 1946, he promised British funds to meet Kachin needs. The chiefs then asked —and still do—for hospitals and schools.

In pressuring the government of the Union, the Kachins use two political instruments: the Kachin National Congress, led by Duwa (Chief) Zau Lawn, a Christian and former headmaster of an American Baptist Mission school, and the Kachin Youth League, led by Sama Duwa Sinwa Nawng, the product of a Buddhist monastic school. Sinwa Nawng led the delegation to the 1947 conference that agreed to set up an autonomous Kachin State within the Burmese Union. Because of his fight against the British, even to the extent of helping the Japanese in the war, he is called the "Aung San of the Kachin State"—Aung San being the national hero of Burma, the martyred leader of the independence movement.[3]

[3] After organizing a student strike in the 1930's and collaborating first with the Japanese and then with the British, Aung San became head of the

The two Kachin leaders are rivals, seesawing in power as elected heads of their State. As hereditary chiefs, they command the loyalty of some Kachins but not of all. For many backwoodsmen defy hereditary leaders, as well as any other authority that tries to rule them. The danger in the Kachin State is not that moderate leaders will want to break loose from Burma; it is that untamed hillmen might tear the Kachin State apart and create dissension from which only the Communists could profit.

[2]

Of all the forces that work for change among the Kachins, and the Shans as well, none has been so consistently underestimated as the Christian missionaries. Their influence over more than a hundred years permeates the borderland. As agents of quiet, nonviolent revolution, they were probably unrivaled.

Their effectiveness cannot be measured in number of Christian converts. In that field, evangelists have reaped only a meager harvest. All Burma with 20,000,000 people counts no more than 350,000 Christians. Of the 2,000,000 people in the Shan State, with its stanchly Buddhist majority, only about 25,000 profess the Christian faith. The Kachin State has about 15,000 Christians among its 300,-000 to 400,000 people. The higher percentage of converts among the Kachins underlines what the missionaries have long known. Most of their recruits are former animists, to whom the Christian faith seems to offer a release from terror of evil spirits.

---

dominant party, the Anti-Fascist People's Freedom League, after World War II. His visit to London early in 1947 resulted in Britain's promise to give full independence to Burma within a year. On July 19, 1947, two gunmen with submachine guns broke into a meeting of the pre-independence cabinet and murdered Aung San and five colleagues. Aung San was only thirty-two; he would have been independent Burma's first Prime Minister. For an admiring appraisal by a Briton who dealt with him, see Field Marshal the Viscount Slim: *Defeat into Victory* (New York: David McKay Company; 1961), pp. 423–8.

The most pervasive of the Christian missionaries in Burma and the outlying hills have been the American Baptists. Before the Japanese burst in to destroy Western works, some 180 Americans were scattered among 1,722 Baptist churches throughout Burma. The number of their postwar replacements has not risen much above forty. The two most remarkable Baptists, the first and perhaps the last of a stalwart line, demonstrate by their differences how the missionaries effected change, and how they themselves changed to meet the new times they had helped create.

Their pioneer, the first missionary ever to leave American shores and the first ever to touch the shores of Burma, was a young New Englander named Adoniram Judson. Two unscheduled events landed him as a Baptist in Burma in 1813. The Congregationalists of Massachusetts had scraped together the money to send Judson, an ardent member of their church, to India. But in mid-ocean a fellow passenger changed the Congregationalist into a Baptist by total immersion. In Calcutta he found the missionary ground already overcrowded, so he sailed on to untouched Burma. Only his ignorance of the country outstripped his zeal. Proselytizing was forbidden by the Burman king, who sent him to prison cages on several occasions. Judson's health broke and his three wives all died young, victims of the tropics. With the few Burmese who had the courage secretly to join his church, Judson started a small school and compiled a Burmese-English dictionary. The school became Judson College, destined nearly a hundred years later to inoculate some of Burma's young leaders with revolutionary ideas about independence.

Following in Judson's footsteps, American Baptists spread into the outlying hills in later, more hospitable days. When in 1890 the British first reached Kengtung, they found that one of them, Dr. J. N. Cushing, had been there for years. He was the first to compile a dictionary and grammar of the Shan language as it was spoken in the southern Shan

States. Baptist missionaries in the far wilder Kachin country had already committed that language to writing for the first time.

With relatively poor results in the field of conversion, some missionaries broadened the scope of their work. Mission schools began to make a dent on ignorance of the outer world. Hospitals and clinics began to teach people health while curing them. Methodist, Anglican, Presbyterian, and Roman Catholic churchmen from many countries competed and added to the ferment of new ideas. Little by little the accent shifted from saving souls to training minds, from teaching Scripture to teaching self-help and local initiative.

The modern missionary may not be as meteoric as Judson was, but he is more apt to be trained for his role. We met him in a village not far from the border of China, a young Illinois Baptist in sports jacket and slacks. "My job here is to make myself dispensable," he said. "I'm training my Kachin successor to take over the church and the school." With some 200,000 members, it would seem reasonable to suppose that the Burmese Baptist Church could run its own affairs and spread the gospel too. Needing American support, it would presumably take American advisers with indispensable skills, but strictly as advisers. In any other capacity, the Western missionary in Burma is no longer wanted.

Not far from the Illinois pastor's mission, another Baptist pastor, a Burmese Karen, leads a congregation of 300. Every Sunday in church, his wife plays a wheezing portable organ, and the congregation sings the hymns in four languages simultaneously: Kachin, Shan, Karen, and Burmese. The pastor is not only a fervent Baptist but also a loyal citizen of Burma. Such men will carry on the work begun by Judson after Western missionaries have gone.

The people of the Kachin and Shan States have among them a Baptist who dwarfs all the rest. Gordon S. Seagrave, perhaps the greatest of all who have worked in Burma, is a medical, not a religious, missionary. He severed his legal ties with the American Baptist Mission just after the war. No one could better illustrate how missionaries have changed Burma—and how Burma has changed missionaries. No one could be farther from Judson in outlook or training. Coming from a background of more than a hundred years of continuous missionary work in Burma, Dr. Seagrave is the twenty-eighth member of his family to serve there. He knew as much about the area, the people, and the problems as any non-Burmese could know when he arrived in Namkham on the China-Burma border with a a new medical degree. "Nobody in the area believed in Western medicine," he wrote, "and only the Kachins were willing to submit to surgery."

The center of his work and the pride of his life is his 300-bed hospital. Built of massive cobblestones and cement, the main structure and its outlying houses crown a hilltop above the palm-thatched huts of Namkham. The hospital serves 5,000 inpatients a year and 10,000 outpatients, most of them from villages where only witch medicine had been known until Seagrave's day. Here come sufferers from tropical plagues and parasites, casualties with faces clawed by mountain bears, and victims of plain filth and undernourishment. Somehow Seagrave and his helpers bring them back to life.

If this were all he did, he would rank with other famous healers in distant lands like Dr. Albert Schweitzer or the late Dr. Thomas Dooley. But Seagrave's legacy to the Shans and Kachins goes far beyond mere healing. The heart of his achievement which radiates throughout northern Burma is his training school for nurses. Seagrave began the training at Namkham in the 1920's, with one Shan girl and one Kachin. In 1961 he had seventeen fully trained teaching nurses on his hospital staff and 125 students in the four-year course. Coming from almost every tribal group, some Christian, some Buddhist, and some spirit worshippers, these students have a single bond: they are not city-bred; the soft life and the bright lights are not for them. They finish training skilled and toughened, either to continue at Namkham or to go out to smaller hospitals and dispensaries throughout the border States, taking new techniques and knowledge with them. They know the importance of clean water and environmental sanitation in preventing disease. They can dress a wound, diagnose and treat an ailment, clean an instrument, read a slide, give a hypodermic and a simple anesthetic. If they marry and have children of their own, as many do, they retire from professional nursing, but their homes inevitably become clinics and dispensaries for their neighbors.

Dr. Seagrave estimated in 1961 that some 700 graduates of his nursing school were at work throughout Burma. In a country where, as Prime Minister U Nu said a few years ago, 85 per cent of the people had never had contact with public health, these 700 have been a revolutionary force. Some have sent their daughters to Namkham to become a second generation in training. Dr. Seagrave, in short, has built a lasting institution. His principles of teaching and training will survive. By demonstrating that the long-neglected hill people can apply modern medicine with skill and devotion, the doctor has enhanced their dignity as well as his own.

With advancing years (he was born in 1897) Seagrave grew impatient of proselytizers and intolerant of pious prudes among the missionaries he saw. A few seemed chiefly interested in draping Mother Hubbards over naked children; others, usually of puritan belief, tried to spread drabness over the color of tribal life. They saw wickedness in heathen festivals; they made the unconverted feel inferior. When the "Old Man," as his nurses call him, becomes indignant about these and other peeves, his language is as sulfurous as the hot springs along the Burma Road. He makes no apology for it.

"It seems to me," he wrote, "that swearing is sometimes a very excellent safety valve and keeps one sane and on the job. At other times it amounts to a prayer and I am convinced God recognizes many oaths as such."

So, unlike conventional missionaries, he swears and chain-smokes; he flies into tempers when fools provoke him—and does not have an ounce of smug superiority toward anyone.

Occasionally Dr. Seagrave's temper is tried by a Communist agent among the Chinese who still come to the hospital for treatment.

"About once a week," according to the doctor, "we get a patient from across the river. I call the police to start a security check, and we put a card on the foot of his bed to show that he has come from China. If he turns out to be a bad character, out he goes. We don't waste any time or sympathy on him." One such "bad character" was rash enough to try to indoctrinate Dr. Seagrave himself. He got a shower of the doctor's swearwords and landed in the police lockup. At the end of 1960 about 300 infiltrators, some of them Chinese Shans or Kachins, were in jail in the Shan and Kachin States, about 1,000 in all of Burma.

China's Shadow

Burma's frontier with China twists for about 950 miles, virtually all of it forming the borders of the Shan and Kachin States. Along the ninety-five-mile Shweli Valley it is a settled frontier; one knows where it is. But no barbed-wire fence or wall marks the exact line. One strolls along the valley road near Namkham and passes a white stone pylon in the middle of a field. Beyond the pylon, a farmer stooping over his flooded rice plants is standing in China.

The frontier is real and visible, too, where a bridge takes the Burma Road across the Shweli River. Trade and traffic along the road are but a trickle of what they used to be. A Burmese Army check point near the bridge and a gate that can be lowered across the roadway show clearly enough where Burma ends. Elsewhere, for long stretches, the boundary has not been defined.

[1]

In 1960 the Burmese and Chinese patched up several long-standing frontier quarrels by a sensible compromise. The Chinese had demanded 187 square miles of land claimed by Burma; they settled for two unimportant tracts totaling 130 square miles. One of these, in the far north-west, included the three Kachin villages and 1,400 families whose transfer, as we said earlier, provoked a protest from the Kachin State leaders. The Chinese also won a patch of wilderness in the extreme northeast of the Shan State. In this jungle fastness, tribesmen known as the Wild Wa used to hack off the head of anyone unlucky enough to come within their reach. It was their way of propitiating spirits. Chinese heads were highly prized; British, being rarer, were more precious still. Why any Chinese should have wanted to risk his head in this area, the Burmese could not fathom.

They were willing to give it up, for in return Burma won clear title to a triangle of eighty-five square miles through which the main road runs from Namkham, in the Shan State, to Bhamo on the Irrawaddy. Because of this important road, the British had obtained the tract for Burma by a "perpetual" lease from the Manchu Empire. When we crossed it by jeep in 1954 and stopped at a village, a dozen tribesmen wearing long knives at their belts surrounded us. Clearly they were not charmed to see Westerners. We found their knives and stares disagreeable, and were glad to be gone. Since then, this village and its surrounding land, called the Namwan Tract, has become officially a part of Burma.

To guard even those stretches of the frontier that are demarcated would daunt a Great Power with half a million border police. Burma possesses no natural shield like India's Himalayan wall or the hundred-mile strait of salt water that protects Formosa from the mainland. If China ever exploded into conquest, its army could pour into Burma and meet little more than guerrilla opposition. What concerns the Burmese more than hypothetical invasion is actual infiltration. Chinese have been moving across the frontier, back and forth, for generations. Bandits crossed habitually from Yunnan to Burma, using the Burmese side as temporary refuge from their pursuers. Hungry peasants trekked southward every winter from eroded, overpopulated Yunnan, in search of work on the farms and in the mines of northern Burma. Before the monsoon rains they wandered north again, to escape the malaria of the valleys. They were no more dangerous than the wetbacks of the Mexican-American border; they gave Burma a pool of labor and constituted no threat to security.

But since the Communists seized control of China, two new kinds of refugees have added to Burma's troubles. Some are genuine, fleeing regimentation at home. Some, without doubt, have been agents under orders to make contact with Communist rebels inside Burma. On such assignments, Shans and Kachins from Chinese territory are useful. The Chinese Communists began organizing and training their Shan and Kachin minorities almost from the moment they took control of Yunnan. Unlike the ethnic Chinese, Shans and Kachins from across the frontier can fade into their surroundings in northern Burma, and Burmese police find it next to impossible to identify them.

The crest of the refugee wave from China washed into the northern borderland in 1958. This was the year the Chinese tried to collectivize the farms of their mountain tribes. They soon abandoned the attempt, and the flow of refugees slowed to a dribble. At one remote point of the frontier, where 200 had crossed in 1958, only eight came in the following year. But in 1961 there were still between 40,000 and 60,000 refugees from Communist China in Burma. Sometimes the police come across an entire village of refugees on a jungle hillside. Since the government of Burma pays homage to the Buddha's gentle teachings, it does not deport refugees who have succeeded in crossing the frontier. Only those actually caught in crossing are sent back to Communist justice.

[2]

As military ruler of Burma, in 1958 and again in 1962, Ne Win perceived that the frontier was also a civilian problem. The government's duty, as he saw it, was not just to punish tribal troublemakers who sheltered Communist agents. Its duty was also to give the tribes their first taste of schooling, preventive medicine, and improved agriculture: in short, to give them a sense of belonging to a Union of which few, probably, had ever heard. Accordingly, he set up a brand-new Frontier Areas Administration under civilian control. He gave it full charge of two frontier strips, each from thirty to sixty miles deep. One of these was in the northeast of the Kachin State, the other in the northeast of the Shan State, the wilderness of the Wild Wa. In these areas, the Frontier Administration has taken over authority from the State governments.

To staff the agency, Ne Win combed the universities and government offices to find teachers and rural sociologists and other civilians who knew the tribal languages. These experts work with Army officers and intelligence agents and get special rewards for hazardous service among the tribes. The closest parallel to Burma's experiment is India's North-East Frontier Agency, in which anthropologists and village workers serve with the Army along the disputed McMahon Line between India and Tibet. When U Nu first took back the reins of power in Burma from the Army, he continued the Frontier Administration unchanged, and he praised it handsomely in a speech to the Parliament at Rangoon. If the new instrument lives up to the promise of its early years, it should strengthen Burma's influence among the hill peoples and help to immunize them against infection from across the Communist border.

A second mechanism was borrowed not from India but from Israel. In General Ne Win's initial term, Burmese Army officers visited Israel to study the new self-defense settlements along the exposed frontiers. They found Israeli soldiers and reservists stationed among the farm families, to help with the crops and to train the farmers for combat if necessary. What they saw was a lesson for Burma. The Burmese government promptly built four Israeli-type communities in the east of the Shan State near the Salween River and another of about forty families in the far north of the Kachin State. An offer of land, tools, and credit attracted selected settlers who had served in the Army. Future settlers were sent to Israel for training in the *kibbutzim*, the communal farms. The government gives high priority to this experiment; it plans to build more and more of the new communities. By such unconventional methods Burma hopes to check small border incursions.

[3]

How interested are the rulers of the New China in stirring up the Shans and Kachins of Burma? Their overt propaganda by radio, strident in the early 1950's, had died down by 1960. Publicly they said nothing to encourage separatism and unrest. But they used less obvious methods. In the Kachin State, Chinese efforts have centered on

Bhamo, the capital, and Myitkyina, of tragic wartime fame. To these towns Chinese Kachins and Shans have come to live in recent years, most of them refugees, some undoubtedly agents. As evidence of its interest in winning converts among Kachins and Shans, the Chinese government set up a "People's Library" in Bhamo, stocked with English publications like *China Reconstructs* as well as with Burmese books picturing the Communist paradise across the frontier. In the Shan State the Chinese maintain a consulate at Lashio, on the one good road that leads from Burma into China. Burma's leaders do not doubt that through this consulate, on instructions from the Chinese embassy in Rangoon, the Communists are wooing the students and particularly the separatists.

In both territories the Chinese face one obstacle above all others. This is the widespread dread and dislike of China, whatever the form of its government. Both border peoples remember with bitter distaste the brief postwar occupation of their towns by Chinese Nationalist troops; they detested the Chinese even more than the Japanese. Since the war the Shans have had equally unpleasant memories of the invasion of the eastern part of their State by the dregs of Chiang Kai-shek's armies. It does not soften their hearts to be told that the Communists are Chiang's enemies. Chinese are as unpopular in the two States as elsewhere in Southeast Asia; any nostrum bearing a made-in-China label is poison.

China's Soviet partners do not suffer from such handicaps. When Mr. Khrushchev visited Taunggyi with Mr. Bulganin in 1955, it was a frolic long to be remembered. The Shans were vastly curious about Mr. Khrushchev. Why should such a powerful world figure take the trouble to visit them? They lodged him in the Government House, built for the British Resident, in a setting of lawns and flowers. (Occupying the adjoining room in 1960, we made certain that our rocklike beds were identical with his.)

The Shan government then took its Russian visitors to Inle Lake, where water people known as Inthes live in villages built on stilts above the waves. The Inthes, darker than the Shans, are said to have come from islands far to the south in the Bay of Bengal. There they evolved a curious watermanship, as the early Venetians did on their lagoons. Although they left no written records, these water people are believed to have followed an eighteenth-century king of Burma in one of the incessant wars of those days against neighboring Thailand. The king retreated into northern Burma, and the Inthes with him. When they came to the broad waters of the Inle Lake, weariness overcame them and they decided to settle on the water, as they had in their ancestral home. The lake people are leg rowers: they stand on the sterns of their long-prowed boats like Venetian gondoliers, crook one leg around the oar, and push backward.

Mr. Khrushchev found their lake "wonderful," as tourists do, and the race of the leg-rowed boats "thrilling." At a banquet in Taunggyi he said he had been "moved and gladdened" by the welcome the Shans had given him. But then Mr. Khrushchev blundered. The only room in Taunggyi big enough for so important a dinner was the assembly hall of Kambawsa College, a private school founded in British days for the sons of sawbwas. The former feudal rulers were on hand to honor this foe of feudalism. In his speech Mr. Khrushchev gaily ripped into the imperialist British for having failed to educate their colonial subjects. His briefing officer had not warned him that among the sawbwas in his audience were old boys of Oxford and Cambridge.

The Soviet leader made at least one other bobble, attributable to inadequate homework. He had heard many references to Aung San, the Republic's hero. Mr. Khrushchev turned to U Myint Thein, the brilliant Chief Justice of the Union. "Who is this Aung San?" he asked. "And what party does he belong to?"

Most of what Mr. Khrushchev said at Taunggyi was better salesmanship. "Yours is a young State," he told the Shans. "You do not as yet have your own engineers, nor the necessary experience. If you need assistance, tell us and we will help you." In his impulsive way, Mr. Khrushchev offered the Shans a 200-bed hospital, grander than any Taunggyi had known. They accepted it gladly, although the government of the Union insisted on paying in rice or other goods for all such "gifts." The Russians sent technicians to supervise the construction, every three technicians requiring two interpreters at Burma's expense. The hospital has two drawbacks. It is two miles outside the city, and it is too elaborate for the Shan State to maintain without money from Rangoon.

In more than one sense the Soviet "gift" serves a purpose. It drives home a lesson in the education of a borderland, the lesson of its inescapable dependence on Rangoon. Moscow and Peking may shower useful luxuries on the Shans, but it is to Rangoon, the capital and commercial center, that they must look for many day-to-day needs. When a businessman requires an import license, when a school principal is short of textbooks, when a shopkeeper must replenish his stock, when a hospital director finds his medicines running low, only Rangoon can fill the need. The capital city is the center of financial as well as political power, and the hinterland is inescapably dependent on it. Every rural society in Asia must look to the metropolis in this way, and Burma's is no exception. Geography, economics, and common sense compel the Shans and Kachins to face southward.

Except for the single thread of the Burma Road into China, their roads, railways, air routes, and rivers lead southward into the heart of the Union. The Kachin State, though farthest from the center, is most directly tied to Rangoon by Burma's best line of communication: the Irrawaddy.

[4]

What the Mississippi meant to the American West when Mark Twain was young, the Irrawaddy means to the new and loose-knit Union of Burma: the wet nurse of its fields, the bearer of its trade, the highway of its people. For the Kachins it provides a natural thoroughfare leading directly to the heart of the nation's political and economic power at Rangoon. Such access to the capital gives the Kachins an advantage rare among borderlands on the Asian continent. In later chapters we shall examine other backwaters whose people would be fortunate if they had an Irrawaddy.

Bhamo, the Kachin capital, prospered in British days as the northern terminus of the "Old Flotilla." This was the flatboat fleet of the Scottish-owned Irrawaddy Flotilla Company. The owners boasted that they ran the biggest service of river craft in the world. You could "hear their paddles chunkin'" all the way down river past Mandalay to Rangoon. The British scuttled their paddle wheelers to keep them out of Japanese hands. Burma's independent government nationalized the company and its partially rebuilt postwar fleet. But "fleet" is a misnomer. In 1954 the entire passenger flotilla serving Bhamo consisted of only five ships. They ran on a happy-go-lucky schedule. Sometimes the government commandeered a couple of them for official use; sometimes one of them went aground and stayed aground. This was the double dilemma during our own journey in 1954 down the Irrawaddy. It explained why the ship that would carry us 297 miles downstream to Mandalay steamed into Bhamo three days late.

Its arrival stirred such excitement that half the town's population, it seemed, flocked to the muddy shore, first to greet it and then to wave it off. To board, we squirmed our way through oxen, porters, children, and cargo. Traffic on the lower deck was further clogged by baskets of fish, sacks of rice, bunches of bananas, and a swarm of milling, shouting people. On the upper deck, 200 passengers had already staked out claims to the few square feet of living space.

Everybody was busy arranging the family bedding and food for three days and nights on deck. Far from complaining, they faced the journey with a gay and triumphant air. For they were aboard, and who could tell when the next boat would leave Bhamo? Wisps of smoke from cheroots and cookstoves began to drift across the deck. We climbed for fresh air and found ourselves on a sloping tin roof behind the ship's bridge. This roof we were to share through most of the journey with twenty-five military police. Between eating, sleeping, doing their laundry, and playing games, these young men guarded the ship from the rebels who have terrorized Irrawaddy shipping ever since Burma's independence. We were glad to have them as companions.

Although the Mississippi seems without question masculine, a Father of Waters or Old Man River, the Irrawaddy is a splendidly beautiful lady. She changes her mind and her direction without notice. She can be tempestuous or lazy, deep or deceptively shallow. Considering that the Irrawaddy is only 1,250 miles long, one fourth of the combined length of the Mississippi-Missouri, it manages to send a lot of water down to the sea. In one memorable flood year (1877) it poured 2,000,000 cubic feet per second into the Bay of Bengal—a third more than the Mississippi ever dumped into the Gulf. In flood, the Irrawaddy discharges forty times as much water as in the dry season; the Mississippi, only twelve times as much. Could there be more conclusive evidence that the oriental lady is wilder, more temperamental, than the old man who just keeps rollin' along?

The Irrawaddy is most headstrong in the three defiles of its upper reaches. In one of these gorges, about twelve miles below Bhamo, where the Kachin State merges with Burma proper, the water is deep and the current swift even in the dry season. Our ship spanked along at a joyous rate; somehow the sunlit water, sweeping through the forested hills, sent *Siegfried's Rhine Journey* surging through our minds. But beyond the defile the shoreline flattened. The engine slowed, and the leadsmen took over.

On the Irrawaddy one cannot move far without leadsmen. They are the men who stand at water level on the bow, measuring the depth of the river with long bamboo poles. After each dip of the pole they sing out the result to the navigator in his wheelhouse overhead. Our leadsman, like the navigator, was neither Burman nor Kachin; he hailed from Chittagong, the main seaport of East Pakistan, the home of the craftiest pilots in all Asia. When the water was deep, his tenor voice sang out *eik-a bum malena!* which means, in a Chittagonian mixture of Urdu and Bengali: "One fathom—can't find bottom!" But as the river shallowed, the cry grew ominous. After a while we could tell from the song just when to worry about the sandbanks and shoals.

Mark Twain would have felt at home on our flatboat. When he described his own river, "whose alluvial banks change constantly, whose snags are always hunting up new quarters, whose sandbars are never at rest," he was describing Burma's river too. He would have understood the leadsman's cry of "mark twain!" in Chittagonian dialect; he would have felt the weight of the pilot's worries.

An Irrawaddy pilot needs X-ray eyes, a photographic memory, and a gamester's spirit. He must decide when to gamble and when to play safe in his battle of wits with the river. He must peer at the swirls and ripples and currents and know what lurks beneath them. To us, as landsmen, the surface of the water told nothing; to our navigator it was a familiar book.

On the second day the river split into a mass of sandbars. Again and again, as the leadsman warned of trouble, the captain brought his ship to a standstill. We watched these cautious probings by hanging over the edge of our tin roof. Suddenly we felt a soft thud. The bells rang a succession of frantic orders. The propeller churned up muddy water at the stern, but the ship did not budge. We were firmly stuck on a sandbar.

For three hours the crew fought to free the ship. The hot sun beat down on the tin roof. Our ship had no wireless; a passing boat undertook to get word of our plight to the nearest pagoda town, half a day's journey away. The nearest road led nowhere but into insurgent territory; the nearest airfield was a hundred miles distant. We began to adjust ourselves to spending a while on an Irrawaddy sandspit. The captain, more sanguine, strained his engines to the limit. The ship swung and shivered. By a supreme effort, he brought the stern around, and we floated into deeper water. Later we learned that rebels had been kidnapping and killing near where our ship had been stuck for three hours.

The Irrawaddy, as we have said, is the only superhighway that links the Kachin State with the Union. It needs more buoys, more lights, more dredges, more ships. The people who depend upon it, Burman and Kachin alike, represent a large segment of the life of the country. They need more protection from rebels and outlaws. The same problems, maintenance and security, beset road transport in both the Shan and Kachin States. Except for the few that are hard-topped, roads degenerate into mud in the rainy season and rubble in the dry. Neglect of maintenance, lack of security: together, these form the vicious circle that is delaying the unity, distracting the people, and stalling the progress of Burma.

Some Observations on Union

We come back at the close of this chapter to the questions we raised at the start: why is the road to nationhood, like

the roads of Burma, so rough and dangerous? Why do
many Shans and Kachins still react to the central authority
with suspicion or fear or violence? Why, in short, do they
behave like border peoples? Old nations tend to forget their
own birth pangs until some deeply buried misunderstanding within their own society erupts into violence. Then
they realize that unity is only the topsoil, to be nourished
and husbanded year after year.

In the early days of Burmese independence, the political
"outs" in the borderlands formed an organization which
they called a "Council of Nationalities," not to be confused
with the upper house of the Parliament in Rangoon. Their
Council issued a statement in 1954 which said, in part:
". . . the states are, in fact, colonies of Burma proper and
the 'governments' which rule them are only puppet organizations." Whether or not they believed it, and perhaps they
did, the borderland dissidents still use that ugly word
"colonies" as a weapon, and hurl it at the very people who
fought and worked bravely for their own independence.
With all the bitterness and irony of the talk about "colonies," there is no serious talk of secession except among the
Shans.

Would separation be feasible? Would it be wise from any
point of view? In theory, an independent "Shanland" is indeed possible. Burma's constitution of 1948, as we have
noted, gave the Shan State (though not the Kachin) the
right to secede from the Union. Legally as well as morally,
the Shan people were thus free to "dissolve the political
bands which have connected them with another." They
could have formed new "political bands" by joining their
ethnic and linguistic relatives, the Thais, to create a Greater
Thailand. Or they could have stepped onto the world stage
as a nation with their own flag, stamps, coins, tariffs, embassies abroad, membership in the United Nations, and all
the other trappings of nationalism.

Why not? More than thirty members of the United

Nations are smaller in area. Almost twenty U.N. members have smaller populations. Moreover, an independent "Shanland" could feed itself, which is more than one can say of many nations. But would independence assure the Shans a good life by their own standards? Could a Shan nation survive? When one tries to answer these questions, the dream of separate nationhood becomes a nightmare. A Shan nation would immediately find itself struggling in economic and political quicksands, as the wiser Shan leaders know full well.

Lacking industries, a Shan nation would have to sell farm products in order to import necessities of all kinds, from tractors to pins. It might supplement its income by selling teakwood and the steadily declining lead and silver of the Bawdwin Mine. But the amounts would be small. Miners would have to be recruited elsewhere, since Shans dislike working underground. Without access to the sea, a Shan nation could only export its produce through Burma, China, or Thailand. It would run the constant risk of all weak and landlocked countries: economic strangulation at the hands of stronger, perhaps unfriendly, neighbors. The only effective outlets from the Shan State are the roads and railroads that lead to Burma proper. These a government in Rangoon could shut whenever it chose.

The political hazards of Shan independence are dizzier than the economic. For the Shans would not necessarily be masters in their own house. As we have seen, they do not form a majority of the people of their State; the majority consists of a conglomeration of Kachins, Palaungs, Was, and other mountain tribesmen. Since Shans shrink from military service, how would their new nation defend itself? Possessing only the rudiments of an effective civil service, how would it govern itself? Though nominally independent, it would constitute, at least for a time, a power vacuum suspended between Burma, Thailand, and China. The Shan nation might easily deteriorate into a satellite of China, a staging area for expansion southward. Its probable fate would, in due course, be full absorption into the Chinese Communist empire, with the regimentation and loss of identity which such absorption implies.

National independence, then, would give the Shans a security about as deceptive as that of an oyster in its shell. Their nation would be born into a pitiless century, one that has little regard for peoples who are mere fragments of ancient cultures, who dream that they can live entirely to themselves.

Are the Shans so different from Burmans that they must be separate? Do they not spring from similar stock? Do not most of the Shans and Burmans profess the same Buddhist religion? If the Burmans were as brutal as the Japanese invaders, one could understand Shan separatism. But Burmans happen to be tolerant, easygoing, and sensible in their dominance. If Shans and Kachins suffer discrimination, it is not because of Burma's official policy. The nature of their 1948 constitution and leadership makes it hard to believe that the Burmans are trying to smother any other people. They are struggling to build a nation, and to make "out of many, one."

Partnership, of course, implies duties for the Burmans as well as Kachins and Shans. It will be up to Rangoon, for example, to provide more training schools so that these border people can manage their own affairs within a Burmese Union. This will require an agricultural college for the Shan State comparable to Mandalay University, and maybe one for the energetic Kachins as well. The Burmese could profit from the example of the University of Hokkaido in what used to be a neglected borderland of Japan. Few Shans and Kachins have qualified and been welcomed in Burma's own institutions of higher learning. What they learn there does not usually fit their needs.

The nearness of China should spur Rangoon to action. The Chinese, inevitably, will push into Yunnan with new roads and railways, with factories and collective farms. In due course the pressure of population will compel them to tame Yunnan's rivers, to reclaim its wastelands, to harness whatever unused resources it may possess. With such transformation almost sure to come on the other side of the frontier, Burma cannot afford to let the Shan and Kachin States stand still.

The kind of change that is feasible on the Burmese side is not what Western economists often recommend. The Shans and Kachins will not let themselves be herded into factories, even if Burma had the money to build them. There is no need to wrench these border peoples out of a farming economy. The northern borderland is primarily agricultural, and so it will remain. The first imperative for the Shan and Kachin States, as for all of Burma, is the restoration of public order. Only when the farmer can take his goods to market without danger, when parents can send their children to school without fear, when the roads and trails are as safe as they were in the imposed peace of British days, can the Shans and Kachins become full members of the Union. Only then will the highways and railways, and the Irrawaddy, serve to knit the Union of Burma together. A second imperative, as we have suggested, is greater opportunity for training. And the third, the most difficult of all, is to heed the injunctions of U Nu.

"We have perpetrated on one another all the distressing sins of disunity," he wrote in his *Autobiography*. "The time has come for all of us to be so united that the dwellers in mansions and the dwellers in huts, the police and the public, the judge and the peasant, are brothers."

4

Edge of Tibet

SIKKIM AND ITS NEIGHBORS

> . . . *nowhere else on the earth's surface can there be found, within so small a radius, a combination of tropical luxuriance, sylvan beauty and mountain sublimity equal to that which meets the traveller's eye among the valleys and highlands of Sikkim and Eastern Nepal.*
>
> —DOUGLAS FRESHFIELD

> . . . *I think that mountains that are as high as that [Mount Everest] are disagreeable.*
>
> —MARK TWAIN

FLYING NORTH from Calcutta, the traveler looks down upon a watery plain. Rivers coil among the rice fields, carrying the silt of the Ganges Valley to the sea. When the rains have stopped, a thousand mirrors reflect the sun, and the shadow of the airplane races across them on its northward course. Then, after an hour and three quarters, the passenger alights at a country airport called Bagdogra. Straight ahead of him, a mountain wall rises out of the plain and into the clouds.

Can there be a man "with soul so dead" who never has let himself be stirred by his first sight of the Himalayas?

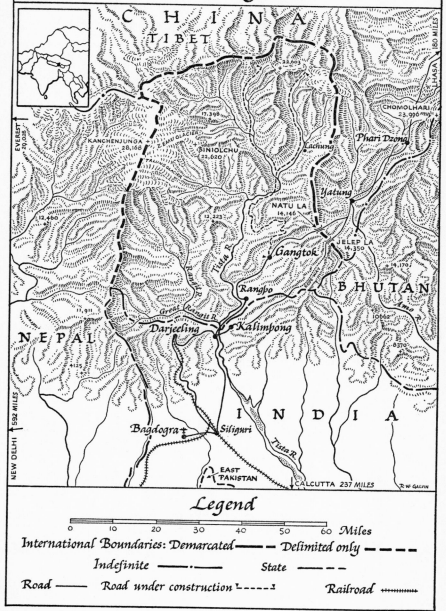

SIKKIM
and its Neighbors

CHINA

TIBET

EVEREST 29,028

KANCHENJUNGA + 28,168

SINIOLCHU 22,620

ZEMU GLACIER

TALUNG GLACIER

17,398

22,603

CHOMOLHARI 23,996

LHASA 180 MILES

Lachung

Phari Dzong

Yatung

12,400

22,223

NATU LA 14,146

Rangit R.

Tista R.

Gangtok

JELEP LA 14,350

1705

17,911

Great Rangit R.

Rangpo

BHUTAN

10662

Amo R.

Darjeeling

Kalimpong

8370

4125

NEPAL

NEW DELHI 592 MILES

Bagdogra

Siliguri

INDIA

Tista R.

EAST PAKISTAN

CALCUTTA 237 MILES

R. W. GALVIN

Legend

0	10	20	30	40	50	60	Miles

International Boundaries: Demarcated ——— Delimited only ― ― ―

Indefinite —·— State ― ― ―

Road ——— Road under construction ∟----⌐ Railroad +++++++

The soldiers and civil servants of British India found renewal in these mountains, and relief from the furnace of the plains. The modern connoisseur of borderlands responds to the Himalayas for special reasons. Behind him, India spreads its tapestry of Caucasoid peoples, Aryan languages, and predominantly Hindu religion. Ahead of him (if he could vault the wall) he would find a Mongoloid people, a Buddhist faith, and an ingrown way of life.

Whoever brings an awareness of geography knows that he is facing not one mountain but a procession of peaks almost twice as high as the Alps and many times more massive. They swing across Asia in a gentle arc for 2,000 miles from Ladakh to Burma. Perhaps 10,000,000 people live within the mountain wall itself. Most of them farm the southern foothills; some grow rice on terraced slopes up to 7,000 feet; a few tend yaks and sheep at heights up to 17,000 feet. A constant flow of transients has kept the mixture churning. Tibetans have driven their mule caravans through the passes to India for purposes of trade. Indian merchants have pushed into the hills with goods for farmers and villagers. Buddhist and Hindu pilgrims have plodded up and down the mountains, leaving their imprint on the entire region.

If the passenger at Bagdogra also brings an awareness of politics, he knows that he is facing one of the most sensitive boundaries in all Asia: the frontier between India and the "Tibet Region of China." Along both ends of the 2,000-mile arc, the territory of India meets that of Communist China on the crest of the Himalayas. Along the center, for about a thousand miles, three mountain states separate India from Tibet. But for purposes of security, India considers their Tibetan frontiers its own, and has undertaken to defend each of them. It will not "tolerate" an attack from the north against the independent Kingdom of Nepal. It guides the defense and foreign relations of semi-independent Bhutan. In Sikkim, the tiny mountain state between the other two, India has taken full control and made it her protectorate.

Why this special concern for Sikkim? Again we call upon geography. This sliver of territory, no larger than Yellowstone National Park, is the shortest corridor linking Lhasa, Tibet's capital, with the heart of India. A convenient cleft in the mountains and two manageable passes have channeled trade between Lhasa and Calcutta for generations past. Thanks to the Tista River which carved the entrance, the traveler at the Bagdogra airport can reach Sikkim in four hours. He jeeps east and north for about fifty miles. At a suspension bridge over a tributary of the Tista, he shows his papers on both sides, and finds himself in the princely State of Sikkim.

If one could create a microcosm of the entire Himalayan borderland and its people, the product would be not unlike this protectorate. Its political system, to be sure, is probably unique; a hereditary prince holds nominal control of domestic affairs, but defers to republican India in all vital decisions. Otherwise, Sikkim provides a fair sample for a study of the borderland. Its extremes of terrain and climate are typically Himalayan; so are its ethnic strains and cultures. Until recently, nobody tried very hard to pull its people, for good or ill, into the modern world. Nobody paid much attention to Sikkim's own resources of timber, minerals, and water power. Here as in other borderlands, we find that modernized Asians—in this instance, Indians— have fallen heir to an unfinished colonial task. They are trying to adapt to a traditional society Western ideas and techniques they learned from Britain. Since Sikkim crowds so much of the essence of a borderland into so small a laboratory, we shall focus our chapter on this corner of the Himalayas.

Lilliput of the Himalayas

It is not only Westerners who look blank at the mention of Sikkim. When an Indian high court judge from the plains was offered duty there, he had to consult a school atlas to discover where and what Sikkim was. When a respected Indian teacher signed a contract to be principal of the boys' school in Gangtok, Sikkim's capital, he asked the authorities in New Delhi where Gangtok was—"and," he reminisced years later, "they didn't really know." The wife of an Indian diplomat in Washington showed her contempt when two Americans told her they were about to go to Sikkim. "If you want to see savages," she snapped, "you don't need to travel so far from home." Does this not have a familiar ring? Is it not the disdain of sophisticated Japanese for Hokkaidoans, of Filipinos for Moros, of Burmans for Shans and Kachins? City-bred Indians are not immune from the temptation to dismiss outlying peoples as uncultured and crude.

Luckily for India, the leaders of its government show more perception. They know that Sikkim's location gives it an importance out of all proportion to its size. They also know the fallacy of measuring in square miles a place where people normally move up and down as often as on the level. Within Sikkim's 2,818 square miles, its elevations range from about 700 feet above the sea in the Tista Valley to 28,168 on the summit of Kanchenjunga, astride the frontier with Nepal.

Suppose one could drop a blindfolded man by helicopter into the rain forest of southern Sikkim. Remove his blindfold, and he would guess that he was deep in the tropics. The evidence would be heat, rain, insects, monkeys chattering and parrots screeching in treetops through which hardly any sun can penetrate. Deposit the same man in an upland valley at 4,000 feet; he would find citrus groves and conclude that Sikkim had a pleasantly subtropical climate. Put him suddenly into Gangtok at 6,000 feet, surrounded by terraced rice fields, prayer flags, and monasteries, and he would wonder whether he had reached James Hilton's Shangri-La. Lift him suddenly into the bare northern highlands, and he would be sure that this was Tibet itself.

Such a wealth of choices has earned Sikkim a band of devotees abroad. The late Frank S. Smythe, who climbed its icy slopes and wrote memorably about them, predicted that Sikkim would become "the playground of the eastern Himalayas." It is not yet that, for it lacks facilities for tourists and requires a permit of every foreigner. But it has long been a happy hunting ground for the few who have discovered it for themselves. They form a world-wide fellowship of climbers and hikers, writers and artists, naturalists and collectors of Buddhist lore. The Sikkim fellowship imposes only these qualifications for admission: its members must love the place, dream about it, and vow they will return.

Sikkim's crowning glory, in more senses than one, is Kanchenjunga, the third highest mountain in the world. Many have tried to climb it, and a few have died trying. This has not surprised the Sikkimese, who believe that the summit is the abode of a temperamental god. When a British-led expedition finally conquered it in 1955, the mountaineers stopped six feet short of the top for fear of offending the god and his people. Other visitors have contented their eyes and souls with a view of the Kanchenjunga range from a hillside above Gangtok, thirty miles away. In the cold before dawn, the peaks stand white and jagged against gunmetal sky. Suddenly the highest point catches fire. The glow spreads to the mountain flanks, as if molten lava were coursing downward through the snows. Presently four other giants are bathed in orange and pink. The nearest, on the viewer's left, is Narsing, 19,130 feet, conquered by Dr. A. M. Kellas in 1921; next to it Pandim,

22,010 feet; then Kanchenjunga, a sovereign among princes. Beyond it Simvo climbs to 22,360 feet; and last of all, on the far right, the fluted spire of Siniolchu, 22,620 feet, variously called the virgin, the princess, and the White Tower of the Himalayas. The mountains keep a decent distance; at Gangtok they do not shut out a slice of the sky as the Jungfrau does at Grindelwald. Yet looking without binoculars from thirty miles away, one can often detect a plume of snow, blown as if by an angry god from the tip of Kanchenjunga. Is it surprising that the Sikkimese fear and revere it as the home of a supernatural being? Soon after dawn, clouds fill the valleys and the white peaks float without support as if they did not belong to the planet.

Even if it had no mountains, Sikkim would repay the hiker by its natural curiosities. The President General of the Daughters of the American Revolution could deck her bosom with a different species of Sikkim orchid every day of the year, and for months longer. In this State, a speck on the world map, grow 450 of the 7,000 known species. Most of them are not the showy kind so dear to the Daughters. They are the dainty ones that shower from tree trunks, so high and small that one sees the flash of their colors before being able to identify the blooms. If the Sikkim government could safeguard and market them in the West, it might earn a tidy addition to its foreign exchange.

Sikkim's 500 species of butterflies offer a lepidopterist a lifetime of work and delight. A retired director of the botanical gardens in Darjeeling believes that Sikkim has no rival in its wealth of butterflies. Sir Joseph Hooker, the British botanist who first came there in the 1840's, saw thousands at rest on a river's edge, "with erect wings, balancing themselves with a rocking motion." He compared them to "a crowded fleet of yachts on a calm day." Among Sikkim's 1,500 species of moths, the Atlas moth attains a wingspread of twelve inches. Its wing-tip markings suggest snakes' heads; its four transparent spots probably look to birds like an enemy's eyes.

The birds themselves are varied enough to make Sikkim an ornithologist's heaven. Between 5,000 and 6,000 species have been identified. Some flit through forests so dense that collectors rarely see or catch them. Of one, known as Gould's Shortwing (*Brachypteryx stellata*), red with a spotted brown and white breast, probably not fifty specimens exist in all the world's museums. Here lives the smallest known woodpecker, the brown Rufous Piculet (*Sasia o. ochracea*), only three inches long, and also one of the world's largest, the Great Slaty Woodpecker (*Mulleripicus p. mohun*), sixteen inches from tail to head not including its four-inch beak. Above the timberline, a bird watcher may be lucky enough to see a dash of blue on the snows. This is another rarity: Hodgson's Grandala (*Grandala c. coelicolor*), related to the American bluebird but somehow choosing the treeless slopes as its feeding ground.

If a Westerner wants to chase birds or butterflies, he had better bring two essentials to the Sikkim forest. One is leggings to guard against leeches, which lie in wait on every bush. These pests will fall or jump with faultless aim and will jab any bit of skin not thickly covered. The other essential is the company of a Lepcha as guide. A shy and gentle people, the Lepchas are as much at home in the Sikkim woods as the Algonquins in the Canadian wilds. They know how much weight a swaying cane bridge will carry. They also know birds and animals, flowers and trees, although not, of course, by their English or scientific names.

The Lepchas are one of the three main peoples of Sikkim. As far as anyone knows, they were the first inhabitants. Where they came from is a mystery; broad faces and slanting eye folds show a Mongoloid origin, perhaps from Assam in northeast India, perhaps from Indochina. In the last two generations, some Lepcha children have gone to school, and a few have achieved distinction. One is a magistrate, another an agriculture officer; others serve in the Maharaja's private guard or work for high Indian officials as domestic servants. One Lepcha flew with his Indian employers to Washington, D.C., the first of his people ever to cross the Atlantic. He spent too much time and money on American movies and was sent back to the Himalayas, a Marco Polo of his people, a fount of knowledge and tall tales of the outer world. But he is an exception. In general, Lepchas remain on the lowest rung of the economic ladder. They are relatively new to farming, and their farms are among the poorest in the State. Many still live in the forests, growing what food they can and hunting what they must, ceaselessly propitiating the spirits that rule their lives. Through intermarriage with the Bhutias, of Tibetan origin, they are slowly dissolving into the society around them, probably a "departing race" like the Ainu of Japan.

The Bhutias, another of Sikkim's three main ethnic groups, began migrating into Sikkim from the north 600 years ago. It is these husky herdsmen and farmers who give North Americans in Sikkim a sense of being back in the Rocky Mountains. Cheekbones, noses, eyes, hair, and build, all suggest the American Indian of the Western range. Young Bhutia women are hoydens who swing down a trail together, shouting, singing, roughhousing with one another and with their young men. These tomboy girls have no trace of the demureness, the deference to the male, that characterizes so many Asian women. With age they lose their good looks but not their uninhibited spirits. Bhutias and Lepchas together number only about a third of Sikkim's 150,000 people.

Virtually all the rest belong to the group that is multiplying the fastest, and may yet take over Sikkim by sheer numbers. These are the Nepalis.[1] Because of their industry, energy, sturdiness, and drive, they are sometimes called the Japanese of the Himalayas. The British first brought or attracted them into Sikkim around the turn of the century,

---

[1] *Nepali* is the local term for a person of Nepalese origin living in Sikkim, Bhutan, or India. We use it to differentiate him from a Nepalese citizen of Nepal.

having found Lepchas and Bhutias unsatisfactory for menial work. Before long the Nepalis had spread through southern Sikkim and Bhutan, and the governments of both States tried to prevent them from overrunning the northern highlands. A good Nepali farmer in Sikkim grows more rice or maize from an acre than any other in the Himalayas. He knows how to terrace fields for rice which look too steep for cultivation. He waters the paddy by an ingenious system of runnels and bamboo pipes leading down from one terrace to the next. Nepali manual workers, men, women, and children, chisel the rock, crush the stone, and pull the rollers for Sikkim's roads. Most of them come from several tribes in the nearby hills of eastern Nepal. Those who are orthodox Hindus do not intermarry with the Buddhist Bhutias or the animist Lepchas. With their darker skin and their clannish ways, they appear to have little in common with the other peoples of Sikkim or with the fighting Gurkhas of their ancestral Nepal. One can identify Nepali women especially by their gold necklaces and earrings as big as saucers, and by the rings they often wear in their noses. Skilled and unskilled, it is the Nepalis who keep the economy of Sikkim running.

On market days in Gangtok, all three groups mingle as neighbors, chattering and bargaining among the stalls. Sometimes a Bhutanese or a Tibetan strides through the crowd; he, too, is accepted as a member of the Sikkim family. Only one group, the Indians, stands aloof. There are not many Indians in Sikkim; most of them are soldiers, technicians, or civil servants on temporary duty. They keep to themselves, perhaps deliberately. The wives of Indian officials shop in the bazaar under parasols held by servants. In their saris they look as self-consciously foreign as did the wives of British officials a generation ago. The Sikkimese, for their part, tend to keep aloof from the Indians. They are not unfriendly, but do not want to be swallowed up among the 400,000,000 people of the Indian Union. To Bhutias and Lepchas especially, the separateness of Sikkim is worth preserving.

[1]

The living symbol of Sikkim's integrity has long been a prince in a Tibetan nobleman's robe of gold brocade. He rules by India's permission, but there is nothing remotely Indian about him. He is a political, social, and personal rarity in the context of republican India, as exceptional as some of Sikkim's birds and moths. The man and his office tell a good deal about the nature of India's control over this bit of the borderland.

His Highness the Maharaja of Sikkim, Sir Tashi Namgyal, looks north rather than south to his ancestral origins. His dynasty was founded as long ago as 1641 by three Tibetan monks who had trekked southward into Sikkim. They converted the people to Buddhism and installed a Tibetan named Namgyal as the first ruler. The Maharaja is a direct descendant; his line has thus lasted longer than the Manchu dynasty in China (1644–1911) or, for that matter, the present royal house in Britain. Nor is this his only distinction. Of all the 500-odd semi-independent princes under the protection of the British Raj, he is the last to have kept even nominal hereditary rights and powers. The Republic of India disestablished all the rest and put them on lifelong pensions. A few were appointed as Governors of new Indian States, but all except Sir Tashi Namgyal lost the paraphernalia of princely rule.

In 1947, when India won its independence, the Maharaja had been sitting on the throne of his thimble-sized State for thirty-three years. By 1960 he had become a patriarch among hereditary princes anywhere. Few of his people could remember when anyone else had occupied the Gangtok palace. A straight, slight figure in his robe and skullcap of gold brocade, wearing dark glasses to hide, it was said, a childhood injury to one eye, His Highness has become almost as much a part of the Sikkim scene as Kanchenjunga itself. A catalogue of his acquaintances would make a Who's Who of Tibetan travel for half a century. Virtually every writer, explorer, and Tibetologist who made the journey to Lhasa stopped to present the traditional silk scarf to the Maharaja on the way. Two Viceroys of India, Lords Linlithgow and Wavell, were among his guests, as well as Prime Minister Nehru and the Dalai Lama. Since he seldom traveled outside Sikkim, such visitors helped to keep him in touch with the world. He liked to talk to them in his palace and show them his superb collection of tankas, or Buddhist paintings, mounted on brocade.

Soft in speech, he gives an impression of otherworldliness. In later years, he scarcely noticed when members of his staff prostrated themselves before him, touching their foreheads to the ground on coming into his presence. His conversation was full of quips, but somehow disembodied, as if he were in tune with those spirits in whom he, like many Sikkimese, believe along with their Buddhist faith. If he took a liking to a visitor, he would wrap his robe around himself and glide into his studio to show his paintings. For this princeling of a mountain hideaway is an amateur painter of talent. His subject is Himalayan scenes, usually close-ups of glaciers and frozen lakes, of snow-bound passes and wind-swept shrines. He applies his favorite whites and blues with a bold hand. Although he has not seen the ice slopes since he climbed on Kanchenjunga as a young man, he still lives among them in his imagination.

An uncommon man, one whom the Indian authorities often found difficult to manage. Many times, especially in the first years of Indian guardianship, they must have been tempted to sweep away the Maharaja and all the trappings of his court. The majority of his people, as we have noted, are Nepali. What could a Maharaja of Tibetan origin mean to them? And what use had the new India for a hereditary prince, surrounded by landowners, an anachronism in a democratic, socialistic republic? The left wing of the Indian Congress Party would have liked to see His Highness tossed into limbo.

Mr. Nehru's government balanced these temptations against the practical politics of using him. Never absorbed into India, Sikkim remained nominally independent under Indian protection. How would it have looked to the Himalayan peoples all along the frontier if India had snuffed out even the fictional independence of an unoffending State? Moreover, the British had found the Maharaja and his advisers useful as a mechanism of indirect rule. Indian officials would assuredly have run into local resistance if they had tried to run Sikkim without intermediaries.

Therefore the Indians contented themselves with keeping the Maharaja and his court as an instrument. It was the government of Sikkim that levied taxes and bestowed benefits, although Indian money and skill usually made the benefits possible. When a new road was opened in southwestern Sikkim, it was called the Namgyal Highway, and His Highness was, of course, invited to cut the ribbon. When a cottage industries center was founded, training sixty girls in arts and crafts, it was named the Palden Thondup Institute, for the Maharaja's heir. When a new courthouse was built, or a new office building for government departments, India was careful to have it designed by Sikkimese, with roof of blue and window frames of black and gold. The Indians refused to impose upon Sikkim's capital any trace of Indian character. Indeed, the one Indian name immortalized in Gangtok is not that of Nehru or Gandhi but of N. K. Rustomji, a popular Chief Minister. As a farewell tribute when he left office, the government of Sikkim dedicated to him a charming deer park on the edge of the Gangtok ridge.

The Indian tactic of deference to the Maharaja has proved its worth. In recent years His Highness and his Sikkimese advisers appear reconciled to Indian guardianship and control. As the head of this miniature State moves through his ceremonial rounds, opening a clinic, inspecting a school, receiving a foreign notable, praying at a monastery, he no longer tugs at the leash held by Indian hands. An observant visitor could find one evidence of the change in the Maharaja's reception room. Until late in the 1950's a photograph of the Dalai Lama stood there, an avowal of Sikkim's cultural and dynastic ties with Tibet. In 1960, after the Dalai Lama had fled into Indian exile, his picture had been replaced by one of Dr. Rajendra Prasad, the President of India.

Tougher independence of spirit survives in the Maharaja's children. They must have acquired it partly from their mother, a strong-minded Tibetan woman. She separated from His Highness many years ago, left the palace for good, betook herself to her native Lhasa, and ultimately returned to live in her own home five miles northwest of Gangtok, on a ridge overlooking the Kanchenjunga range. Sorrow struck hard at this otherwise favored family. The eldest son, Paljor, was killed while training with the Royal Air Force during World War II. The youngest daughter, Pema Choden, had to live in Switzerland as an invalid. But two of the children remain in Sikkim as assets to their own State and, indirectly, to India.

One of them is Princess Pema Tsedeum, which means "lotus-life-light" and accurately describes her radiance. She is a born princess in every sense, with her smooth cheeks, laughing eyes, and lustrous black hair, and her regal Tibetan dress. A sleeveless brocade gown, worn over a long-sleeved blouse of contrasting silk, the dress acquires special brilliance from the Tibetan apron that blazes with horizontal stripes.

But Princess Kukula, as she is called, has never been content to be just a fashion plate. Schooled in a Catholic convent in nearby Kalimpong, married to a Tibetan Buddhist nobleman, she is at home among educated people of West and East. She has sophisticated views on literature and world affairs, as if she had grown up in a world capital instead of the Himalayas. Lately the laughter has faded from her eyes. The aftermath of the Tibetan uprising in 1959 overwhelmed her. She gave herself to organizing the care of refugees, pleading with the government of India to do more for them, trying to make outsiders conscious of the tragedy at Sikkim's door.

In coming years the family leadership will pass to the Maharaja's son, Palden Thondup Namgyal. As the crown prince, or Maharaj Kumar, this strong-willed young man illustrates the alchemy of modern and traditional in the borderland. Born in 1923, educated in the exacting standards of an Anglican school north of Delhi, he is contemporary even when he wears Tibetan robes. His looks and charm would melt the snows on Kanchenjunga. From boyhood he has been a radio "ham," picking up signals from India and the world beyond. Long before India gave attention to the economic needs of Sikkim, he was agitating for roads and a ropeway (a freight-carrying cable) to unlock the forest treasures of his State. His personal life has been an inner struggle between tradition and his urge to smash it. His wife was chosen according to the tradition of importing a highborn girl from Lhasa. Soon after bearing a child in 1958, this delicate princess bowed low in obeisance to her father-in-law, knocked against a table, and died of an internal hemorrhage. In choosing a second wife, the young widower broke spectacularly with tradition. Late in 1961 he slipped an engagement ring onto the finger of Miss Hope Cook, a twenty-one-year-old student of Sarah Lawrence College. The Kumar, as he is called, had met her in Darjeeling and had invited her to Gangtok for the family's approval. It took six months for the government of India to consent to an American princess on the edge of Tibet. The Maharaja's Buddhist advisers decided that 1962 would not be "auspicious" for the marriage, and no date was set. Meanwhile Miss Cook was schooling herself in Buddhism, the religion of the Sikkimese court.

In spite of his Western tastes, the Kumar has sought increasingly to make himself a leading secular voice of the Tibetan branch of Buddhism. Who could play the role more appropriately? With the Dalai Lama in exile, with the Panchen Lama a Communist puppet, with the Maharaja aging and frail, the crown prince stepped into the breach as a nonpriestly leader of his religion. The government of India encouraged him. It found him effective in advertising India's tolerance toward all religions (except toward Islam in Indian-ruled Kashmir). India invited him to the annual Republic Day festivities in New Delhi, when the Union's mosaic of peoples takes living form. It also permitted him to go to Moscow for an orientalists' congress, to read a learned paper on Buddhism in Sikkim. He represented Sikkim also at the commemorations in Japan of the 2,500th anniversary of the Buddha. This time he read a paper on *Buddhism vis-à-vis the Industrial Civilization of the World,* insisting that the eternal truth of Buddhism would stand untouched by industrial revolutions, scientific progress, or "anything that the mind of man can devise."

> The conquest of space with the rocket and jet plane [he said], the conquest of anxiety with tranquilizing drugs, the conquest of man with bigger and better bombs, the conquest of the spirit with propaganda and advertising, these are the conquests of which he [man] is so proud, strangely forgetting or happily ignorant of the saying that "Though one should in battle conquer a thousand men a thousand times, he who conquers himself has the more glorious victory."

At a ceremony in Sikkim, in the presence of the Dalai Lama, the young heir apparent paid this graceful tribute

to India, the nominal protector and actual ruler of his
country:

> It is indeed in the fitness of things that India
> should, at this time of need, come forward to nour-
> ish and give fresh life to the faith that was child of
> her flesh, and we are confident that the closer cul-
> tural contacts that will develop as between India,
> Sikkim, and Tibet . . . will enrich the lives of all
> their peoples alike, that the child will give support
> to the mother that brought it to light, and that, in
> the course of time, the reunion will give birth to a
> newer life wherein the spirit will be purged of evil.

To Indian ears, what melody could have been sweeter?
Here was a son of the Himalayas, Tibetan in origin, Buddhist in faith, acknowledging Mother India, predominantly
Hindu, as the protectress of Buddhism. Well might Indian
officials plume themselves. Their policy of preserving and
using the princely house of Sikkim had begun to pay divi-
dends.

India is allowing Sikkim to be used also as a safe-deposit
vault for what can be salvaged of Tibetan culture. One
evidence is a massive library and research center of Ti-
betology, newly built on a ledge 1,500 feet below Gangtok.
Named, of course, the Namgyal Institute as yet another
gesture to the Maharaja and his family, the center was
financed partly by Sikkim and partly by India. Fittingly, the
twin-towered stone building faces Tibet. The Tibetan books
on its shelves are unbound sheaves of paper, kept in boxes
like those of old-time pianola rolls. A scholar can find Tibetan translations of ancient Sanskrit texts and other rare
manuscripts and printings of Buddhist Tibetan literature.
Whatever may happen in Tibet, these treasures are safe—
as long as Sikkim is safe. Prime Minister Nehru did not fail
to visit the Institute during its construction; his govern-

ment contributed sacred books and a Bengali scholar as curator.

[2]

The signs and symbols of Buddhism pervade Sikkim as though it were the faith of the masses instead of the State religion of a minority. Sikkim flaunts its Buddhism more exuberantly than that most Buddhist of all our borderlands, the Shan State of Burma. The faith practiced by Sikkimese is more sensuous than that of Southeast Asia and Ceylon; it is the Mahayana, or northern, version, overlaid with symbolism borrowed from India. A Shan who visits Sikkim would hardly recognize its Buddhism as his own. Indeed, he would despise it as a corruption of the faith of his fathers. To be sure, he would find certain familiar things: wall paintings and statues representing the Buddha, and monks wearing dark red robes in place of the orange of the southern Buddhist lands. If he stayed with a Sikkimese Buddhist family, the Shan would find his hosts entertaining the monks on important family occasions, as the good Buddhist family does in the Shan State. But there the resemblance ends.

"Take yourself no external refuge," the Buddha told his disciples when he knew he was about to die. Yet his present-day followers in Sikkim seek refuge in prayer flags, prayer wheels, and sacred objects without number. Living where they do, they crave supernatural shelter from snow and wind, from flood and landslide. As islanders often fear the sea, so the Buddhists of Sikkim tremble at the thought of the wrath of the mountain gods.

White prayer flags fleck the hillsides, festoon the bridges, and flutter outside the monasteries to ward off evil. On the crests of the passes leading into Tibet, hundreds flap in the wind like the wings of roosting seagulls. Some are strung like ships' bunting across bridges. Others are hung on poles and inscribed with prayers. On flags, rocks, and walls, inscriptions repeat the mystic Tibetan words *Om Mani Padme Hum!* This formula is usually translated, inadequately and inaccurately, as "Hail to the Jewel in the Lotus!" Whatever its metaphysics may mean, in Sikkim one sees and hears it interminably. When monks repeat it in unison, the words lose their identity and the voices drone like the buzzing of bees.

Much of this might mystify a Shan from Burma. So would the sight of a monk or wayfarer on a Sikkim trail twirling a cylinder on a stick. This cylinder is called, again inaccurately, a prayer wheel. Inside it, a yellow bag bears the magic inscription of the *Om Mani.* Inside the bag itself, as many as 500 prayers are imprinted on a roll of paper. With a single whirl of the cylinder, one says all the prayers at once, surely a labor-saving device as ingenious as any of Edison's. Himalayan and Tibetan Buddhists are not content with a portable cylinder that turns with a flick of the wrist. They have fashioned giant prayer wheels, sometimes eight feet tall, usually built into monastery walls. A true believer walks past a line of such drums and sets each one spinning with a stroke of his palm. When all are revolving together, it would take a computer to count the number of prayers being said at the same time.

Inside a monastery in Sikkim, a southern Buddhist is far removed from the sunshine and gold of his own pagodas. As his eyes adjust to the semidarkness, two discoveries would shock him. One is a sculpture of two figures in erotic embrace near the altar. The pose is vaguely like that of Rodin's *The Kiss,* but the faces are those of fiends. Seeking an explanation, one learns that the male represents compassion, the female, knowledge, or (another version) that the male is a god who has thrown off energy personified and incarnated in the female. The second shock for the southern Buddhist would be the multitude of saints and godlings, ghosts and demons, portrayed in wall paintings. One face that appears repeatedly is strange to Burma: the eighth-century missionary known in India and Nepal as the Padma Sambhava, in Tibet as the Guru (teacher) Rimpoche, and in Sikkim as either. It was he, a Buddhist St. Paul, who journeyed from India into Tibet preaching a mixture of Mahayana Buddhism and Hindu legends known as *tantras*. Thus he founded that amalgam of symbolism and mythology called tantric Buddhism, the version now universal among Buddhists of the Himalayas.

To the uninitiated, its symbolism is a maze that has no exit. There are two clues to the maze: first, this religion is filled with beings that personify human emotions, passions, virtues, and failings; and second, the devilish faces in its pantheon are nothing but masks to frighten enemies. One enemy, as we have said, is the god who sits atop Kanchenjunga. He comes to life in the mystery plays, called devil-dances by Westerners, which are performed in monastery grounds. One masked dancer represents the god when he is angry, another when he is benign. The angry one is a concentration of hideousness: its teeth like tusks, its cheeks and lips contorted with hate and fury.

Southern Buddhists disown the tantric version as materialistic, superstitious, corrupt, and carnal. Yet is it more materialistic than, for example, the Shwedagon Pagoda in Rangoon, coated and recoated with acres of gold? Is its animism different, in essence, from the worship of *nats*, or spirits, which often dilutes the "pure" Buddhism of Burma and Thailand? In 1961 the government of Burma, the guardian of a supposedly austere Buddhism, appropriated money for the building of two *nat* temples. In Sikkim, outsiders are wise not to make comparisons or to let tantric Buddhism shock them.

Beyond their tantric symbols, the monasteries of Sikkim offer much that is genuinely religious. In the Maharaja's temple next to his palace, the brilliance of ornamentation suggests a joy that rightfully belongs to worship. And at the hilltop monastery of Enchay, along the trail that leads to Tibet, wall paintings glow with the simplicity and wonder of Italian primitives.

One of the saving graces of Sikkimese Buddhism is the absence of a large priestly caste. In pre-Communist days, perhaps 40 per cent of the entire male population of Tibet and Mongolia lived in monasteries. In Sikkim, on the other hand, most monks are part-time workers for their faith. Like lay preachers in the West, they marry, raise families, till their farms, and appear in the monasteries only on ceremonial occasions. Enchay Monastery, for example, serves as the headquarters of 200 monks, but only fifteen constitute a permanent staff.

For Sikkim, this is a blessing. It means, for one thing, that a State with only 150,000 people can use its man power for productive ends. It spares Sikkim the kind of bottleneck which kept secular education and modern techniques out of Tibet for centuries. Tradition lives on, but reform and change are not stifled. In any event, the monks could never be dominant in Sikkim where Buddhism is the religion of a minority.

The census of 1951 showed only 39,397 Buddhists, compared with 97,863 Hindus, more than two thirds of the population. The Buddhist minority includes what a Marxist would call the "ruling circles," together with most of the people of Tibetan or Bhutanese descent. The Hindu majority consists almost entirely of Nepalis, the "masses."

How does it happen that socialistic, predominantly Hindu India should maintain Buddhism as a State religion along with a hereditary prince in Sikkim? Why should it not govern through Sikkim's energetic Hindu majority, the Nepalis? To understand why the Indians rule their new inheritance as they do, we shall have to see how India came to acquire it.

India's Inheritance in Sikkim

Before the coming of the British in the seventeenth century, India did not shape the history of Sikkim. Its only influence on the Himalayan enclave was the indirect light of Buddha, "the greatest Indian that ever lived." [2] Sikkim's early centuries were beset with pressures from east and west, not from north or south. At the start of the eighteenth century, Bhutanese invaded from the east; Tibetans threw them out. Toward the end of the eighteenth century, Gurkhas invaded from the west. So far neither British nor Indians had been heard from. Nor had the Manchu Empire, whose agents sat in Lhasa.

But it was bound to happen—sooner or later some English explorer, trader, or soldier would try to penetrate the Himalayas. The first to do so with a serious purpose was Warren Hastings, one of the few magnificent men in the "long stiff line" of British proconsuls in India. In 1774, after a brush with Bhutan, he sent an emissary through the Bhutanese passes to make friends and trade agreements in Tibet. The route through Sikkim was still unknown. To Hastings it appeared that he might recoup the fortunes of his virtually bankrupt employers, the East India Company, by opening a Tibetan trade route through Bhutan.

He knew that his negotiations would depend on a third party, China. The Manchus of Peking were not only in virtual possession of Lhasa; they also extended a supervisory control over the whole Himalayan area. Theirs was not direct rule. They controlled the Tibetans and the outlying Himalayan peoples by dispensing pats of approval and slaps of annoyance, like a governess in a nursery of disorderly children. At first the Manchu officials in Lhasa

[2] The estimate was Prime Minister Nehru's, in a press conference on April 5, 1959. In the same statement the Prime Minister said: "Tibet, culturally speaking, is an offshoot of India."

smiled on caravan trade with India. But they frowned
when Hastings suggested building a road through Bhutan
into Tibet. And when those vocational warriors, the Gurkhas, invaded not only Sikkim but Tibet itself, the Manchus sealed off Tibet to all trade with India. Then as later,
they were suspicious of Europeans. They felt sure that the
British and Britain's Indian subjects had been encouraging
the Gurkhas. Having blocked British trade through the
passes, the Manchu armies promptly drove the Gurkhas
from Tibet and from Sikkim as well.

This did not stop the British from probing into the Himalayas. The East India Company's conquests on the plains
had been simply a means to an end. Its objective had been
trade and profit. Why else would a Chartered Company
have sent private navies and armies halfway around the
world? When the soldiers had done their work, a small but
effective corps of civilians carried it forward: clerks, doctors, geologists, and naturalists among them. These were
the handy men of empire building. But for them, British India might never have breached the Himalayan wall. Their
endurance matched their curiosity to know what lay within
the mountain barrier. To name just a few, it was Brian
Hodgson, an ethnologist and zoologist, who penetrated Nepal; Campbell, a physician, who developed the hill station of
Darjeeling as a "sanitorium" for fever-stricken Britons from
the plains; Hooker, the botanist, whose explorations disclosed what lay along the shortest route to Lhasa.

Step by step, the British moved into effective control of
Sikkim. In 1817 they made an alliance with the Raja (as
the ruler was then known) and restored to him those parts
of Sikkim that had been taken by the Gurkhas. Next the
British persuaded him to part with the mountain ridge of
Darjeeling, as well as a strip connecting it with the plains.
For this they paid £300 a year. Few more stunning bar-
gains had been struck since Peter Minuit paid the equivalent of twenty-four dollars for Manhattan Island.

The snipping of territory continued. When the Sikkimese maltreated Hooker and Campbell, the British retaliated by taking more territory in 1849, and by setting up a protectorate over what remained. A treaty backed by bayonets in 1861 made it clear that Britain henceforth would be the master of Sikkim in fact if not in name. A few hundred Tibetan troops tested this supremacy in 1888. They built a fort on Sikkim soil. The British promptly sent a force all the way to the Jelep pass to push them out. There a "battle" was fought at 14,350 feet. It was no more than a few volleys fired at the backs of Tibetans running madly downhill, but since it was a clash between armed men, it ranks as probably the highest battle in history.

By this time the British knew that they must station an official in Sikkim itself, not, as before, merely at Darjeeling. This decision brought John Claude White onto the scene, to rivet Sikkim firmly to India.

[1]

White was one of those men, little regarded or rewarded in England, who left a lasting imprint on the fringes of the Empire. An engineer by training, a pioneer by temperament, he was well cast for the role he played for twenty years as Political Officer for Sikkim. The handlebars of his mustaches, replicas of Lord Kitchener's, alone would have supplied the majesty befitting an agent of the Queen. To them White added a dignity that seldom bent and never broke. He understood, moreover, the imperial importance of "face." Building a residence at Gangtok, his new post, he chose a hilltop overlooking the Maharaja's palace and monastery. In a silhouette of the Gangtok ridge, the home of Britain's Political Officer perched at the highest level. Below, in the hierarchy of "face," stood the houses of subordinate British officials; still lower, the palace; and far down the slopes, the homes of Sikkimese officials.

White made his status-seeking pleasant for himself and

his successors. He designed his official home as a gabled English country house. A countryman at heart—and what upper-class Englishman is not?—he took good care to surround it with English lawns and gardens in which something would always be blooming. The house commanded a stupendous view of the Kanchenjunga range. It was, and is, a bit of England, and of heaven too. It remains English to the tips of its eaves, although it has become the official residence of the Political Officer of the Republic of India.

With no precedents to guide him, White faced a twofold task: political and administrative. His political assignment, broadly speaking, was to make Sikkim a dependable outpost, secure against intruders from the north. For this purpose, White had to wheedle good relations—that is, friendly compliance—from the Maharaja and other notables. When he took up his new post, he found the Maharaja insubordinate and, on orders from Calcutta, sent him into a two-year exile on British Indian soil. In a few years he won compliance and friendship too. No ripple disturbed this friendship when, in 1904, the British sent an army under Colonel (later Sir Francis) Younghusband through southeastern Sikkim, over the Jelep La to Lhasa. Using Sikkim as a corridor, the expedition hunted a Russian menace in Tibet which turned out to be a myth. In the classic pattern of British indirect rule, White deferred to the Maharaja, flattered him, and even chaperoned him at a glittering durbar in Calcutta. It was, in a sense, the coming-out party of Sikkim's ruling family. In a formal coat and a high stiff collar, defying Calcutta's heat, White carried off his ceremonial duties with style.

But externals were poor clues to John Claude White. He wanted to make Sikkim more than a mere vestibule to Tibet. He took an engineer's interest in the State and its people. When he first rode up the Tista Valley in the late 1880's, there were no roads and only a few mule tracks. The bridges were terrifying contraptions of cane and rope. The only schools were those in the monasteries, and they hardly deserved the name. White set out to provide the essential underpinnings of a British colony: roads, police, and revenue. When he left Gangtok after twenty years of service, a cart road connected the capital with the railhead in India, and others crisscrossed the region nearest the Indian frontier. He had created a well-trained police force; he had also built a jail, but law and order were such that it seldom had more than three or four inmates. A few missionary schools and dispensaries had appeared. White even launched two or three rudimentary industries: apple-growing in the northern highlands, weaving and carpet-making in Gangtok. Instead of draining Sikkim, he sought to build it.

White would have done more if the imperial authorities in Calcutta had let him. In the treks that took him to almost inaccessible areas, he had found copper. The people had been working it, in a primitive way, in pre-British days. Prospectors invited by White also found iron, tin, zinc, aluminum, lead, gold, and silver. And who could travel in Sikkim without being aware of its untapped forest wealth? Who could fail to notice its water power that tumbled, unused, down the boiling Tista? Repeatedly White begged the government of India to let Sikkim be developed. But the guardians of the Raj turned deaf ears. What did Sikkim matter to an empire that ruled a fourth of the globe and more than a fourth of its people? Higher authorities told White that they were reluctant "to destroy the simplicity of an Arcadian little state." The psychology of the museum curator triumphed, as it had in North Borneo and other colonies. In spite of his political successes, White retired in 1908 a disappointed man. He felt that the economic possibilities of Sikkim had not been tapped.

[2]

The Britons who succeeded White had no compelling interest in the northern borderland. They did make the road to Gangtok motorable, thus bringing Sikkim's capital within five hours' drive (landslides permitting) of the railhead in Bengal. They also placed a Punjabi engineer of near-genius, named Chand Jali, in charge of laying out and building a caravan road from Gangtok to the Natu La, the route to Tibet. Starting from a height of 6,000 feet at Gangtok and ending at 14,146 feet twenty-seven miles away, he aligned the road so skillfully that the grade never rose more than 350 feet in a mile. This was a boon to Sikkim; other improvements and changes were few.

The industries White had started soon languished and all but died. One of his successors ascribed their failure to the lack of competent supervision. A truer explanation was the failure to train skilled workers and managers. The mealy bug and other pests blighted the small crops of oranges and apples. Malaria killed or disabled thousands every year. Tapeworm was universal. Kala azar fever, a parasitic scourge, ravaged the Tista Valley and other low-lying areas. One traveler in 1936, a year of epidemic, reported passing through a hamlet where sixty-three persons had been living six months before. The only survivors were two children whose grandparents had taken them away to the mountains in time. The British authorities built a temporary 250-bed hospital of bamboo at Rangpo on the Tista. But the hospital could only relieve; it could not prevent. Preventive medicine required, first, techniques of spraying not yet known in the 1930's; second, a program of educating the people to ward off disease at its sources. This kind of training the colonial regime never undertook. The British brought peace, justice, security, and order to Sikkim, but they left the mass of the people unschooled, unequipped for survival in the modern world.

India in Britain's Place

When the British Raj walked off the Himalayan stage in 1947, independent India stepped into well-polished English shoes. It was a new experience for rulers and ruled. For Indians had never governed or controlled these mountain peoples before. Indian kings in pre-British days avoided the Himalayas and took little interest in their people. Only Asoka, the great emperor of the third century B.C., spread his power a short distance above the base of the Himalayan wall into what is now the Katmandu Valley of Nepal. The rest of India's empire builders—the Guptas of the fourth century A.D., the Delhi sultans of the thirteenth, the Moguls of the sixteenth to eighteenth—all were content to stop at the foothills. It was Britons, not Indians, who first pushed the borders of an Indian empire to the crest of the Himalayas.

Thus it was a new responsibility for Indians to guard the Sikkim vestibule. Yet Indian civil servants took over their unaccustomed duties with the aplomb of men brought up in the British imperial tradition. Sikkim retained nominal charge of its internal affairs; a standstill agreement temporarily continued the previous arrangements with the (British) government of India until a new treaty could be fashioned.

Free India was by no means sure what to do with its inheritance. Would it absorb Sikkim into the Indian Union, make it a district of the State of West Bengal, perhaps give it one spokesman in the national Parliament at New Delhi? Would it introduce elections and the democratic process? Or would it use local leaders and old-time institutions, as the British had done in the princely States of India and in colonies around the globe? The Indians would have liked to postpone decisions; they were beset by Hindu-Moslem massacres in the midst of nation-building. But they had little time. It was not long before trouble bore down on Shangri-La.

The State Congress, an offshoot of the all-powerful Congress Party in India, wanted to see the hereditary privileges of the Maharaja abolished. It also wanted a start toward land reform and representative government. Predictably, these demands collided with the wishes of His Highness in the golden robe. In February 1949, local Congress leaders were clapped into jail. When their followers marched on Gangtok, the Maharaja temporized. He agreed to set up a stopgap government with the Congress leader as Chief Minister, but without power. At this point the new Indian Political Officer, the canny Harishwar Dayal, warned New Delhi that Sikkim was threatened with disorder. India rushed a Deputy Minister of External Affairs to Gangtok; he recommended sending troops and appointing an Indian as Chief Minister to keep order. Both were done. Although the Indians professed that their rule would be temporary, they had, in fact, taken the first effective step toward political control of the route to Lhasa.

Soon it was time for the next step: absolute, unquestioned military control. The next year, 1950, the Chinese Communists marched into Tibet. The government of India hastened to strengthen its authority along the entire border, all the way from Kashmir to the wild northeast frontier near Burma. After concluding treaties of "peace and friendship" with Nepal and Bhutan, the Indians were ready to clamp their hold upon Sikkim with a tighter treaty.[3] Events in Tibet compelled Dayal, the chief Indian negotiator, to twist the arm of the reluctant Maharaja. The day before the treaty was rushed to signature on December 5, 1950, the Dalai Lama fled Lhasa (for the first time) ahead of the Chinese invaders. The day after the signing, Mr. Nehru

---

[3] For the official Indian texts of the three treaties, see *Foreign Policy of India, Texts of Documents, 1947–59* (New Delhi: Lok Sabha Secretariat; 1959), pp. 17–19, 31–3, 37–40.

confessed to his Parliament that "it did come as a surprise to us and a shock" to learn of Chinese troops marching to the "liberation" of Tibet. At the time, Sikkimese leaders around the Maharaja were bitter at Dayal for having virtually forced them to sign. Before many years they were to feel grateful to him, and to India, for military protection.

[1]

The treaty was ironclad. It gave India the right to station troops anywhere in Sikkim and "to take such measures as it considers necessary for the defense of Sikkim or the security of India, whether preparatory or otherwise, and whether within or outside Sikkim." India demanded and got full control of arms brought into Sikkim, free entry for all Indian goods, sole conduct of Sikkim's foreign relations. In addition, India obtained the sole right to build strategic roads and handle Sikkim's communications. The Indian negotiators thought of everything. They even insisted on the right to issue warrants for tracking down any "fugitive offenders"—for example, spies—if the Sikkimese should dilly-dally in bringing them to justice. For all these benefits, India agreed to keep the Maharaja on his throne and to pay his government a subsidy of 300,000 rupees ($60,000) a year. Some of the Maharaja's advisers wailed that this was a paltry sum and the treaty a cruel bargain. Sikkim still kept a measure of separateness as a protectorate; it had averted being swallowed by the vast and alien Indian Union. Actually India's control was more sweeping than that of the British in imperial days.

Now the pattern was set. India had what it wanted. In return for the reality of power, it would leave the Maharaja the fiction. Though His Highness was an archaic survival, he would have his uses; Indians could govern Sikkim behind him. Buddhism could remain as the State religion. Sikkim was not ready for representative democracy; elections would do no more than choose some members of a council to advise the Maharaja. A free press was, and remains, unknown. Land reform was enacted on a limited scale. Previously the State had leased the land in large tracts to landlords who managed them, dispensed justice, collected taxes, and paid the State annually. Now the leases lapsed, and farmers held their land by State permission. If a farmer could not cultivate a large tract himself, he could let it out to a secondary holder, who paid half his crop as rent. A few hundred-acre holdings remained, but these were exceptional. The average holding became ten acres, and 95 per cent of all the farmland in Sikkim was directly cultivated and paid for in cash. To this extent, at least, Sikkim bowed to the winds of reform that were blowing through India. But former landlords remained as His Highness's closest advisers.

In the Ministry of External Affairs in New Delhi, there were men of vision who said: "We must prove that life on our side of the frontier is better than on the other." As Chief Minister of Sikkim, India appointed John Lall, a brilliant civil servant trained at Oxford, a thinker as well as a doer. From Gangtok he and others pleaded with New Delhi to extend India's first Five Year Plan to Sikkim. But India's attentions in those years were otherwise absorbed.

In contrast to its military alertness on the frontier, New Delhi was courting the favor of Peking and accepting a *fait accompli* in Tibet. This prolonged kowtow to China was enough to inflict a backache on the Indian diplomats involved. Deference reached its ceremonial depth on April 29, 1954, with the signing of the Sino-Indian agreement on Tibet. Dealing with what it called "the Tibet Region of China," the agreement began with the famous Five Principles, the first of which was "mutual respect for each other's territorial integrity and sovereignty." It then sought to regulate the age-old traffic of traders and pilgrims across the Himalayas. Sikkim, of course, was directly affected, since the traffic over the passes provided employment for Sikkim and customs revenue for India.

[2]

This was the period when India and China edged closer together like two large birds in a clumsy love dance. It was as if an ostrich and a vulture were spooning. Good-will delegations shuttled back and forth between New Delhi and Peking. They formed a cross section of the educated top layer in both countries: civil servants, engineers, teachers, and a goodly proportion of arty-crafty types. The Chinese Olympic soccer team came, trounced Calcutta's local champions, and drew ecstatic praise from Indian sports writers. "Cultural" troupes of Chinese dancers, singers, and actors were so busy in India that one wondered how any "culture" could have remained in China itself.

The early years of the love dance brought a sudden windfall to Sikkim. While the Maharaja and his advisers waited for Indian development funds, China sent a request to New Delhi which was to mean employment, at relatively high pay, to hundreds in Sikkim and the neighboring regions. The Chinese needed a rice reserve for their troops in Tibet, estimated at that time to number between 20,000 and 30,-000. No road yet crossed the wastelands between Lhasa and the railhead in western China. (A road linking Lhasa with Peking has since ended Tibet's dependence on the supply route from India.) In 1953 the only practicable route was by sea from China to Calcutta, by rail to Siliguri in the Himalayan foothills, by truck to Gangtok, and then by the mule trail over the Natu La to Tibet. Would India please consent to the shipment? The Indians pondered. Reports of famine in Tibet had reached New Delhi. Chinese troops were said to be living off the land and raiding the food reserves of Tibetan monasteries, where it is cold enough, in the high plateau, to store grain unspoiled for fifteen years.

Thus rice for the army might indirectly relieve the people's hunger. The Indian government therefore gave its permission. To emphasize its humanitarian motives, it waived the usual customs duty on non-Indian goods going through India to Tibet.

The rice amounted to about a thousand tons. A single freight train could have carried it with ease. But in the railless, roadless frontier country, transportation of a thousand tons was, as Mr. Nehru recalled later, "a terrible job." A mule can carry, at most, 160 pounds, slung in two sacks from its back; it needs perhaps ten pounds of feed a day. No less than four days were required to bring a mule load forty-four miles from Gangtok to Yatung, the nearest Tibetan town. The trail twisted upward to 14,146 feet and then downward, more steeply, into the Chumbi Valley of Tibet on the other side.

But steep trails mean nothing to the people of the borderland. Muleteers flocked into Gangtok, attracted by the promise of months of employment. One man could handle a caravan of nine mules; with perhaps 12,500 individual loads required, the rice shipment was a bonanza. Most of the drivers were Tibetans, big men in boots and fur-trimmed hats of gold brocade; some were Sikkimese Bhutias of Tibetan origin; all were quick with a smile, however weary, on the trail. They strapped the sacks onto their mules at a loading ground below Gangtok. The head of the lead mule was decked with a scarlet yak tail; bells hung from its neck and flanks. Gay and bustling was the scene as each caravan took to the uphill trail. By the time dawn streaked Kanchenjunga, many had already climbed to the high ground far above Gangtok, the muleteer striding alongside the last mule to guard against stragglers. Traffic downhill was just as busy. Tibet made good use of these rice caravans to send India bales of wool, for rough carpeting, and loads of yaks' tails, to be made into Santa Claus beards. One New York importer used to sell this specialty. But the

United States embargoed yaks' tails and wool when the Chinese Communists seized control of Tibet; and new markets had to be found in Europe, India, or China itself.

[3]

Mules were not the only carriers. Porters by the score converged on Gangtok to take goods on their backs over the pass to Yatung. Hundreds of them were broad-faced, tan-skinned Sherpas, whose ancestors had migrated from Tibet into a remote corner of northeastern Nepal. Their grandfathers had drifted into the British hill station of Darjeeling about the time of World War I, in search of jobs. Strong, resourceful, intelligent, brave, they soon made their fame world-wide. Himalayan mountaineers for thirty years had depended on the Sherpas as human conveyor belts, to carry their food and oxygen, their tents and tools, to heights where man had never stood before. It was a Sherpa from Darjeeling, Tenzing Norkey, who climbed with Sir Edmund Hillary to the untrodden summit of Everest; another, Ang Tharkey, shepherded the French up Anapurna.

The boom traffic to Tibet gave employment in the slack season not only to Sherpa men but to a hundred of their women. Porters earned thirty-five rupees (seven dollars) for carrying a load to Yatung. The Sikkim government limited each human load to eighty-two pounds, usually encased in a wooden crate. With a strap around the forehead, each porter hoisted the load onto his (or her) back and started up the trail on springy bare feet. Above Gangtok, a Sikkimese policeman checked the cargo to make sure that it contained no ammunition, opium, or other forbidden goods.

Many hiked the forty-four miles to Yatung in three days instead of the usual four. Some Bhutanese and Sherpas did it in two days and thus collected full pay for half the time. Occasionally they rested the load on a T-shaped stick. They rested again at four check points maintained by the Indian Army on the trail to the Natu La. At the frozen crest of the pass they rested once more, long enough to throw a rock for good luck onto the cairn that marks the summit. But money and pride pushed them on.

At one time during this rush hour on the Tibet road, 3,200 porters were registered for the traffic, although the number actually employed was much lower. Trade with Tibet broke all records. In six months of 1953, Indian exports to Tibet by all routes, not including the rice shipment, totaled 11,119,000 rupees, or about $2,250,000. The busiest of all the trails on the entire northern frontier were the one over the Natu La and the longer, slightly higher, companion route over the nearby Jelep La. Most of the trade consisted of cotton textiles, tea, and other foodstuffs; smaller items included hand tools, kerosene, flashlights and batteries, and miscellaneous consumer goods.

Profitable though it was, the trade with Tibet gave Sikkim no more than a shot in the arm. For benefits that would last, the Sikkimese had to wait. In July 1954, the extension of India's Five Year Plan to Sikkim was still being debated in New Delhi. But by the end of that summer the pace of decision-making had quickened. Twice, on July 17 and August 13, Peking complained that Indian troops had "intruded" into Tibet. India denied the charge, and accused Tibetan officials of trying to cross into Indian territory in the same general area. Unknown to the public until 1959, this was the start of a succession of incidents along the Tibetan frontier. Infiltration and "aggression," arrests, and killings on supposedly Indian soil began to preoccupy the government of India.

There is no proof that any specific border incident spurred India into spending money in Sikkim. The first quarrel took place almost 600 miles from Sikkimese territory, northwest of Nepal. The later, more serious, incidents occurred in desolate Ladakh, 1,000 miles farther to the northwest, and along the McMahon Line which starts 300 miles to the east of Sikkim. Nevertheless, the coincidence remains. By the autumn of 1954, only a few weeks after the first border dispute, the Indian government had made up its mind to catch up with past neglect in Sikkim. In March 1955, the Maharaja officially announced a new development plan, wholly financed by India, and asked his people to co-operate in "this great adventure."

[4]

Sikkim's development is worth a close look, for it serves as a test and an example of India's tutelage along the Himilayan frontier. The first plan called for spending 22,500,-000 rupees ($4,500,000) during seven years, in addition to the annual subsidy. To evaluate it in terms of money alone would be misleading for two reasons. First, Sikkim is so microscopic on India's map that a million rupees would go a long way. Secondly, money is never a reliable guide to the effectiveness of a development program. What matters is the use of the money and the philosophy behind it.

By these standards, India and Sikkim planned well. They set aside half the money for nonmilitary roads, bridges, and public transport. By 1960, they had built 148 miles of new motorable roads and 263 miles of smaller farm-to-market roads. It used to take a farmer three or four days to get his cash crop to the place of sale. By 1960 the time had been cut to a day or two from almost any of the cultivated areas.

Other segments of the plan showed equal insight. One of its guiding principles was the training of managers and leaders. Before 1953, it had been almost impossible for a Sikkim boy to win a scholarship for higher or vocational education in India. Sikkim felt discriminated against; in a single year early in the 1950's, the government of India granted scholarships to 212 boys from neighboring Nepal, but not one from Sikkim. Thanks to the new program and to Indian funds, 400 Sikkimese had won such scholarships by 1957. Many of them went to an agricultural school at Shillong, in Assam, where conditions approximate those of

Sikkim more closely than on the Indian plains. By 1960 some of these scholarship winners had supplanted Indians in administrative and technical posts in Gangtok.

Another principle, often overlooked in development plans, was the processing of local products wherever possible. Sikkim's products are few, their importance in world trade negligible. But they can earn revenue for a hard-pressed State government. Thus a fruit processing plant was opened in 1957, chiefly to bottle orange and apple juice for the Indian market and to cut down India's spending of foreign exchange for them. A small whisky distillery made use of Sikkim maize, barley, and mountain water. A Scot, tasting it, might conclude that Kipling had been right, after all, about East and West. But Sikkim's liquor is not brewed for Scots; it is for those Indians who are not prohibitionists. Even so, who knows? It may yet appear as a curiosity in Western liquor shops along with Turkish *raki,* Japanese *sake,* and Greek *retsina* wine. Other Sikkim products may also reach the outer world. Carpet-making and other arts and crafts, first promoted by Sir John Claude White, have been revived in the new cottage industries institute. Handmade paper from Sikkim spruce, wool from Sikkim sheep, furniture from rare Sikkim woods—such are some of the fruits of the government's new concern for processing local resources. As for minerals, which White and his successors tried in vain to develop, the governments of Sikkim and India have joined in providing 10,000,000 rupees ($2,000,-000) of capital for a Sikkim Mining Corporation. The Maharaj Kumar, of course, is its first President.

By 1960 a new emphasis on education had begun to show results: 151 schools compared to eighty in the preplan years; 335 teachers at work; and 7,500 children in school. Other public services usually, but wrongly, classed as "welfare" showed headway. Malaria, which had struck one out of ten Sikkimese as recently as 1955, was being wiped out. Dispensaries were being built and staffed so that every Sikkimese could find medical help within five miles of his home.

One veterinary hospital had been built at Gangtok, others planned for remoter areas. Stud bulls, pigs, and poultry were imported to improve the breeds. As for pests in farms and orchards, Sikkim was at last getting the better of them. Before the development plan was launched, farmers could get little help in combating the mealy bug and dieback which blighted the orange groves and the white ants that infested their potatoes. Not until the plan got under way could the State agricultural officer supply the farmer with the right insecticides and practical guidance for using them.

The planners, taking their cue from India's own community development, have paid attention to the "felt need" in helping a rural population to help itself. To learn what the farmers and their families wanted most, the Maharaj Kumar and his officials called a series of meetings with local headmen. They discovered that drinking water held first priority. The farmers suggested channeling mountain streams through bamboo pipe systems to their homesteads. Roads and schools came second and third.

In general, the development program started well. Whether it will deepen the Sikkimese people's trust and friendship for India, which financed it, one cannot say. Financing does not buy gratitude, and gratitude does not assure friendship, as India should know full well. This much India can say: more economic and social progress was achieved in the few years after 1955 than in half a century before. Like the Japanese in Hokkaido and the Americans in the Philippines, the Indians were not content to harness Sikkim's physical resources. They set out also to develop human resources. For this enlightenment, much of the credit belongs to Indian officials assigned to Sikkim: to John Lall, Chief Minister in the formative years of the plan; to his progressive-minded Indian successors, N. K. Rustomji and Baleshwar Prasad; and to those in New Delhi who saw the

need and met it. No small part of the credit should shine
upon the Sikkimese, notably the young heir apparent. But
in a perverse way, some of the credit could be claimed by
the rulers of Communist China.

The Prod of China

As annoyances multiplied along the 3,000-mile Himalayan
frontier, as the Chinese sought to weld Tibet into their system, the rice shipments through Sikkim dwindled and
stopped. India stepped up its financing of Sikkim beyond
what it had promised, and embarked on the boldest of all its
military projects. This was the building of a Y-shaped road
to the far north of the State, almost to the Tibetan frontier.
The road would have been about eighty miles long if each of
its three prongs could have been straight, but hairpin bends
made it much longer. Its chief purpose was to bring troops,
supplies, and light weapons from Gangtok to the northern
limits of Sikkim in a single day. An incidental purpose, admittedly incidental, was to help apple growers on northern
hillsides to get their cash crop to Calcutta markets within
two days of picking.

Had it not been for overriding military needs, no one
would have been rash enough to carve a road through such
terrain. For northern Sikkim is crumpled by ridges, chasms,
and mountain torrents. Much of the roadbed had to be
hacked and blasted out of cliffs. To cross one torrent, the
engineers had to design a single-span steel bridge 400 feet
long and 500 feet above the water. There was no room for
bulldozers and other modern equipment. Ledges had to be
cut away virtually by hand. Compressor drills and dynamite
could be used in some places, but many of the cliffs were
too steep and the trails too narrow for anything but human
labor.

By 1960 about 8,000 men, women, and children were at

work on the northern road. Most of them were Nepalis, living in huts of bamboo and palm alongside their work. Some
were drilling holes for explosives with sharp-pointed "jump-
ing crowbars." Others were splitting the rock with mallets
for the road base and the retaining walls. Seen from across
a valley, the swarms of workers looked like termites boring
into a temple wall. Chipping and tapping, heaving and pant-
ing, they had finished forty-five miles of road by the end of
1960, except for two difficult bridges.

This northern road, like others in the Himalayas, is in
constant danger from landslides. When the monsoon rains
hit, sometimes with a yearly fall of 200 inches, rocks are
loosened and calamity strikes below. Landslides have buried many villages and left gashes on many mountain slopes.
Rare is the summer and autumn when Sikkim's roads are
unblocked. Because of the shifting rocks and the rains, the
northern highway will be hard-topped as soon as its base
has settled. Although only twenty feet wide for most of its
length, and twelve feet on the cliffside stretches, it will require more maintenance per mile than a superhighway in
the West.

The "North Sikkim Highway" was a military as well as
an engineering risk. A prudent nation does not ordinarily
oblige a potential invader by building a paved road to the
points from which he might come. An invasion of Sikkim,
however, is not what Indians fear. The pattern of recent
years, elsewhere on the Tibet frontier, has been one of minor incursions. A few soldiers have violated the border;
more often Chinese spies and agitators pretending to be de-
fectors have infiltrated. Against such violations, the road
will be invaluable.

[1]

The only invasion of Sikkim up to 1962 was of a kind the
Indians had not planned for. This was the influx of thousands of refugees during and after the Tibetan uprising

in 1959. Singly, in scores, sometimes in hundreds, they trekked across the high passes to save their own lives and those of their animals. On the wind-swept northern pastures of Nepal, Sikkim, and Bhutan, Tibetan herdsmen created a desperate problem. Sikkim found itself playing host not only to the refugees but to the 25,000 sheep they had brought with them. The sheep could not go south; in the heat and humidity of the valleys they would sicken and die. Reluctantly the government of Bhutan agreed to take 20,000 sheep plus 1,000 Tibetans to care for them. The solution was dangerous. In the lush pastures of northern Bhutan, Tibetan flocks accustomed to the sparse growth of their own plateau would probably eat themselves to death.

Tibetans who escaped without animals faced different problems. Ragged, hungry thousands made their way south toward Gangtok in search of food. Almost two thousand were given work on the North Sikkim road at high wages of from five to seven rupees a day. The experiment failed. Many quit, some saying they had left Tibet to escape building roads. Tibetans generally are not manual laborers by temperament or training; they are farmers and nomadic herdsmen. Unhappy, often unwell in low altitudes, most of the refugees congregated in a camp organized and maintained under the devoted leadership of Princess Kukula.

Other thousands of Tibetans poured into northern India. With the help of private organizations, including the American CARE, India set up reception and training centers for them. Outside Darjeeling, more than 500 children of lowly families were put to school to learn reading, writing, and useful trades. Sons of Tibetan nobles and merchants enrolled in the celebrated St. Joseph's College, a Roman Catholic school that has taught future leaders of the Himalayan borderland for generations. Here they pursue a forlorn hope of somehow helping to liberate their country.

Whenever the risk was not too great, refugees used the old caravan routes into India as channels of escape. From

Lhasa, the shortest and most direct of these routes led to Kalimpong, the Indian hill town close to the Sikkim border.

[2]

No discussion of the eastern Himalayas can ignore Kalimpong, the most cosmopolitan of all borderland communities. It has absorbed more foreign influences than Zamboanga, drawn more strange personalities to it than Hokkaido, and, as we shall see, served almost every kind of borderland purpose. As the southern terminus of the trail to Tibet over the Jelep La, Kalimpong was bound to be flooded by refugees. Monks took over a local monastery. Nuns in russet robes with close-cropped heads were billeted in a school. Families boarded everywhere. Few of them escaped intact, and their stories of a husband tortured, a child lost in flight, of monasteries pillaged and burned, spread revulsion among the people of Kalimpong. These were not impersonal horror stories; they concerned friends and families, former homes and other traditional links with Tibet. How such stories, told in Sikkim and other parts of India, were affecting the borderland peoples and their habit of looking northward, is still to be assessed.

For Kalimpong, the burden of refugees was not only heavy but apparently permanent. Where could these cold-climate, high-altitude Tibetans go? They suffered from Kalimpong's low level of 4,500 feet and its subtropical warmth; they probably would go on suffering there, one more drain on the already impoverished townspeople. Within fifteen years, Kalimpong had lost the two main sources of its prosperity and leadership in the borderland: the trade with Tibet, and the resort patronage of Britons.

Until 1955, when the Chinese began to create difficulties, thousands of mules streamed back and forth across the Jelep La each year, carrying Tibetan wool and Chinese brocades southward, and Indian cotton goods and household articles northward. The long street leading down to Kalim-

pong's loading ground was lined with well-stocked Tibetan
and Chinese emporiums. The lower town around the bazaar
was the trading area of Indian merchants. Most of them
were Marwaris from the Arabian Sea coast, the sharpest,
most detested of all the trading castes of India. When a Chinese trader faced a Marwari, an irresistible force met an
immovable object. Yet trade and barter flourished, with an
average turnover of 1,200,000 rupees a month. In the boom
years of the China-India love dance, it was estimated as
high as 12,000,000 rupees a month. After 1955, the stream
of commerce receded and gradually dried up, the victim of
the Tibetan rebellion and its cruel aftermath. The Marwaris
shuttered their shops and departed. The mule bells, the
chatter of muleteers and traders fell silent. Kalimpong's
streets emptied like a Hollywood set from which the cast
and cameramen had gone.

Kalimpong might have survived in fair shape without
Tibetan trade if it had not already lost its British patronage.
Before independence, the British who ran India had made
it not only a thriving summer resort but a center of missionary work. A square church tower recalls those days. English
villas still dot the ridge above the town, but they are mostly
dilapidated and their gardens overgrown. So are the two
missionary establishments founded by a remarkable Scot,
the late Dr. John Anderson Graham, the first missionary
ever elected Moderator of the General Assembly of the
Church of Scotland. Just as Dr. Seagrave's influence permeates northern Burma, so Dr. Graham's shines through this
part of the Himalayan borderland. His "homes" for needy
children, started in 1900, his school for boys, his colleges
for teachers and nurses, his hospital and leprosarium, these
survive as monuments to British philanthropy and Dr. Graham's indomitable energies. A few Scottish teachers and
doctors remain. But most Britons and the other foreigners
have left, and with them much of the money that made Kalimpong hum.

[3]

One business flourishes and keeps Kalimpong in the public eye: intrigue. The Chinese Communists honored the town by calling it the command center of the 1959 uprising in Tibet. A visitor once told Mr. Nehru that there were probably more spies in Kalimpong than the rest of the inhabitants put together. "That is an exaggeration," said the Prime Minister. But he acknowledged that many people came in various guises, "sometimes as technical people, sometimes as bird watchers, sometimes as geologists, sometimes as journalists. . . ."

In the Himalayan Hotel, an old brown chalet on a hilltop among tall camellia trees, guests size up one another with more than casual interest. On any evening, the informal circle around the living-room table, sipping whisky or warm Tibetan beer, might have included the following: a retired British civil servant, silently deploring the collapse of civilization; an Indian botanist whose special enthusiasm was the Lepchas of Sikkim; an American student collecting Buddhist scrolls for a California professor; Miss Tashi Dorji, accomplished sister of the Prime Minister of Bhutan; Prince Peter, an anthropologist of the royal house of Greece and Denmark; the Buddhist son of Nicholas Roerich, the Russian painter of central Asian subjects; and Mr. Wong. Mr. Wong was known simply as a Chinese businessman, silent, unobtrusive, and courteous to all. A visitor returning to the hotel in 1960 missed Mr. Wong and inquired for him. "Dear Mr. Wong! He was recalled to Peking," was the answer. "He was a spy, you know. Such a nice man! We hated to see him go."

Without doubt the star of the Himalayan Hotel cast is Mrs. Annie Perry. Of Scot-Tibetan-Nepali origins, she manages the family hotel, the refugees, and much of Kalimpong besides, with a light hand and a warm heart. Her father, David Macdonald, served in Tibet for twenty years as British and Indian trade agent. He retired to the hotel which had been his home, to write his memoirs and translate the Bible into Tibetan.

How many agents the Chinese keep in Kalimpong nobody could guess. In 1960, the Indian police arrested the alleged leader of the Chinese Communist apparatus, charging him with having instigated the murder of a Tibetan refugee monk. The arrested man turned out to be a highly respected Kalimpong citizen. When he confessed that sixty of the townsfolk were working for him, Annie Perry said firmly that she would never trust anybody any more.

Perhaps the least popular of the permanent foreign residents is the Chinese trade agent, admitted under the terms of the 1954 treaty between India and Communist China. Probably the most popular is the Prime Minister of Bhutan and his family, who make Kalimpong their unofficial winter capital. The Prime Minister, Jigme Dorji, welcomes visitors to his villa on the ridge above the town and startles them by his resemblance to Yul Brynner, the actor. His head is shaven, his eyes sparkle, his speech snaps with incisiveness. In flawless English, he dissects the handicaps which his Bhutanese people face as a result of their long seclusion. By Himalayan standards they are prosperous and well fed, but illiterate and defenseless against attack. A new road connecting the heart of Bhutan with India will bring people out, but Mr. Dorji will police the traffic carefully. He has no intention of letting Indian or European education spoil his younger generation for honest work for Bhutan. The Prime Minister knows that Chinese maps claim a slice of Bhutan's ill-defined northern frontier. By 1961 he was not yet ready to allow India to station troops along that frontier, as it had done in Sikkim. Yet India, pledged to defend both States, was understandably worried about the exposed position of Bhutan.

[4]

Worries, however, are relative. At the beginning of 1962, after fifteen years of independence, Indians could not point to any part of their 2,000-mile northern borderland and say: "Here, at least, we are safe." In dispute between China and India were 51,000 square miles of Himalayan territory. Chinese soldiers were sitting on 12,000 square miles of soil which India claimed as her own. Indians stationed in the Himalayas, patrolling, guarding, and administering, were prone to the fatalism of Italian farmers on the slopes of Vesuvius. They knew that anything could happen along the line from the wastes of Ladakh in the northwest to the tribal areas governed by India's North-East Frontier Agency, much of which Peking's maps label "China."

For several reasons, Nepal was a special source of anxiety. Its king had signed an agreement with the Communist Chinese, settling a disputed boundary and providing for the first road from Tibet into Nepal. Internally, Nepal was none too stable and, moreover, was rumbling with anti-Indian sentiment. "This is what we are getting," said Mr. Nehru in 1959, "in exchange for all the friendship and help we have given in the last ten years or so." It was a complaint that Americans could treasure and remember.

In Sikkim, at least, the Indians could feel relatively satisfied and secure. The Chinese had not disputed the Tibet-Sikkim frontier, which they and the British had settled by treaty in 1890. It followed the watershed between the Tista and Tibetan rivers, and dipped below 17,000 feet at only one point. In the long boundary negotiations with India in 1960, the Chinese never challenged this line, though they refused to confirm or even discuss it. India's military posture in Sikkim was as strong as it could be in such terrain; for this, the authors of the 1950 treaty were partly responsible. India's political relations with Sikkim were reasonably good; for this both Indians and Sikkimese could thank their joint efforts to bring the State along. Wise leadership and restraint on both sides had helped to ease the inevitable frictions. For this, in all fairness, Mr. Nehru should have pinned a large gold image of the god of Kanchenjunga on the chest of Chou En-lai himself.

5

Beyond the Hindu Kush

AFGHANISTAN'S NORTHERN BORDERLAND

In Afghanistan there may yet be time to rediscover, reconstruct, revive, and reinterpret old values in modern terms before superficial imitation of the West has gone beyond the point of no return.
—**PROFESSOR W. H. GRIFFIN**

NEGLECT is one indignity that the land and the people of northern Afghanistan have not had to bear for long. Freedom from attention has rarely plagued or blessed them. For this reason alone they qualify as an eccentric among borderlands. On the relative merits of neglect and attention, one should not attempt a judgment; what matters, of course, is the kind, and the northern Afghan borderland has attracted almost every kind of attention.

It served, for one thing, as the most trodden stretch of the highway between Europe and Asia, in the great migrations westward and the armed invasions both east and west. It had the ill luck, for another, to figure as a pawn in the nineteenth century power game between the Russian and

British Empires. And finally, it emerged in our own time as the more strategic and richly endowed half of the country called Afghanistan. These are the kinds of attention that will concern us in the most fussed-over of our borderlands.

[1]

Why should men on the move have used this particular strip of Central Asia as a main thoroughfare between Europe and the Orient? Across the south, the borderland is walled off from the rest of Afghanistan by a geographical barrier, the massive ranges of the Hindu Kush mountains. Standing in the northern foothills of the Hindu Kush and looking northward, one faces a high, dry plateau. It slopes gently downhill for a hundred miles to the subtropical valley of the Oxus River. Flowing westward, the Oxus forms for 680 miles the modern political barrier between Afghanistan and the Soviet Union. Again looking north, from the Oxus, one faces desert, then forest belts, then tundra all the way to the Arctic Sea. No obstruction intervenes, nor any other major, dependable source of water for men and beasts crossing Asia. There we have the clue to the volume of human traffic through the valley of the Oxus. Conquerors with their armies, their captives, and slaves; nomads with their flocks; traders and pilgrims with their caravans; the homeless and the hungry—all trampled and lived off the lush valley, scaled the bare brown hills, and usually moved on. Marco Polo passed this way bound for Cathay. After traversing what is now northern Turkey and Iran, the teen-age son of a Venetian merchant noted such "rich herbage, fine pasturage, fruit in plenty, and no lack of anything" that "armies are prone to loiter here because of the abundance of supplies." Marco found "the best melons in the world in very great quantity." (In this respect, at least, nothing has changed in 700 years.) Beyond the once-splendid city of Balkh, which Marco found ravaged and looted by the Tatars, he rode twelve days "without finding any habitation

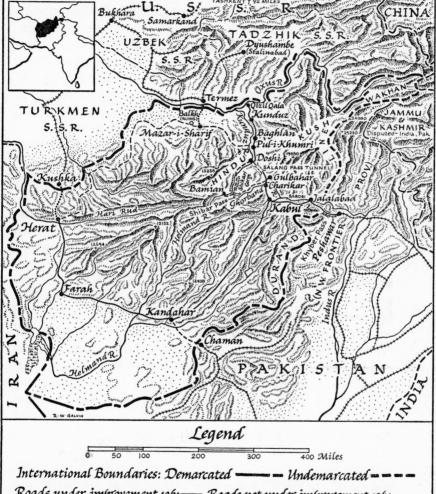

Landlocked
AFGHANISTAN

Bukhara
Samarkand
U. S. S. R.
TASHKENT 92 MILES
CHINA

UZBEK
S.S.R.
TADZHIK S.S.R.
Dyushambe
(Stalinabad)

TURKMEN
S. S. R.

Termez
OXUS R.
WAKHAN

Balkh
(RUINS)
Qizil Qala
Kunduz
JAMMU
&
KASHMIR
Disputed- India, Pak.

Mazar-i-Sharif
Baghlan
Pul-i-Khumri
24080
25230

Kushka
Doshi
19880
SALANG PASS TUNNELS
HINDU
KUSH
PROV.

Bamian
Gulbahar
Charikar
Hari Rud
Helmand R.
Ghorband
SAROBI
Kabul
Jalalabad

Herat
Shibar Pass
13856
12152
12654
D. U. R. A. N. D.
Khyber Pass
Peshawar
N. W. FRONTIER

Farah
12438
Indus R.

Kandahar

IRAN
Chaman
Helmand R.
PAKISTAN
INDIA

R. W. GALVIN

Legend

0   50   100   200   300   400 Miles

International Boundaries: Demarcated ——— Undemarcated ----
Roads under improvement 1961——— Roads not under improvement 1961----
Main roads projected 1961·········

because the people have all fled to mountain fastnesses for fear of the bandits and invaders who used to molest them."

Darius I broke ground for Alexander the Great, who planted Greek ideas on both sides of the Hindu Kush. Then Genghis Khan scorched the earth that Alexander had sown. Between these two, five big invading armies and many smaller ones ravaged what is now called Afghan Turkestan. A few stayed to found Herat, Balkh, Mazar-i-Sharif, and other centers of religion, trade, and learning, to see them wrecked, and sometimes to rebuild them from the ruins.

Meanwhile the people of the Hindu Kush fell under the sway of two great Asian religions. Buddhism seeped across the Afghan hills from its birthplace in northern India, bound for China by the best caravan route. In the second century of the Christian era missionaries stopped in a valley of the Hindu Kush to carve two outsize statues of the Lord Buddha out of the rock walls of the vale of Bamian. As with the building of a European cathedral, the patient chipping away at these beloved images went on between invasions for perhaps 300 years. In A.D. 630, a Chinese pilgrim named Huen Tsang passed through the Bamian Valley and counted ten monasteries and at least a thousand Buddhist monks living in man-made caves surrounding the statues. The pilgrim saw Bamian toward the last of its great days as a Rome or Mecca of the Buddhist world. Soon after, Arab invaders rolled through the valley welding the Afghan peoples solidly into the Moslem world where they are today.

It is a wonder that, between invasions, the dust ever had time to settle; much of it still hangs in the air. After the Oxus Valley had taken the main onslaught, some of the conquerors drove their men and beasts south through the passes of the Hindu Kush and across the Indus River into northern India, which they ransacked and usually abandoned in the end. (Genghis Khan quit India, it is said, because he could not bear its scorching heat. In this respect he showed less stamina than the British who followed.)

Has any people or piece of the earth ever survived so many intrusions or so brutal a beating? There is perhaps a parallel in the history of Poland: trampled by Huns, Slavs, and the very same breed of Tatars that dipped south into the Oxus Valley on their way west. Northern Afghans, like Poles, have shown a gift for absorbing and outliving invaders. The experience seems to have encouraged in both peoples a stubborn pride in their identity. Each has drawn strength from a demanding religion. But parallels of this kind quickly diverge. Poles look back more than a thousand years to the beginnings of their nation-state; Afghans, a little more than 200 years.

Even into the 1960's, the human traffic is as varied and brisk as through an international airport. On a leisurely day's ride northward from the Hindu Kush, one can encounter the following people: two Polish road engineers, a German industrial engineer, an Austrian ditto, a white Russian civil engineer, an Italian hydraulic engineer, four Chinese foresters (Communist), one Chinese agronomist (Nationalist), a Turkish malariologist, an Indian entomologist, a team of French archaeologists, an undetermined number of Russian road builders. All these, too, can be classed as transients. They probably came last year; they will probably be gone next year. Others will take their places. They reflect the current importance of the borderland to the people who govern Afghanistan from the capital in the southeast of the country. Kabul's interest, for reasons which we shall explore, centers on roads, factories, and farms, and on foreign technicians who can help to hasten the development of all these.

[2]

Among the comings and goings through the centuries of men of passage and men of prey, a population gradually took root in Afghan Turkestan. Who were the people who stayed behind? Each invader made his contribution of captives, slaves, and military garrisons. Centuries of Greek rule left a sharp imprint in the Graeco-Buddhist art of the area and in the faces of people. Out of Persian sources developed a large tribal group, the Tajiks, numbering about 2,000,000 modern borderlanders. Tall, swarthy, and reputedly clever, the Tajiks have made themselves a strong trading as well as farming class. Various tribes of Turks, uprooted by the Mongol hordes, found their way west and south to settle on both sides of the Oxus River. Thus today, Uzbeks, Turko-mans, and a smattering of Kirghiz and of smaller tribes of Turkic stock constitute the second largest group of border-land peoples. Uzbeks are not only herdsmen; they are said to be the best cotton farmers of Central Asia.

Genghis Khan is believed—there is no proof—to have left a garrison of a thousand in the Hindu Kush. If this is the true origin of the Mongolian Hazaras who live there now, they must have found wives among the people already on the spot, for they have somehow multiplied to more than half a million. They congregate in the wild valleys of the western Hindu Kush and usually venture out only to earn money to take back. In the cities, one finds these sturdy peo-ple with broad, cheerful faces doing the rough work: shov-eling snow off the rooftops, pulling heavy carts, and baking the flat loaves of whole wheat bread, the staple diet on both sides of the Hindu Kush.

It is natural for northern Afghans to turn their backs on the Hindu Kush and face north. The country slopes to the north; the rivers run northward from the melting snows of the mountain watershed. When the Central Asian people of the borderland stand on the shore of the Oxus and look across, this is what they see. Afghan Tajiks can look across the border to the Tajik Soviet Socialist Republic where 1,000,000 or so of their distant cousins live under Commu-nist rule in a state about the size of Wisconsin. Afghan Uzbeks, perhaps 750,000 people, can almost wave to their neighbors of the Uzbek Soviet Socialist Republic, the 5,000,-

000 Uzbeks living in a state that suggests the size and shape of California. Moving westward along the boundary, a Turkoman on the Afghan side can see the bare brown desert of Soviet Turkmenistan, the home of 1,000,000 Turkomans, at least five times as many as on the Afghan side of the border.

One should not infer that northern Afghans are straining their eyes and ears northward. Far from it. For one thing, their own land and way of life could hardly suit them better. They have not only room but the freedom to move around which is necessary to them and which has been denied to their kinsmen north of the Oxus. For another thing, the Afghans tend by nature and experience to mind their own local affairs with a healthy concentration of self-interest. They have learned, moreover, that trouble is usually what comes from outside. Although this traditional judgment may be in process of revision, it has strongly guided their actions for a long time. Both in tsarist days and since the Bolshevist revolution, northern Afghanistan has received and sheltered refugees. In Baghlan, the capital of Kataghan Province, one can meet the family of the last Emir of Bokhara, a fugitive of 1920 from the Russians who deposed him. In this sugar-mill town of the borderland, the Emir's family lives in comfort and safety less than a hundred miles from the Soviet border. Along with refugees from the Russian side of the Oxus came news of the nationalization of land (in 1922), of animals confiscated and left to die on the steppe, of the mobilization of Moslem women to work in textile mills. The Oxus border was virtually closed, and well guarded from the Soviet side. There was no chance to go to Russia, little need to trade with Russia. Borderland products traveled south across the Hindu Kush to Kabul. From there, exports left the country via Pakistan and India, at least until 1950. Then the borderland people began to sense a change. The Oxus border began to open for two-way trade, and this meant that northern Afghanistan could once more become a passageway, a focus of attention from both north and south, a development to make the borderland people wary.

For the old maxim that attention from the outside spelled trouble could apply to the south as well. Northern Afghans are ruled from and by the southern half of the country. Whatever comes from Kabul must be looked at with caution. To understand why, let us follow a delegation of borderland leaders to the capital, on a summons from the King himself.

[3]

When the King of Afghanistan wants a vote of confidence or a reading of the temper of his subjects, he summons a *Loe Jirga*. This is the traditional Great Assembly of tribal and religious leaders from all over the country. Small local jirgas are common as a means of conducting tribal affairs. But a *Loe Jirga* in the capital city of Kabul is rare. It convenes only at moments of grave decision. It met only five times in the first sixty years of the twentieth century.

For the fifth Great Assembly, toward the end of November 1955, we were on hand. The air of Kabul at nearly 6,000 feet tingled like iced Riesling in the early morning. As delegates began to stream into the city, white tents sprang up within the walled gardens of palaces and public buildings. On dark red Afghan carpets inside the tents, servants opened their bundles and prepared the bedding for their weary masters. Some of them had been trekking for more than a week, first by yak, camel, or horse, then by car, bus, or small plane. (Afghanistan, a country the size of Texas, has no railroads and had, in 1955, less than fifty miles of hard-topped roads.) A few of the delegates had come all the way from the snowy Wakhan, Afghanistan's extreme northeast province bordering Chinese Turkestan; others from the Oxus Valley; still others from the sun-baked mountains of the south and east, near India and Pakistan.

Bearded, turbaned, and robed in long, loose coats of wool or quilted cotton, they strode into the modern quarter of Kabul as the cast of one of de Mille's historical extravaganzas might invade Whitehall or Constitution Avenue. Their hosts, the King's bureaucracy, were "Kabul men." Superficially, at least, a different breed of Afghan, beardless, wearing European suits and gray karakul caps, they busied themselves with the hospitality due their guests. For the opening session of the jirga, the King's own guard and brass band lined the courtyard of the Foreign Office. Scarlet buses, just delivered from Russia, conveyed the delegates from their quarters. Trumpets blared the national anthem as the King, in uniform, drove up in the royal limousine. Through the open windows of the hall came the voice of His Majesty as he delivered the welcoming address in a shy monotone. Applause at the end was decorous. The jirga deliberated for almost a week, longer than had been expected. It ended with a resolution expressing modified confidence in the policy of the King and his ministers. Then the delegates feasted, packed their bundles, turned their backs on Kabul, and began the long journey home.

What use can a constitutional king, however autocratic, possibly have for a tribal assembly? Should it be rated as a puppet show, a sop to tribal leaders who have lost their real power? To write off the jirga as mere pageantry would be to misunderstand its purposes and the political realities that keep it alive. Although Afghanistan's written constitution provides for an elected lower house and makes no mention of tribal institutions, the jirga is still the most representative of all national gatherings. Although the King maintains an army (with Russian training and equipment), a third of the tribal leaders present at the meeting in Kabul could have mustered enough rifles seriously to threaten the monarchy. They had done so many times in the past. In short, Afghan society functions on two levels. After 225 years of almost unbroken family rule, Afghanistan remains a confederation of tribes still in the painful process of becoming a nation. The jirga of 1955 laid bare still another fact of life. In both human and geographical terms, it revealed a country split right across the center.

Out of the 368 delegates, 238 (almost two thirds) came from the southern half of the country and represented the dominant tribes. These are the Pushtuns,[1] and historians have fallen into the habit of taking them at their own valuation and calling them "true Afghans." "True" or not, they produced the family which has held power almost continuously for 225 years. They are fighters in a society where rifles, and the willingness to use them, count. They make their own rifles and tote them into the fields with their flocks and plows. Pushtuns, moreover, are the irreconcilables of the area, as the British discovered, first on the northwest frontier of India, and second in their ill-considered forays into Afghanistan. Not the least of the troubles of Afghan kings have stemmed from their own kind, the rival and quarrelsome Pushtun chieftains. "True Afghans" have always pursued tribal and clan feuds with the tenacity of Scottish Highlanders and Kentucky mountaineers of the past. They not only pursue feuds; they hand them down from generation to generation until family honor is cleansed either by revenge in kind or a satisfactory money settlement. A Pushtun feud can outclass the kind that Huckleberry Finn learned about from his friend Buck:

> . . . a feud is this way: a man has a quarrel with
> another man, and kills him; then that other man's
> brother kills *him;* then the other brothers, on both
> sides, goes for one another; then the *cousins* chip
> in—and by and by everybody's killed off, and there

---

[1] *Pushtun* is one of several commonly used versions of the name. Others are *Pakhtoon* and *Pathan.* The British have adhered to the Indian version *Pathan,* rejecting the Afghans' own *Pushtun* as they reject *Iranian* and *Thai* and adhere to *Persian* and *Siamese.* The chances are that *Pathan* will survive as long as there's an England.

ain't no more feud. But it's kind of slow, and takes
a long time.

Suitably, the Pushtun family home is a square mud fort
with watch towers manned by riflemen. These faceless
brown boxes flank the roads of southern Afghanistan. "This
is a residential district," the Afghan explains to the puzzled
foreigner. Every guest is safe within the fortress. But his
immunity may end in an ambush when he steps outside.
Thus hospitality, like revenge, is a cornerstone of the Pushtun code. Written contracts between Pushtuns are rare,
partly because a spoken promise is sacred and partly because so few Pushtuns can write. "You are quite safe," the
traveler is told on entering Pushtun country. "The tribesmen have a gentlemen's agreement not to shoot across the
road before sunset."

It was to rally support for an old and deeply cherished
Pushtun cause that the King and his ministers called the
jirga of November 1955. The issue concerned not the
6,000,000 or so Pushtuns inside Afghanistan, but a like
number left outside, in territory conquered by British India
and then inherited by independent Pakistan. The British
contended that these mountain Pushtuns had "spilled" over
into the plains, and in 1873 a British proconsul, Sir Mortimer Durand, drew a boundary line that sealed them within
British India. The Durand Line not only separated Pushtun
from Pushtun; it also saddled the British rulers of India
with frontier tribes they could never pacify or rule. However irrational, there the Durand Line was, and Pakistan
was not disposed to discuss it. In 1955, the Afghan government was still crying over "spilled" Pushtuns; it was also
agitating among them for a mythical free state called *Pushtunistan*. The issue had just about wrecked trade and diplo-
matic relations between Afghanistan and Pakistan. The
shattering blow to Afghans was the decision of the United
States to build up Pakistan's military strength. Since Ameri-

can military aid was tied to an alliance, the Afghan government refused it, and turned to Russia.

Were the tribes of the north ready to go along with the Pushtuns? Was it in their interest to pursue the feud with Pakistan to its bitter end? This, in effect, was the question which the government put to the 1955 jirga. The delegates gave their approval in subdued, almost somber words. The fact that the northerners did not dissent or rebel in public, at least, seemed to register a political triumph for the monarchy. It suggested that the two sides of the Hindu Kush were perhaps more reconciled to the idea of nationhood. This idea, first put forward in practical form in the eighteenth century, has taken a long time to gain even tentative acceptance.

Beginnings of a Nation

Just as the militant Prussians pulled the German nation together and dominated it, so the fighting Pushtuns set out to consolidate and rule what is now Afghanistan. Historians like to date the birth of the "nation" in the middle of the eighteenth century, for it was in 1747 that a *Loe Jirga,* meeting in the southern city of Kandahar, elected the first amir or king. Then for the first time a local family, the Durrani, not a foreign invader, undertook to bring traditionally separatist tribes under a central authority. Ever since then, the rulers have been Pushtun; the country has been dominated from the south where Pushtuns live, and run from Kabul. The tribes north of the Hindu Kush had to be brought into the fold by means of strong and—on the whole—rational leadership from the south. The tribal composition of that time (1747) was not essentially different from what it is today: predominantly Pushtun south of the Hindu Kush; predominantly Uzbek, Tajik, and Turkoman in the northern borderland.

With a single interruption (in 1929) the rulers of Afghanistan have come from two branches of a single Pushtun clan, which is something of a record for royal continuity in that part of the world. To appreciate a little of what this continuity has meant, one might go back to the court of Richard III in England of the fourteenth century. The atmosphere of perfidy that pervaded the Tower of London under the House of Lancaster was no more foul than that which poisoned the Bala Hissar fort in Kabul under the Durranis. Custom prescribed that power be kept within the clan, but dictated no rule of succession or legitimacy. The practice of polygamy made for large and variegated families. The great Amir Dost Mohammad, who reigned for twenty-nine years of the mid-nineteenth century, had forty-two sons and thirty-six daughters, which was not considered an outstanding achievement. Thus a Durrani who managed to mount the throne was likely to find himself hedged about by a brigade of brothers, half brothers, cousins, and uncles (not to mention nonrelated rivals and enemies) dedicated to unseating him and taking his place. Sometimes they did it with a bullet or a dagger or, if the mood was merciful, by burning out his eyes. Sometimes they retired to the provinces, raised an army, and marched on Kabul. If by luck a king died a natural death, it was the signal for a general fraternal scrimmage ending with the fastest or the strongest at least temporarily on top of the heap. After 150 years of such unpleasantness, the atmosphere cleared somewhat. Of the five Durranis who have sat on the Afghan throne in the twentieth century, only two met violent ends; a third died of natural causes in exile. A coalition of five brothers fought its way to power in 1929, when the throne stood empty and dilapidated. In defiance of tradition, the five promptly and peacefully chose one of their own number to be king, and summoned a *Loe Jirga* to ratify the choice. When this admirable ruler, Nadir Shah, died of an enemy's bullet four years later, the unconventional brothers quietly slid his nineteen-year-old son Zahir onto the throne and stood by their nephew as benevolent advisers and regents. Thus the wicked-uncle stereotype vanished from the Afghan scene for a generation at least.

By any royal standards, East or West, the Durranis must be rated high in leadership, perhaps because the rigors of reaching the throne insured the survival of the fittest. In order to survive, they had to be both crafty and ruthless. The barbarity of their punishments provided horror stories for British writers of the nineteenth century. In those days, chopping off hands and ears were not the worst of the penalties inflicted, for example, on petty thieves. Yet, with all their severity, Afghan rulers tried to use their power for large purposes: to weld an independent nation out of scrappy tribes; to extend authority and security across the Hindu Kush; to govern with a firm but not too heavy hand; and, finally, to "catch up" with the time in which they lived. If they have not realized any of these goals, neither have they abandoned them. With luck and a little freedom from attention they might have done better. Both were denied to them.

The Great Game

The nineteenth century brought Great Britain and Russia into rivalry all across Asia from the Caucasus to the borders of China. Both powers were on the move, probing and reaching out to absorb new territories as an amoeba absorbs its prey, until inevitably they found themselves face to face and glowering across the territory of the Durrani kings. This century-long expansion, confrontation, and rivalry are commonly called "The Great Game."

Afghans had never been pampered by security. Nevertheless, the ordeal of watching not one but two avaricious European powers creeping up on them from opposite directions could hardly have been reassuring. From the south

Bound for the loading ground, "muleteers flocked
into Gangtok, attracted by the promise of months
of employment" on the Sikkim-Tibet trail.

The Gangtok loading ground. "Tibet made good use of the rice caravans to send India bales of wool for rough carpeting."

XVIII

A mule caravan leaving Gangtok (Sikkim), bound for Tibet. "A mule can carry, at most, 160 pounds, slung in two sacks from its back."

"Mules were not the only carriers." Sherpa porters, carrying loads up to eighty pounds, start up the Sikkim-Tibet trail "on springy bare feet."

His Highness the Maharaja of Sikkim: "an impression of otherworldliness."

Princess Pema Tsedeum of Sikkim "has sophisticated views."

A Bhutia in Sikkim gives Americans a sense of being in the Rockies. "Cheekbones, noses, eyes, hair, and build, all suggest the American Indian of the Western range."

A Lepcha in the Maharaja's private guard in Gangtok. "The Lepchas are one of the three main peoples of Sikkim. As far as anyone knows, they were the first inhabitants."

"It is the Nepalis who keep the economy of Sikkim running." On the main street of Gangtok, this young man runs a Swiss sewing machine to make white shirts for muleteers.

Before refugees began pouring into Sikkim, Tibetan beggars (or spies) like these trudged southward into India.

On Mount Kanchenjunga lives "a temperamental god," often wrathful but occasionally merry, as in this mask.

came the British, having swallowed, state by state, the Indian subcontinent, until, in 1849, the gentlemen of the East India Company crossed the Indus River and established military outposts in Pushtun tribal territory. From the north the Tsar's armies swept down into Central Asia, overrunning thousands of square miles of Kirghiz, Uzbek, and Turkmen tribal territory. The two imperial powers were darkly suspicious of each other's motives. Englishmen believed that the Russians had their eyes on India; Russians had no doubt that British tentacles were about to strangle the rich trading centers of Tashkent, Samarkand, and Bokhara. In a final spurt, the Russians took all three centers, and in 1884 stood at last on the northern Afghan border. If the tribesmen of the Hindu Kush had been able to read English (most could not read at all) they might have appreciated a stanza of the Victorian poet Alfred Lyall, who warned that

> *The Afghan is but grist in their mill, and the*
> *waters are moving it fast,*
> *Let the stone be upper or nether, it grinds*
> *him to powder at last.*

From a British diplomat we have this rationale of the Great Game:

> The civilized must, for the sake of their own preservation, overrun and absorb into their dominion the uncivilized on their borders, for if they do not do so they will themselves be overwhelmed. . . . So they [the British] moved steadily forward across the great plains of India, and as they moved they reached out beyond their boundaries, seeking to safeguard the territories they had conquered by probing into the secrets and the policies of those which lay ahead . . .[2]

[2] Sir Kerr Fraser-Tytler, British Minister in Kabul until 1941, in *Afghanistan* (London: Oxford University Press; 1958) p. 76.

in the last event, the Afghans. The British impulse to push the edges of Empire constantly outward became known as the "Forward Policy."

In London, the policy was controversial. Most Tory governments espoused it; Whig and Liberal governments reversed it when they came to power, shifting gears into what they called, in all seriousness, "masterly inactivity." Thus it is not surprising that thirty changes of government during the nineteenth century kept the pendulum of policy swinging. What concerns us here is that the Forward Policy swung Englishmen into two invasions of Afghanistan. The first invasion, launched in 1837 during the Whig stewardship of Lord Melbourne, was designed to replace Dost Mohammad with a puppet less friendly to the Russians. As the British declaration of war phrased it: "The welfare of our possessions in the East requires that we should have on our western frontier an ally who is interested in resisting aggression and establishing tranquility in the place of chiefs ranging themselves in subservience to a hostile power. . . ." To keep their puppet on the throne in Kabul required an army of occupation. Against this occupation, the tribes rose with rare unity of purpose, and massacred the whole British force of 16,000.

One man, a Scottish doctor, lived to tell of the horror. Forty years later, with the Tory government of Beaconsfield in power and the Forward Policy in favor, the lesson and the memory had faded sufficiently to try another invasion. Dispensing with an amir altogether, the British this time took control of the country as far north as the Hindu Kush. But the word "control" has little meaning when one is sitting on a nest of wasps. Again the tribes made the conquest untenable and even inflicted a rousing defeat on the forces of Queen Victoria. This time most of the British managed to leave the country alive if not with dignity. The British Raj suffered one of its few deep humiliations in the East. Afghans have never stopped boasting that in two wars they "defeated" the mightiest empire in the world. To Americans they will say solemnly but with a twinkle: "You and we are the only ones who ever threw the British out."

The two attempts seemed to prove that a foreign occupation acted as an emetic in the body of Afghanistan. This was something new: that tribesmen who in the past had tolerated and even absorbed invaders, such as the Greeks and the Mongols, now compulsively disgorged them.

[1]

One of the sidelights on the Great Game that added to its verve and style was the assortment of lone players roaming the field. How such people edge their way into the game, what cloaks they wear, what daggers they carry, what lore they learn and write,[3] entitle them to far more attention than we can give them here. In Central Asia, it was the Englishman, thinly or not at all disguised, who got himself most often into the middle of the melee. One of these, Charles Masson, stands high for his knowledge alone. Masson turned up in Afghanistan in the 1820's after defecting from the army of the British East India Company. His real name was James Lewis, but in escaping from India, he changed it and also palmed himself off as an American. The Company caught up with him in Kabul and let him off on condition that he would stay there and spy for England. From then on, he wore Afghan habit, learned Afghan languages, joined caravans, sat around tribal campfires, and lived to publish in 1844 his four volumes filled with priceless insight into the people of the Hindu Kush, as well as vitriolic attacks on the British Forward Policy. The man who appears to have taught Masson to talk like an American was an even more improbable player, the

---

[3] A doorway to this literature of adventure is Fitzroy Maclean: *A Person from England and Other Travellers to Turkestan* (London: Jonathan Cape; 1958).

solitary American on the scene. He was Josiah Harlan of Pennsylvania, who, though he had no medical training, served the British East India Company for three years as a surgeon. Resigning in 1826, he went to work successively for three rulers who hated one another bitterly: first Ranjit Singh, the Sikh leader of the Indian Punjab, then the Afghan rivals, Shah Shujah and Dost Mohammad. In 1838, Dost Mohammad made the versatile American a general of his army and sent him northward across the Hindu Kush to annihilate a scavenger chieftain, the Prince of Kunduz. With 1,400 cavalry, 1,100 infantry, 2,000 horses, 400 camels, and one elephant, he set out for the north, "and there upon the mountain heights unfurled my country's banner to the breeze under a salute of twenty-six guns." On a pass 12,000 feet above the sea, wrote Harlan, "the Star-Spangled Banner gracefully waved amidst the icy peaks and soilless rugged rocks of a sterile region, seemingly sacred to the solitude of an undisturbed eternity." Did President Van Buren know about this gesture in the peaks of Central Asia? If not, he found out when, back in Philadelphia in 1842, Harlan published a book of memoirs.

Harlan brought back a detailed report of the borderland. Kunduz was a death trap of "miasma and marsh fever." The Prince of Kunduz, a brigand and slave trader, held up caravans passing through his territory and collected from them transit duties of over 100,000 rupees a year. The feudal chief of those days, Harlan observed, lived well. He had horses for riding and hunting, dogs and slaves, warm clothes and good food. Most chieftains ruled moderately; the one at Kunduz was an exception who punished his people by selling them into slavery. A rich caravan trade passed through the borderland, plying between India and Russia. From Moscow and Bokhara came tea, loaf sugar, chinaware, gold thread, velvet, hardware, cutlery, sheet copper and iron pots, raw silk and paper; from India salt, piece goods, and cashmere shawls; from Kabul wheat, maize, fruits, lambskins, camels, and sheep.

Harlan spent his next twenty years in the United States promoting schemes that would take him back to Afghanistan. First he tried to persuade the United States Army that it needed the Afghan one-humped mongrel camel which he found "patient, quiet, tractable." (The experiment was, in fact, tried in the American Southwest, but ended disastrously. American horses and mules could not adjust themselves to the strangers and bolted on seeing them.) Next Harlan suggested an expedition to bring back Afghan grapes for an American wine industry. He failed in both attempts, and ended his days far from his beloved Hindu Kush, in San Francisco.

[2]

Returning to the arena of the Great Game, we find the Russians pursuing their own forward policy. For a candid explanation of it, we are indebted to the Tsar's own Chancellor, Prince Gorchakov, whose memorandum of November 21, 1864 stated: "Our August Master has directed me to explain succinctly but with clearness and precision, our position in Central Asia." With Russia, as with all "civilized states," said the prince, "the interests of security on the frontier, and of commercial relations, compel the more civilized state to exercise a certain ascendancy over neighbors whose turbulence and nomad instincts render them difficult to live with." He went on to describe accurately the process of expansion which has no end, since each new conquest exposes the "civilized" state to a new frontier with troublesome neighbors. The state must choose either to live with a disorderly frontier, or to "plunge into the depths of savage countries, where the difficulties and sacrifices to which it is exposed increase with each step in advance." This, added the prince sympathetically, had been the dilemma of "the United States in America, France in Algiers, Holland in her colonies, England in India—all have been inevitably drawn into a course wherein ambition plays a smaller part than imperious necessity, and where the greatest difficulty is in knowing where to stop." The Russians, however, had found a place to stop, a stable frontier, the memorandum concluded. They would fortify it and concentrate on "domestic development." With this promise and an assertion that Russian policy was serving the interests "of civilization and humanity at large" ended a most instructive manual of the Great Game.

Alas for Prince Gorchakov's promise. Within three years, "imperious necessity" forced the armies of the Tsar again to sweep southward, this time to secure for the Empire the commercial prizes of Tashkent, Samarkand, and Bokhara. This final lunge, as we have seen, brought Russian power to the Oxus, within gun range of the Afghan borderland tribes. Although the possibility did not seem to occur to Gorchakov, it is arguable that the tribesmen found the Russians more "difficult to live with" than the Russians found them. Indeed, the next sixty years were to teach the Afghans many things about living with difficult neighbors on both their frontiers.

One of the clichés of the Great Game pictured Afghanistan as a British-made buffer state. Nobody heeds the Afghans' claim that by rebuffing two aggressive neighbors they made themselves a buffer. The British did, however, replace their unrewarding Forward Policy in 1881 with a new Buffer Policy.

[3]

The first rule for making a buffer state is to proclaim its independence and then to find ways of controlling it. This the British accomplished through a bargain with the "wily Amir," as they called him. Abdur Rahman handed over the conduct of his foreign affairs to British India, and received in return money and arms for his army and a promise of British aid if he were attacked from outside. The second step is to demarcate borders all around the buffer state. After agreeing to a joint boundary commission for the north, the Russians proceeded to play the familiar trick of staking out a forward claim to disputed territory as the commission was being organized. In 1885, the Tsar's forces occupied the Panjdeh oasis on the northwest Afghan frontier, precipitating the only pitched battle in history between Afghan and Russian armies. The Russians won, causing a momentary scare of general war. Neither Britain nor the Amir was in the mood to accept the challenge. The boundary commission met to confirm the Russian victory. Whom should we find as a leading British member but that zealous empire builder, Colonel West Ridgeway.

Ridgeway did one of the few respectable jobs of boundary drawing in that part of the world. By 1887 the Afghan-Russian frontier was fixed, and no one has seriously challenged it since. Two small but crucial tasks remained: to make of the lofty Wakhan in the extreme northeast a thin tail to the Afghan buffer, thus keeping India and Russia forever separate; and marking on the map—for ice and snow prevented the last six miles from being done on the spot—the glacial meeting place of Afghanistan with China in the easternmost Hindu Kush. With all this completed in the summer of 1895, the British felt they had erected a "framework of stability in Central Asia." Such faith in the strength of boundaries—a European faith characteristic of settled peoples—the pastoral and nomadic tribes of northern Afghanistan could not share. But the Amir Abdur Rahman, who had spent eleven years as an exile in Russia, knew enough about boundaries and about national feeling to accept the northern border, while protesting bitterly the eastern boundary imposed by the British in 1893. This was the Durand Line, cut deliberately through the middle of Pushtun tribal territory so as to create a

fortified buffer strip between the Afghan border and the
northwest frontier of India. Thus Sir Mortimer Durand,
an imperial servant of even less luster than Ridgeway—
under orders, of course—sowed the dragons' teeth that were
to sprout in *Pushtunistan* and shape Afghan history in the
1950's.

Two happenings far distant from the Hindu Kush gave
Britain and Russia incentives to call off the Great Game.
One was the complete defeat the Russians took from
Japan in 1905; the other was the rising power of imperial
Germany. An Anglo-Russian Convention of 1907 settled,
in the manner of the period, the fate of the weak countries
and borderlands for which England and Russia had competed. Persia they split into northern and southern spheres
of influence; Tibet they consigned to Chinese suzerainty;
Afghanistan was to stay in Britain's orbit but not to become
her property. Russia, at least on paper, renounced all influence over the Amir's realm. To this paper the Amir
Habibullah was expected to put his signature. He had not
been a party to the convention, considered it a thieves'
bargain, and refused to sign. Was the Great Game really
called off with the signing of the 1907 agreement? Or did
it simply lower the curtain on one act of a political drama,
to be continued as the Cold War? If so, then Stalin and
Khrushchev simply picked up the work of expanding Russian power where the tsars left off, and the United States
shouldered some of the responsibilities which Great Britain
unloaded after two debilitating world wars.

Soon after World War I, Great Britain relinquished her
forty-year control of Afghan foreign relations. It took a
third Afghan War to bring about this concession, a thirty-
day affair which the Afghans proudly call their "War of
Independence." To empire-minded Britons the concession
seemed an act of weakness, a surrender of the keys to the
defense of India. But it was an act in tune with the times.
The cry of self-determination was echoing through Europe

and around the world. Now the country was on its own, free on both sides of the Hindu Kush from the stern eye of the English tutor. But now people on both sides had to pay and pay again for the years of buffer-state isolation, when to close the windows and draw the blinds had seemed the best defense against demanding neighbors.

It could be argued that the forty years of isolation provided the Afghans with a necessary surcease from being hauled and mauled about. This is half the truth; the other half is that the closed society stagnated. Into it no modern notions about health or social welfare or a liberal education or a scientific spirit could penetrate. No railroad tracks had ever been permitted to cross its borders. Roads for wheeled traffic had yet to replace caravan trails. Over this Moslem stronghold the twentieth century had laid as yet only a light hand. In the forty years after 1921, the hand was to spread but never to crush the underlying layers of past centuries, which somehow managed to survive and coexist with the twentieth. It was as if the first eight strata of ancient Troy all went on living and functioning as the ninth stratum was gently superimposed on them.

The Nomads

The coexistence of many centuries, a fact of life taken for granted in most of Asia, comes as a surprise to a Westerner. Meeting a band of Afghan nomads, for example, he may feel that he is suddenly back in Biblical times. He is wrong; nomadism belongs to the twentieth century no less than to the first. In Afghanistan, the nomad is called a *kuchi*, which is the Persian word for marcher. Whoever asks about the number of such marchers will get a ready answer: "About two million." How this figure was arrived at is a mystery. There has never been a count of Afghans, let alone nomads who have baffled census takers always. Who shall say how many starlings there are in a migratory flock, or how many ants in a procession? Moreover, the term *nomad* is open to several meanings. The Afghan nomads earn their living in one or more of these ways: as stockmen who breed, pasture, and sell flocks; as carriers of goods on the backs of animals; as traders, buying in one part of the country and selling in another, or across the border. It is not unusual for a sizable family of nomads to own land and grow wheat or barley in addition to conducting a mobile business. Even without owning land or a house, the nomad may be a man of property, movable for the most part. Of the country's animal population (estimated also loosely at 3,000,000 cattle, 14,000,000 sheep, 6,000,000 goats, and 4,000,000 Karakul sheep) a large share belongs to nomads. It is this wealth that sets the well-defined pattern of their wanderings. They must find mountain pastures in the summer and valley pastures in the winter.

Those who work primarily as traders or carriers of goods move from farm to market or between towns. Much of the export trade of the country has traditionally been carried on by nomads, crossing and recrossing into Pakistan with a casual disrespect for boundaries. A modern equivalent of the old caravans, the nomad train serves as one link and source of news between Afghanistan and the world.

Nomads began to show respect for the northern border as the Russians tightened their hold on the country across the Oxus River. When the Bolshevists took over from the Tsar, they closed and patrolled the border, and traffic dwindled. But farther east, some venturesome Kirghiz tribesmen still wander across the high passes into China, in search of upland pastures.

All through the year nomads are on the move on some Afghan roads and trails. They travel in small independent trains of from twenty to perhaps 200. But several contingents may be found sharing a halt at a watering place. Old and young, they travel on foot, usually barefoot. Only babies ride—atop the great load on the back of the mule or camel. Securely strapped to the peak of the load, the child rocks with the motion of his mount, either sound asleep or glassy-eyed like a seasick passenger. Rarely is a nomad baby heard to cry or complain. The procession sweeps down the dusty road, usually with a man in the lead. Then comes the child aloft on his camel. Alongside swings the mother and a couple of small sisters. Then another camel with load and baby, then perhaps a few goats driven by small brothers, followed by the grandmother, toothless, wiry, and full of bounce. This order may be varied and repeated several times to make a *kuchi* caravan.

The daily trek starts in chill darkness before dawn. After breakfast around small fires, the family goes into action like a team of stagehands, folding tents, loading beasts of burden, rounding up flocks. In the dim light, it would be easy to overlook something, but the *kuchi* family cannot afford to lose a single piece of clothing or a household utensil. A good day's march is about fourteen miles, but it can end only where there is water and a bit of green pasture, and where the nomads can camp without fear of being chased away by a landlord or farmer. Gradually, over the years, the relative rights of the *kuchi* and the landowner have been staked out and recognized. By mid-morning and before the heat of noon, the day's march ends. In making as in breaking camp, each member knows what to do. The men unload; the boys drive stakes into the ground and spread the black felt or brown burlap tents. Using her shawl as a bag, the grandmother collects animal dung left behind by other tenants of the campground. The children help her mix the precious dung with straw and pat it into cakes the size of dinner plates. When the cakes are dry, they make the best and usually the only fuel for cooking and warming in this almost treeless land. By midday, the rice or barley is steamed, the camels and goats are grazing beside the stream, the older people are resting in their tents, and the children are clambering over boulders in the field across the road from camp.

Nomad trains are always swinging through the streets of Kabul and other towns, but they keep aloof from city people and from the "authorities." When nomad women with babies strapped to their backs go shopping for tea or cloth in the bazaars of Kabul or Charikar, they are as shy as deer. They have their own well-organized world, far from the city. In 1954, a European anthropologist, Prince Peter of Greece and Denmark, reported that he had found deep in the Hindu Kush a great nomad bazaar called "The Abul Camp." This is apparently the main trading post where each year, between May and July, some 60,000 nomads congregate to buy and sell their wares, including everything from tea and grain to secondhand American clothing. Two *mirs* or rulers preside over the camp, dispensing justice and maintaining order. One introduced himself to Prince Peter as a rich landlord, the other as an arms merchant. The traders came without their women; they were heavily armed with rifles, pistols, and cartridges, which they stacked on entering the camp, a city of white tents beside a shallow river.

Thus in the Turkestan of 1962 the nomad walks, the farmer rides a mule, the rich landlord and trader a horse. Of those who habitually walk or ride mules, a couple of thousand have recently learned to drive trucks over the few hundred miles of road for wheeled vehicles. On the half-dozen airstrips, a few score newly trained Afghan pilots land planes. The average man and woman of Turkestan have never seen the inside of a school. Perhaps one boy in ten has learned to read, write, and recite the Koran from a village priest or *mullah,* but the childhood introduction to literacy fades through disuse. A city man may be better equipped; his sons are almost sure to be. They have access to new elementary schools and, if they show special promise, to secondary school and even to university training in Kabul. Although Kabul University, founded in 1932, graduated only 1,142 students in its first twenty-seven years, its mere existence suggests the urge to catch up and to modernize that in some degree motivated every one of the five Afghan rulers of the twentieth century.

To Modernize a Nation

In trying to modernize a nation of unruly tribes, the Afghan rulers have had to keep in mind two questions: first, "How fast can I push my people ahead and still stay on my throne?" and second, "Where can I get help from abroad without compromising Afghan independence?"

Abdur Rahman, who died in 1901, perhaps the most farsighted of Afghan kings, was the first to ponder these questions. (One evidence of his wisdom: he broke the tradition of violent succession by naming his eldest son as his heir, giving him a thorough training in government, and disciplining his other sons to serve the heir apparent.) About the risks of looking abroad for aid, he wrote in his memoirs:

> If it be considered necessary and advisable that concessions should be made to any foreigners, such concessions must be given in small portions and to nations whose countries do not touch the boundaries of our own dominion—for instance to Americans, Italians, Germans. . . . If a very large number of Europeans, such as engineers and the like, be required for the service of our government, preference should similarly be given to the people of those countries already named.

The well-trained son and heir, Habibullah, heeded his father's advice during his eighteen-year reign. He imported from Germany the first metal water pipes and hydroelectric machinery ever to come into the country, and from the United States the first hydraulic engineers.

Thus began with the Kaiser's Germany an association that was to outlast Hitler's *Reich* and to provide Afghanistan's most useful link with the world of industry and science. For more than fifty years, Germans have been the best-liked and trusted of foreigners both in Kabul and in the Turkestan borderland, where, as we shall see, they helped to change the face of the Kunduz River Valley.

[1]

It remained for Habibullah's son, Amanullah, to demonstrate what happens when an Afghan ruler tries to catch up without regard to the question: "How far and fast can I move and still stay on my throne?" Amanullah was a small, tubby man with a mustache; unlike most Durrani rulers, he wore no beard. Like others of puny physique, he seemed to compensate with a bumptious energy and charm. In the triumphant moment of Afghan independence, he set out to remake his country along Western lines. The manner of the enterprise was about as foolhardy as trying to cross the Hindu Kush on roller skates. A slip or a slide meant oblivion, as the King was to learn. Indeed, his ten-year reign deserves to be studied as a demonstration of how not to modernize a tribal system based on a rural economy within a Moslem state, all rolled into one land-locked Asian kingdom. The trouble was not with the Amir's intentions, the honesty of which have not seriously been questioned, but with his wild miscalculation of his own power, both civil and military. Following Abdur Rahman's advice, he imported European technicians by the score but neglected to plan work that would keep them busy. Scrapping his grandfather's precepts, he invited Russian engineers to survey new roads which never got built, and thirty Russian pilots to train an air force which never got off the ground. He imported a French architect to design a grandiose new capital three miles outside Kabul; he carved out a connecting boulevard as wide as the Champs Élysées and laid trolley tracks alongside it. (Thirty years later these monuments lay empty and in disrepair. Nearby stood the skeletons of two trolley cars, the only objects on rails in this still railless domain.)

But these follies were minor. In 1923 Amanullah approved an administrative code declaring the equality of women before the law, and in 1924 he prescribed compulsory education for girls as well as boys. There followed the first open tribal rebellion, which the Amir managed to put down with the help of two English planes manned by German pilots. A jirga thereupon canceled women's rights and limited the schooling of girls to those under twelve.

The King ignored warnings. In 1927 he embarked on a tour of Europe and the Middle East. The enterprise not only took him away at a crucial time but stripped the national treasury. The return from Europe by way of Turkey and Iran probably spelled his undoing. For in these two Moslem countries he found dictators smashing traditions and, in Turkey, tossing fezzes and veils onto the refuse heap. That both Riza Shah and Atatürk backed their reforms with guns and used them ruthlessly seems not to have penetrated the Afghan King's unmilitary mind.

Back in Kabul, he summoned another jirga unlike any in Afghan history, for Amanullah ordered the tribal chieftains into Western dress. In their hastily sewn frock coats and soft hats, they looked like miserable "caricatures of non-conformist clergy." To this unhappy assembly, Amanullah announced new reforms. Women were to shed their *burqas*, the traditional shrouds into which little girls disappeared at puberty. The experiment lasted for three dizzy months.

"People got used to it rather quickly," a middle-aged Afghan recalled twenty-five years later. "At the start, we boys used to hang around the girls' school to watch them

come out. But after a month we took them for granted."
The tribal elders and the Moslem clergy, however, did
not. They were outraged. In 1929, with the tribes and the
mullahs rising against him, and the army which he had
neglected fading away, Amanullah fled the country.
Women disappeared into their shrouds, and with them went
the brave hopes of a new era. Into the power vacuum
jumped a figure even more bizarre than the exiled King.
A successful outlaw seized the throne and held it for nine
chaotic months. He was not a tribal chief, not even a
Pushtun, but a Tajik bandit on a shooting, looting spree.

Between May and October 1929, little was left of the
Afghan nation, even less of the buffer state. Either the
British or the Russians might easily have intervened, but
neither did. Probably neither cared to encounter the army
of the other on a pass in the Hindu Kush. Instead, the old
Durrani clan once more picked up the pieces.

[2]

The rescuers were four brothers, distant cousins of
Amanullah. The eldest, a military man, managed to recruit
enough Pushtun tribesmen to march on Kabul, capture the
usurper, and take over the throne. He became King Nadir
Shah. His brothers became respectively his Prime Minister,
Minister of War, and envoy in London. A fifth brother represented the country in Moscow. By all the rules of royal
behavior, the five should have plotted to destroy one
another, but these were unconventional men. Throughout
their French schooling, they had apparently cherished a
devotion to their own country and a dedication to it. They
found it without an army, police, or money in the treasury. The southern tribes were in ferment; the northern
provinces had virtually seceded. It took almost two years
and an army of 40,000 to pull the country together again.
The brothers re-created the traditional autocratic monarchy. Nadir Shah wrote its first constitution, which bowed

to the forms, if not the reality, of representative government. The King headed a benevolent autocracy staffed by
his brothers and close friends. Strongly nationalistic, they
gave their attention to setting up better communication
with the northern borderland.

Nadir Shah was murdered in 1933 and had little chance
to see the flowering of his work. Those who watched it
credit him with more than a touch of genius. In perspec-
tive, one of the King's most inspired acts was probably the
building of the Great North Road.

To realize the meaning of this road, one must visualize
the Hindu Kush: a complex of mountain ranges, not just
high but thick, not just snow-capped but craggy and bare,
cutting the country in half almost from end to end. The
most accessible of the passes through which armies and
caravans labored were more than 11,000 feet high and
snowbound for six months of the year.

No wheel could ever negotiate these trails. Where the
melting snows had cut deep gorges through the mountains, even feet could not find a way. It was believed always that no river-level passageway existed through the
Hindu Kush. The first ruler to refuse to accept this thesis
was, characteristically, Amanullah. He employed Russian
engineers to find such a passage and to cut a road through.
The attempt was both an engineering and a financial fiasco,
for the Russians chose and pushed up the least likely gorge.

Nadir Shah had the boldness as well as the stamina to
try again. The political need for the link between the south
and the borderland spurred him on. But it was part luck,
part intuition, and part knowledge that forged the link.
There were two geological questions to be answered. Which
of the many passes was actually the watershed, the true
divide between north and south? And which of the winding
rivers came out on the northern side of the mountains?
The undiscovered divide turned out to be the familiar
Shibar Pass on the old and well-worn silk road, south of the

main ridge. Following this old route from Kabul, one crosses the Shibar Pass, and on the far side meets the Bamian River. At this point the river turns north and flows downstream to emerge, after forty miles of winding and seemingly impenetrable gorge, on the Turkestan plain. But until 1931 wayfarers had always missed this turning point. They had chosen the hard way up the Bamian River and over the high passes instead of following the river downstream and through the narrow cleft. Somehow Nadir Shah sensed that here was the crucial point, as Lewis and Clark had instinctively chosen the southern fork in their search for the Missouri and the way through the Rockies. Whether the King had knowledge of a decisive clue, we do not know. At that time, Sir Kerr Fraser-Tytler, an ardent sportsman, had discovered that brown trout were plentiful on one side of the Shibar Pass but not on the other. These were the *Salmo oxianus*, the delicious brown trout of the Oxus Valley to the far north. In other words, a mountain stream held, for any fisherman or road engineer, the secret to the waters that flowed north to the Oxus. And the secret was brown trout!

The men who cut through the Shikari gorge had, if not knowledge, certainly a powerful faith. Fraser-Tytler tells of going in 1932 to "where a thousand workmen were cutting, digging, and blasting their way along a steep shale slope with the river roaring fifty feet below them." He spoke to the foreman in charge:

"Where are you going?" I asked.
"To Turkestan," he replied.
"When do you expect to get there?"
"Khuda Midanand (God knows)," he said. "We're just going on till we do."

[3]

Faith and steady nerves are useful even today to anyone who travels the Great North Road. Our first attempt came to nothing. It was during one of the frequent times of tension between Afghanistan and Pakistan, and the Kabul government was not in the mood to give travel permits to foreigners. A few years later, the climate was not at all chilly. The government not only encouraged us to travel north, but the newly appointed Minister of Tourism had for hire a car, a driver, and an English-speaking guide. At six one August morning, we set out to conquer the Hindu Kush in a new Volga, a sturdy little Russian sedan. Our objective was Kunduz, a cotton-milling town less than thirty miles from the Oxus and the Soviet border. We had heard of the bold incision through the mountains, of the comparative riches of the northern borderland. But nothing prepared us for the mountains themselves or for what lay beyond.

Snow peaks materialize on the horizon about thirty miles north of Kabul, as the paved road runs through the pleasant Kohdaman plain, lined with mulberry trees and flanked with vineyards. This is the best grape country in Afghanistan. What look like square mud forts with narrow slits in the walls are raisin barns. The wind sweeps down from the mountains through the barns and dries the grapes without the help of blistering sun. The road takes on early-morning life. Boys in black pinafores lugging schoolbags converge on new white schools in market towns. Open trucks packed with workers rattle toward Kabul. A young farmer with a black beard and gleaming turban leans back on his ambling donkey and plays a piercing tune on his flute. A family of nomads swings down the road with three camels, a few sheep, and two dancing monkeys.

At the fortieth mile stands Charikar, a town linked by shadowy history with the capital built by Alexander the Great. Shops along the muddy main street (there is no more paving) have been unboarded. Turbaned merchants sit cross-legged and indifferent among their wares. We stop to stretch and inspect the wares, for Charikar has long been famous for its finely tempered steel knives, hand honed. Within a minute, the strangers are enclosed by a crowd of little boys and a wrinkled man leading a mangy donkey. Within two minutes a policeman has roughly dispersed the children and the old man. A merchant is persuaded to sell one of his sharpest knives in a crude leather sheath for twelve afghanis (seventy-five cents).

The Kohdaman plain ends at Charikar and now the dusty road follows the valley of the Ghorband River westward into the foothills of the Hindu Kush. Although the road has not yet departed from the ancient caravan route, and will not for another eighty miles, the traveler finds in the Ghorband Valley evidence of Nadir Shah's genius. The King ordered a piece of the valley floor to be carpeted with a forest of alders and laced with rivulets of fresh water from the rushing Ghorband River. In an almost treeless country, a forest appears in the heat of midday like a mirage. One turns off the dusty highway, into the shade of the alders. One puts his water bottle and a melon to cool in the stream of melted snow. Here begins the country of the melons about which Marco Polo sang. Although they are supposed to grow sweeter as one approaches the Oxus Valley, no melon of our experience ever surpassed the one chilled in melted snow and eaten under the alders. The melon is, to our way of thinking, the only sound reason for exploring the Afghan countryside during the summer. Heat and dust can be blinding; water, even from a mountain stream, can be lethal. But there is no need for thirst while ripe melons are to be bought from roadside stands along the way north.

The Ghorband Valley narrows to a thread, and rocks overhang the road as it winds up the Shibar Pass. Travelers for thousands of years have known this summit, 9,800 feet high, but nobody until Nadir Shah recognized it as the Great Divide. This is understandable, since the pass cowers below the main ridge of the Hindu Kush to the north, and stays open all winter. Not until the traveler has dropped down the other side, through a dark and winding canyon, does he reach the place of decision where Nadir Shah's road builders turned their faces northwest and said they were going "to Turkestan." At the 130th mile from Kabul, the old caravan trail meets the Bamian River flowing toward it.

How many thousands of weary men must have paused here at the turn of the rushing river! How many tried to follow it through the narrow canyon, but turned back! Now a signpost stands at the fork, pointing up the narrow road: "Pul-i-Khumri 124" it proclaims, "Kunduz 209," and "Mazar-i-Sharif 259." In other words, "down hill all the way to Turkestan!" From here on, the road is the breathtaking masterpiece of Nadir Shah.

There are moments ahead when even the most trusting traveler begins to wonder where he is going or whether he will arrive. For four hours he is enclosed by sheer walls. The stream tumbles far below a road hacked and blasted out of rock. Sometimes the cliffs above are serrated; often the sides of the canyon swoop down to the river bed as slick as a bowling alley. Of the Hindu Kush mountains, there is no sign. They are all around, but invisible. The only sounds are of rushing water and, in competition with it, the brave horn of the Russian car. One wishes it were a siren, for there is traffic just around the bend. A hundred fat-tailed sheep are in possession of the road, and even if they wanted to move over, there is hardly room. Or an International Harvester truck (almost all Afghan trucks are ancient I.H. models) overloaded with fruit, bales of wool or cotton comes charging around the rock wall, racketing to a stop miraculously just where there is space to pass. What will be waiting around the next twist in the gorge? Another question begins to obsess the mind: what becomes of all this precious water, roaring down to Turkestan? Will it be caught, stored, and doled out to the starved earth of the northern plain?

Answers to both questions come as the sides of the gorge gradually give way to a barren valley bounded by red cliffs. Finally at the 200th mile from Kabul, among irrigated fields of rice and cotton, the traveler has cut through the main ridge of the Hindu Kush without ever seeing the giants themselves. He has made the transition to Central Asia. The plain on which he stands slopes northward without interruption to Siberia and the Arctic. The hot wind in his face sweeps down from the steppes. A lone horseman gallops across the plain. On the rim of the northern horizon, an undulating thread becomes a caravan of more than a hundred camels, driven by Uzbeks wearing embroidered skullcaps. They are heading for their homes, a cluster of round tents by the side of the river. On the opposite hillside, a flock of brown and black Karakul sheep grazes on stubble of tough grass. The shepherd turns out to be a young Pushtun from the far south, near Kandahar. Two years before, the government had offered him land if he would settle in the north.

The valley broadens into a patchwork of green and gold fields, laced with canals. At the 224th mile from Kabul lies Doshi, a town with a future. If all goes according to plan, it will be not 224 but only 124 miles from the capital. For the Afghans are boring a great tunnel through the Hindu Kush, with the help of Russian engineers and money, a three-mile tunnel that will come out near Doshi and bypass Nadir Shah's passageway altogether. From Doshi for about 140 miles northward, an improved road, paved for the first time, will complete the link between Kabul and the Soviet border. Afghan-Russian traffic and trade will become comparatively swift and easy for the first time in history. By Nadir Shah's route, a truck could, with luck, make the round trip from Kabul to the Russian border in a week. So rough was the road that the life expectancy of a truck was not more than ten such trips. With the tunnel cutting off about a hundred miles and the road paved, the round trip would take a couple of days, and the truck's life would be indefinitely extended.

These are exciting prospects for the people of the northern provinces. Their melons, raw wool, cotton, and lambskins will reach Kabul markets in better shape and command higher prices. But whoever supposes that the paved road and tunnel will "open up" untouched country to the factory and the power plant is in for an awakening.

Venture Capital in the Borderland

Even as rocks and dirt were flying in the Shikari Gorge, the promise of a Great North Road was sparking new ideas in Kabul. The planner this time was not a king with a vision of unifying his country, but a merchant with a dream of tapping new wealth and reaping boundless profits. Abdul Madjid Zabuli was a young man from Herat in the northern borderland. He grew up unburdened by formal education, tradition, or family connections, and made a fortune for himself trading wool, karakul skins, and other Afghan products. He lived in Russia for a time, married a Russian girl, and traveled in Western Europe. Coming back to his native land with knowledge of the industrialized West, he had the further advantage of not being a Kabul man. His mind could leap the Hindu Kush either way. It was a mind that defied tradition. For when Abdul Madjid thought of larger profits, he thought not in the conventional Afghan terms of trade but of industry. Even more unusual, when he thought of industry he looked north to the province of Kataghan toward which Nadir Shah's road was crawling day by day. Instead of investing a fortune abroad, as most wealthy Afghan merchants were in the habit of doing, let us, he said, invest in the soil and people of our own country.

But why north of the Hindu Kush, under the Soviet nose?

Why the province of Kataghan, where no factory chimney had ever befouled the clean sky, where no tribesman had ever handled a mechanical or powered tool? Why Kataghan, on the direct invasion highway of ancient days? Afghans of the 1930's could not imagine a modern invasion. They had grown used to the Soviet presence just across the Oxus. Except for the incident at Panjdeh in 1881, Russians had crossed into Afghan territory only once, and then in pursuit of a fugitive from the law. On that occasion, in 1930, the Afghans had chased him back into Russia.

Abdul Madjid foresaw large and quick profits offsetting any political risk. The province of Kataghan had good soil; it had water and nearby coal, all of course still to be surveyed and put to use. The water would have to be harnessed for power and channeled for irrigation. Known coal deposits had to be mined. Much land had to be reclaimed from marsh and sown with cotton and sugar beets. The province was already rich in wheat and rice. Some farmers would have to be taught how to grow the new crops; others would have to be moved into new towns and trained to man machines. The first step was to organize capital.

[1]

In 1932, with his ideas still untested, Abdul Madjid persuaded a few other venturesome merchants to put their private fortunes into a new industrial bank, the first ever known in Afghanistan. Madjid talked the government into supporting the new Bank-i-Melli with a long-term, interest-free loan. But he also got sanction for the principle of interest on investment, always secretly abused but never admitted in this Moslem society. Finally, the royal family itself became shareholders of the bank. It was no ordinary bank, but a mechanism to carry development through all its complicated steps: promotion, surveying, organization of capital and labor, production all the way from the raw material to the finished product; experimentation, training, and finally, marketing of the products. The mechanism was largely one man. At every point in the process, so new to the country, Abdul Madjid injected imagination and drive. He set up offices of the Bank in Munich and in Hamburg, then the European entrepôt of the karakul trade, Afghanistan's largest earner of foreign exchange. He went shopping for engineers, technicians, and managers all over Europe and in the United States. In Germany and England he bought gins, spindles, and looms. The Skoda works of Czechoslovakia equipped a new sugar mill. Finally, Madjid launched the first systematic program for training young Afghans in economics, finance, and industry. All the young men had to travel to the West, since Afghanistan in the 1930's had no facilities for training.

The Bank-i-Melli next mobilized these resources and turned its attention to the valley of the Kunduz River in the borderland. Paralleling the Great North Road, the river emerges from the Shikari Gorge onto the sloping plain of Turkestan. It is simply the enlarged successor of the Bamian River, rushing north to join the Oxus at the Soviet-Afghan border. Its valley, especially the lower half, is well suited for growing cotton. The growing season, March through October, is warm and almost rainless. Pests are virtually unknown. A dry harvest is moderately certain at the end of September, but one must irrigate through July. Only a little cotton had been grown in the valley when the Bank took its projects north. In addition to reclaiming new land, a system of canals had to be dug. At Pul-i-Khumri, the site chosen for the first cotton mill, the river had to be dammed for light and power. Long wooden sheds were built and filled with the new ginning machinery as it arrived, after moving up the Great North Road from Europe. Farmers and shepherds had to be induced to leave their familes to work in the mill for their first small but steady wages. Coal mines to the west had to be opened and the fuel brought on the backs of camels to the factory furnaces. The process worked. Between 1937 and 1942 the new industries began to function and grow. Bales of cotton and rolls of cloth jolted through the Shikari Gorge to Kabul. Around the sheds and the dam at Pul-i-Khumri, there grew up a thriving company town. The owners of the mill laid out wide streets and built arcades, shops, and adobe houses, first for the top officials, later for about a quarter of the mill workers and their families. The mill has tripled its capacity, adding 30,000 spindles. The company contributed a factory kitchen, a dining room for 800, a hospital with ninety-five beds and three doctors. Workers receive one free meal a day, free work clothes, free rent and medical care. Eighty-five miles down the river, another cotton town mushroomed at Kunduz, near the Soviet border.

By 1957, the tribesmen of the borderland valley were growing, ginning, and weaving almost half the cotton cloth used by the entire country. The 12,000,000 or so Afghans were using (according to a fairly reliable statistic) more than 131,000,000 yards of cloth annually. Afghans consume prodigious amounts of cotton cloth. One lone item illustrates an irreducible need. Almost every Afghan man or boy wears a turban and owns at least one spare. The turban of light cotton cloth measures seven and a half yards long by about half a yard wide. Thus the Afghan male head alone demands about 90,000,000 yards of cotton at all times—not to mention the rest of the stalwart Afghan form, covered by voluminous cotton pantaloons and long cotton shirts.

The Bank-i-Melli learned to diversify. In connection with the cotton industry, it set up plants to extract vegetable oils and make soap. It showed the farmers that they could profitably grow sugar beets for the plant at Baghlan, twenty miles north of Pul-i-Khumri, on the Kunduz River. After refining the yield of about 10,000 acres planted in sugar beets, the mill sends the waste to its experimental dairy farm, where 500 cattle, 700 sheep, and a few score horses, mules, and camels feed on beet pulp mixed with molasses. Since the mill can operate only a few months after the beet harvest, the sugar company sponsored another subsidiary industry, sericulture. Mulberry trees flourish in Turkestan. Silkworm breeding by the farmers, and weaving by their women and old people, provides the family with a second source of income. The sugar company promoted the experiment and gave it technical guidance. Ideas radiate from the company town of Baghlan, with its neatly laid-out streets, its arcaded bazaar, and its modern company guest house surrounded by flower gardens. It would be hard to find a more cheerful example of the Madjid formula: pioneering and paternalistic enterprise.

The small group of promoters who presided over the expanding empire of the Bank-i-Melli had no intention of stopping with cotton, sugar, and their secondary products. They obtained monopolies of the imports of sugar, tobacco, and tea, and of the exports of wool and karakul. Most of Afghanistan's precious Karakul sheep congregate in Maimana Province to the west of the Kunduz Valley. Estimates of the Karakul population vary between 3,000,000 and 4,000,000. In summer they graze on the sagebrush and rough bunch grass of the foothills of the Hindu Kush. In winter they migrate north to the warm valley of the Oxus. The best of their skins are sheared, dried, baled, and shipped to New York by way of Kabul. The industry is said to involve the labor of more than a million borderland people. Afghan karakul has met stiff competition from Russian, Iranian, and South African sheep, but it has survived. Its real enemies are, first, a steadily declining fur market, and second, mink. These two combined between 1946 and 1955 to halve the American market.

But the Bank-i-Melli's interests were too far-flung to be

seriously hurt by one declining market. For twenty years its enterprises flourished. They had the protection of royalty, specifically of the young King's uncles, Hashim and Mahmoud. The Bank's principals amassed large and untidy fortunes. They did more. They enriched the borderland with skilled European managers and teachers; they educated scores of young Afghans abroad in engineering and business administration; they turned a barter economy into a cash economy over a large part of the north. In short, they transformed the province from a stagnant, malarial backwater into a farmland dotted with market and industrial towns. An old Afghan motto: "Go to Kunduz to die," became: "Go to Kunduz to get rich."

By 1952 the Bank was promoting projects south of the Hindu Kush, among them a hydroelectric project at Sarobi and an ultramodern cotton mill at Gulbahar, both near Kabul and both German-engineered. The Bank had a finger, too, in the mammoth Helmand Valley scheme which treated the Afghans to their first large dose of American capital and skill. It was Abdul Madjid Zabuli, as Minister of National Economy, who obtained a loan for the Helmand in 1950 from the Export-Import Bank of the United States.

But the pre-eminence and power of the Bank-i-Melli were ending.

The new Prime Minister, Sirdar Mohammad Daud, the King's first cousin, who took over in 1953, did not approve its ways and would not tolerate its power. The Bank's enemies accused it of behaving like a "state within a state." Daud dismissed Abdul Madjid from the Bank's directorate and from his post of Minister of National Economy. He created a new State Bank which took over many of the assets of the Bank-i-Melli, and smaller banks to serve the farmers. Madjid retired to Germany and—of all places— Nahant, Massachusetts.

The Great Gamble

The decline of the Bank-i-Melli was just one signal that power had passed from the capable old hands of the royal uncles and the Bank's Tajik founder into younger hands of the King's own generation. King Zahir Shah had grown up in France with two cousins; one of them, Prince Mohammed Naim Khan, became his Foreign Minister, while the other, Prince Daud, took on the post of Prime Minister. When they were youngsters, Daud had always been the dominant personality. The story goes that he bossed and bullied the other two without mercy. Whether or not this was true of childhood days, Daud took the dominant position in 1953 and held it. No more than Abdur Rahman could he escape the question of how to modernize his country without risking its independence. In shaping his own answer, he showed himself both reckless and resourceful: reckless in inflaming the feud with Pakistan over the Pushtuns inside its border; resourceful in exploiting Soviet help when the feud forced Afghanistan to turn north. Afghans did not relish their dependence on Pakistan for their only direct outlet to the Western world. Pakistanis did not appreciate the Afghan claim to a large slice of their territory and some 6,000,000 of their people. The quarrel simmered all during the 1950's; on occasion it boiled. Twice, in 1955 and 1961, the border was closed so that all trade and communication stopped. This made no difference to Pakistan, except the loss of transit and port revenues; to Afghanistan the closing was nothing less than disastrous. It not only dried up the mainstream of trade; it cut several hundred thousand nomads off from their winter pastures and their livelihood. Daud's decision to close his only direct door to the West and to open the alternative door to the Soviet Union has been aptly called "the Great Gamble." It was to reinforce this decision that the King called the *Loe Jirga* in 1955 and received a cautious mandate to grasp Russia's eagerly extended hand.

One could read some of the results in the trade figures and see others with the naked eye. Between 1952 and 1959, Russia rose from third to first place as the supplier of goods to Afghanistan, Japan from fourth to second place, the United States from fifth to third. By 1959, the Afghans were looking to the Soviet Union for almost three fourths of their petroleum, virtually all of their sugar imports, and three fifths of their machinery. As for Afghan exports, however, Russia was by no means the largest buyer. India still held first place as a market, with the United States and the Soviet Union alternating for second place. With the Pakistan border shut in 1961, the Soviet Union was buying the grapes which would otherwise have gone south, and was also taking Afghan wool at a price above that of the world market.

Outward signs of Soviet helpfulness were not limited to Kabul where the ruling Pushtuns could admire them. Across the Hindu Kush, in Turkestan, the earth really began to move. Among the eye-catching monuments to Soviet good will were three oil storage plants in the north, all convenient to the Soviet border, three silo-bakeries, and a cement plant with Czech engineering and equipment. The Russians drafted the Czechs for three other projects: a second cement plant and a fruit cannery in the south, and development of coal mining north of the Hindu Kush.

As their trade turned northward, the Afghans naturally asked the Russians to pave the 470-mile road from Kabul to the Soviet border and to cut a tunnel which would shorten the old route by a hundred miles, bypassing the Shikari Gorge altogether. From Doshi, which was to be the northern exit of the tunnel, north to Kunduz, the work of grading and widening the old rough road was hurrying forward. Russian dump trucks had deposited heaps of gravel down the middle of the new foundation. Paralleling the Kunduz River, the highway was raised above the flood-land, for two-lane truck traffic, but without shoulders. If the Russian and Polish engineers in charge had thought about breakdowns or nomads or caravans of camels or flocks of Karakul sheep, they had kept their thoughts secret. The half-improved highway did not provide for such contingencies.

The year 1960 brought the first important discovery of oil in Afghan Turkestan. The prospectors were Russian; their technicians were Rumanian and Czech. The find climaxed a twenty-four-year search, first by an American company which reported "promising traces" in 1936, then by a French firm in 1952 and a Swedish contractor in 1955. Four years later, the Afghan government relaxed its former taboo and invited Soviet engineers into this sensitive area. What they found near Mazar and Kunduz gave the Afghans hope that they might someday drill enough oil to take care of their own rising needs and have some left over to export, the dream of every nation striving to modernize and arm.

Oil, coal, hydroelectric power, machine shops, factories, and roads—these by no means complete the list of Russian projects that dot the Afghan landscape like mushrooms after a night of rain. Under discussion was a scheme to harness the Oxus River, a joint venture something like the St. Lawrence Seaway.

Meanwhile, Soviet technicians dispersed to their posts around the country. Rumors that they numbered a thousand civilians and a hundred military could not be verified. Moscow's workers were hardly to be seen, much less counted. Reports that they "lived with the people" had no basis in fact. They kept strictly to themselves, renting downtown quarters in Kabul, occupying modern flats or villas in Kunduz, Pul-i-Khumri, and Baghlan. As in other parts of Asia, Russian experts did their jobs and went home, leaving behind neither friends nor foes. Others came to replace them. The new co-operation gave every sign of permanence. Even if Soviet aid should end, trade would have to continue on a massive scale. For Moscow was not offering gifts, but a series of barter and loan agreements, calculated to keep Afghan goods flowing northward. Barter began in 1950, with Afghan raw wool and cotton in exchange for Soviet oil, cement, sugar, and cloth. Borrowing began four years later. Its first fruits were storage tanks for oil, silos for wheat, and the paving of Kabul streets. But these looked niggling beside the Russian offer in 1955 of a $100,000,000 line of credit, to be repaid over thirty years at 2 per cent. By 1962, this and other credits from the Soviet Union and the United States had persuaded the Afghan government that it was time to declare a moratorium on borrowing. On the basis of past commitments, the Russians were believed to be spending for Afghan aid at the rate of two dollars for every American dollar.

There is probably no better example of how sadly this conventional yardstick of aid can mislead. Afghans were not yet locked, as the figures implied, in the Russian embrace. True, they had mortgaged a large part of their future trade to repay Soviet loans. But at the same time Prince Daud was taking care to diversify his risks. Germans, still the best-liked foreigners in Afghanistan, were kept as advisers at Gulbahar, at Sarobi, and in Kabul itself, where they built an automatic telephone exchange for the capital. On a prominent corner in Kabul, the Siemens Company of Hamburg opened a new showroom filled with the latest electrical gadgets from air conditioners to washing machines. France, which for two generations had educated Afghan rulers, was invited to send doctors, mining engineers, geologists, and experts in atomic energy. Japanese, who had helped to dig Helmand Valley canals in the 1930's, returned to equip a ceramic factory and train Afghan girls newly employed there. On one of Kabul's tree-

lined avenues stands an international house, the headquarters of United Nations technical assistance. Between
1949 and 1961, specialized agencies of the United Nations
had sent 379 specialists from forty-one countries into
Afghanistan, on errands that affected almost every phase
of development from telecommunications to health. Moreover, these were the experts one encountered in the
provinces and along the Great North Road. In a country
that had nursed an almost pathological suspicion of foreigners until a generation ago, the United Nations' presence in
many parts of the country suggested a new openness and a
measure of insurance in the Great Gamble.

For its largest single development scheme, as well as
many smaller ones, the Afghan government enlisted
American skill and capital. The Helmand, one of the three
main river systems of Afghanistan, drains an area about
three times that of the Tennessee Valley. Beset with frustrations ever since it began in 1946, the Helmand Valley
development program will eventually transform the southwest of the country from a desert to a prosperous farm and
factory area. By 1975, it should fulfill its purpose: to serve
as the chief counterweight in the south to the natural
wealth and industrial head start of the north. For political
and economic reasons, Prince Daud knew that the south,
peopled by Pushtuns, could not be left behind.

A good deal of mistaken judgment also beset the American share in the Afghan road-building program. While
the Russians undertook to improve two main roads to their
own frontier, the United States undertook to improve two
truck roads from Kabul to Pakistan, one by way of Kandahar. Both American commitments sank into bureaucratic
molasses, and after four years of delay had to be rescued
by the Corps of Engineers of the United States Army. By
1960 the work had finally passed the surveying stage.

Although it appeared that Prince Daud had made a rough
division of Russian and American labor between north and

south, there were major exceptions. Both Russian-built roads dipped south of the Hindu Kush, one to Kabul, the other to Kandahar. The Communist bloc had also built factories, an airfield, and a large hydroelectric installation in the south. At the same time Americans had gone into Turkestan to make an aerial survey, to supervise the Afghan civilian airline, to equip airports at Herat and Kunduz, and to develop coal deposits.

In one major field, Prince Daud deliberately failed to diversify his risks. For advice in the crucial task of building a modern education system, he turned in 1952 to the United States. Rarely had an American aid mission been faced with so difficult a challenge or handed so important an opportunity. Afghan leaders were bent on modernizing their country. They professed a faith in education as the means by which the people could take part in the modernizing process. How could their leaders communicate this urgency to the people and put in their hands the tools of learning? The country had little on which to build. "Education" in the modern sense existed only in cities. Even that little was poor and out-of-date: in Kabul four private schools for boys and a "university" that did not merit the name. In the provinces, Herat, Kunduz, Mazar, Kandahar, and Jalalabad each had a secondary school of sorts. In the rest of the country, schooling was in the hands of the Moslem clergy. The mass of the people whom Prince Daud wanted to draw into the developing life of the country were illiterate; there was no mechanism for reaching them or their children. It must be created. This was the challenge.

Did the strong, often reckless Prime Minister truly want American advice for this purpose? If he did, then here was the chance to help Afghans think anew and design for themselves a philosophically sound system that would meet their specific educational needs. As one of the Americans who worked on this problem said, Afghanistan needs "a plan that concerns itself not only with the number of schools that will be opened each year, but also with the kind of country Afghanistan is trying to become; not only with the printing of additional textbooks but also with the kind of person the textbook is intended to develop." In short, the Afghans would have to submit to the discipline of setting their sights not five but twenty or thirty years ahead. And some uncommonly wise Americans would have to be on hand to help them. This was the opportunity.

If the problem was ever considered in these terms, the results did not show for the first ten years. The United States aid mission imported three teams from the universities of Columbia, Wyoming, and Illinois. The first helped to start teacher training at the primary level; the second to set up vocational high schools, and create departments of agriculture and engineering in the existing University of Kabul; the third drew up plans for an elaborate new university. All the projects are in Kabul. Educated Afghans may have asked to have them there. The effect, however, was to widen the gap that already yawned between Kabul and the provinces. Even more than in other Asian countries, the hoarding of knowledge and scarce technology in the capital has stunted Afghan progress. Either the Afghan leaders or their American advisers or both were unwilling to meet the problem boldly. Belatedly, in 1962, a more rational approach was being considered in Kabul. The American aid mission was ready to help with a nation-wide school program that would stress agriculture and mechanical arts in the rural areas. The Afghan government seemed ready to make the effort. But one can only wonder how real is the government's interest in its people when it budgets for education only 2 per cent of its annual spending.

Out of the Shroud

Prince Daud's decision to clasp the helping hand of his Russian neighbor is generally rated his most dangerous gamble. Perhaps it was. What may have required cooler political courage was his unheralded resolve to de-veil the Afghan woman. It happened in a quiet, deceptively casual manner during the independence festival of August 1959. Like a man who takes the fuse out of a live blockbuster, the Prime Minister quickly and smoothly disposed of one of the most explosive issues in modern Afghan history. He knew well the experience of his cousin exactly thirty years before. King Amanullah, it will be remembered, scandalized the Moslem clergy and the tribal elders by ordering women out of their veils and announcing that girls would henceforth go to school. Coming on top of other reforms, this one blew him out of the country.

Had basic attitudes softened since Amanullah's day? The Prime Minister must have estimated they had. Moreover, he had confidence, as a military man, that the high army officers would support him in so radical an act. In secret talks with generals and key officials, he was credited with asking them: "How can we progress when six million of our people are kept in the darkness of *purdah?*" The word *darkness* was accurate. In no other countries except, perhaps, Saudi Arabia and Yemen were women imprisoned by their religious and social systems as in Afghanistan. The Afghan woman's veil, known as a *burqa,* covered the whole body like a shroud. Feet gave the only clue to the person beneath, revealing anything from cardboard sandals to spike-heeled French pumps. From inside the shroud, she had to peer at the world, and dodge traffic in the streets, through a patch of latticework embroidery across her eyes. The *burqa,* according to one Afghan doctor, caused poor eyesight, vitamin deficiencies, and skin diseases.

But its penalties were more than physical. The system of *purdah* confined a woman to her immediate family and her feminine friends. Her chances of getting to school were poor; as recently as 1955, perhaps one Afghan boy in ten entered school, but there was only one girl for every seventeen schoolboys. *Purdah* thus barred all but a few women from education, from the chance to earn a living (in the towns, at least), and from professional life. The only professions open to women were nursing and teaching. Most parents frowned upon both. It was this stalemate that Prince Daud set out to break. The first intimation of the great break came a few days before *Jeshun,* the annual festival of independence in Kabul. Four hostesses of the civilian Afghan Ariana Airline walked out of the Kabul airport building in natty uniforms. These young women, trained in Lebanon, were the first of their kind and the first to unveil. The airport crowd simply gasped. After this prologue, the drama continued on August 25 when without proclamation or fuss the royal family, the Cabinet, and the leading generals brought their wives and daughters, unveiled, to the festival and entered the Prime Minister's pavilion. This time there were gasps from foreign diplomats and, some say, cheers from the crowds. The women, about thirty in all, wore loose black coats and black head scarves. Except for dark glasses, their faces were bare. They cowered together in one corner like a flock of frightened penguins. The decisive moment, according to one observer, came when the chief *mullah* strode into the pavilion with his wife, dressed like the other women, on his arm.

There followed innovations just as startling. Always in the same uniform, women began to appear in streets, restaurants, and cinemas. They accompanied their husbands for the first time to foreign embassies, public meetings, and lectures. Gradually their black uniforms gave way to gray or tan coats and head scarves of white or pastel shades. The dark glasses disappeared.

By August 1960, the first anniversary of the Great Break, young women had begun to trickle into the economic life of Kabul and other cities. Several hundred held clerical jobs in government departments; other hundreds were doing semiskilled work in textile mills, shops, and banks. Fifty-eight were enrolled in the medical school of the University of Kabul. An Afghan woman dentist, the only one then holding such a degree, was practicing in the clinic of the new automated textile mill at Gulbahar, fifty miles north of the capital. Most of her patients were men.

Generally the older women clung to *purdah*. Nor were all the younger women in Kabul ready to move into the sunlight. To have been able to cut even a small slit in the curtain, without bringing the whole structure crashing onto his head, proved the Prime Minister's power as well as his skill. The deeply conservative Moslem structure of the country held together. There was no joyful shout of release from the women. They had to be ordered out. Those who obeyed the order did so uncertainly, as prisoners suddenly pushed out of dungeons and told that they are free. In the first weeks of deliverance from *purdah* they stood blinking in the light or, as in a dream, startled to find themselves in a nudist colony.

For city women this was a genuine revolution. Only in the cities had *purdah* taken extreme form. Tribal women, in the borderland and elsewhere, had never been completely shrouded or secluded. (Hazara women wore no veil of any kind.) Ironically, a daughter of a poor Pushtun farmer or an Uzbek shepherd could look forward to a freer life than her richer, more privileged city cousin. Because she was needed for work in the fields, she could breathe the air and lift her face to the sky. Only when strangers came near would she quickly pull her cotton headcloth across her face. Like most farm daughters and wives, hers was the dignity of contributing to the family livelihood, as well as bearing children and keeping the home.

Thus the freeing of city women did not turn the life of the countryside upside down. But its indirect effects could be deep and lasting throughout the country. Now city girls can go to school; they can join the productive and creative life of the nation with their husbands and children; they can enter the professions. In time, as nurses, teachers, and doctors they may reach the borderland villages and towns. They are sorely needed. In 1960 only six doctors served a million people in the northern province of Kataghan. Kabul could supply more, but they would have to be drafted for service. Doctors and other professional men are unwilling to leave the capital for the borderland. If Afghan women develop a greater sense of social responsibility than the men, which is not unlikely, they may help to narrow the gap between the capital and the borderland.

About three months after the break at *Jeshun*, there were organized protests and riots at Kandahar. They were ruthlessly put down. After that nobody appeared to be trying to turn the clock back. Many Afghans were old enough to remember the fate of Amanullah and his reforms; they marveled at the changes that thirty years had wrought.

Amanullah's final gesture was well timed to remind his people, old and young, of what he had wanted for them, too fast and too soon. On April 25, 1960, eight months almost to the day after the unveiling, the exiled King died in a nursing home in Zurich. The official announcement in Kabul said: "The King received the news with deep concern and prayed for the soul of the late Prince." Two memorial services were held, one for men and one for women, and both were attended by members of the royal family. Amanullah's body came home to be buried in state in the royal vault at Jalalabad. Inspired editorials in the Kabul press laid down the line for the history books. Amanullah, they said, "ranked among the great and highly revered leaders of the country" because he had won its independence. His attempts to reform and modernize the country had been sabotaged "from outside." This referred to the British in India, whom Afghans have always accused of plotting against Amanullah because he was friendly with Russia. The charge has never been proved; the British were probably innocent this time.

When Prince Daud's Great Gamble opened the doors to Russia, the northern borderland ceased to be a dead-end street and became once more a through road. How this about-face would affect Afghan independence, whether the north would again become an invasion highway, were subjects of gloomy speculation among Westerners in Kabul. Those in charge of the country said, in effect: "We know how to handle the Russians." In a measure, they were already making adjustments, as others on the fringe of the Communist bloc had to do. Although Moscow did not tell the Afghans how to conduct foreign relations, Prince Daud knew quite well what Moscow did not want him to do. Without the need for invasion, the Soviets had achieved a twentieth-century equivalent of the kind of sphere of influence over Afghanistan which the British had imposed in the nineteenth.

This arrangement could only focus closer attention on the north and make it more than ever an eccentric among borderlands. As evidence of Kabul's concern, thousands of Pushtuns were moving north across the Hindu Kush, to settle among the Uzbeks of the Oxus Valley. The transplanting of these "true Afghans," of the royal family's own tribe, could only be explained as a security measure.

The central government, moreover, was planning all

kinds of improvements for the area north of the Hindu Kush. Abdul Madjid's early innovations in the Kunduz Valley needed refurbishing. Rising demands for water and power called for a storage dam on the Kunduz River. Its dilapidated irrigation canals were already being rebuilt and equipped with modern diversion structures. There were plans to bring more acreage under cultivation for cotton, to improve the cleaning and grading of cotton and wool, the handling of karakul skins. There was even a project in view to vaccinate the nomads on every well-traveled route in the north.

Making allowances for the tendency of officials to equate plans with performance, the prospects for economic progress in the borderland were fair. Roads, oil, trade, and new techniques held out promise of change. How much of this would reach the individual farmer and herdsman, one could not foretell. For centuries he has worked hard, moved at will, and expected little. He may be forgiven if he watches the growing interest of Kabul and Moscow in his land with a certain cynicism. From his ancestors he has learned, first, to ask: "How can I make a little money out of this?" and, second, to shrug and sigh: "This too will pass."

6

This Side of Ararat

TURKEY'S EASTERN
PROVINCES

*If the people living in Turkey today are poorer and
more backward than others it is not because of the
climate of the country nor the character of the individuals. It is because of the lack of education. . . .
The improvement and development of the Turkish
soil depends on the development of the people living
on it. No development project which does not start
with educational development can succeed.*
    —REPORT OF THE TURKISH NATIONAL
COMMISSION ON EDUCATION, 1959

EVEN NOW, he glares at his people as if reproaching them.
He has been dead since 1938, but they cannot shut him
from their sight. From thousands of picture frames and
pedestals, he fixes them with cold, uncompassionate eyes,
the trace of a scowl on his forehead. This, of course, is
Atatürk, regenerator of his country, a titan among all the
Turks who ever lived.

In death he has become a Great Stone Face; in life he
was a dynamo of change. It was one of his obsessions to
hustle his people into the modern Western world. He for-

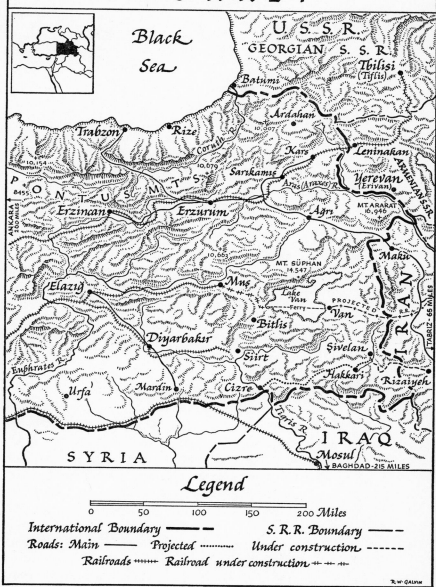

Easternmost
TURKEY

Black
Sea

U. S. S. R.

GEORGIAN S. S. R.

Tbilisi
(Tiflis)

Batumi

Ardahan

Trabzon   Rize   10,907

Çoruh R.   Kars   Leninakan

10,679   Sarıkamış   Yerevan
(Erivan)

P O N T U S   M T S.   Aras (Araxes) R.   ARMENIAN S.S.R.

10,154   Erzincan   Erzurum   Ağrı   MT. ARARAT
16,946

8455   ANKARA 200 MILES   Makü

10,663   MT. SÜPHAN
14,547   IRAN

Elazığ   Muş   Lake   PROJECTED
Van   Ferry   R.R.   TABRIZ – 65 MILES
Van   Van

Bitlis

Diyarbakır   Sivelan

Siirt   Hakkari   Rızaiyeh

Euphrates R.

Urfa   Mardin   Cizre

Tigris R.

SYRIA   I R A Q

Mosul
↓ BAGHDAD – 215 MILES

Legend

0   50   100   150   200 Miles

International Boundary ——— —   S. R. R. Boundary ——— -

Roads: Main ———   Projected ··········   Under construction - - - - - -

Railroads +++++   Railroad under construction +—+—+—

R·W·GALVIN

bade polygamy, stripped Islam of its privileges, ordered men to discard their fezzes, encouraged women to shed their veils. He commanded his people—those who could read—to learn a Latinized alphabet in place of the Arabic. In theory, at least, he made five years of schooling compulsory for girls as well as boys. In a single generation he transformed a decrepit empire into what appeared to be a young and vigorous modern state.

Nothing like it had been seen since the metamorphosis of Meiji Japan. In the cities of western Turkey, already stirring with change, Atatürk's shock treatment jolted his people into a new energy, a new patriotism, a new outlook. To be up-to-date and "European"—these were among the impulses that drove the urban Turks ahead. But the electric currents of reform did not travel as far as Atatürk had hoped. The cities leaped into the Western twentieth century; the countryside did not. In most of the rural hinterland, the current all but failed, and reform shed only a feeble light. The revolution was incomplete.

Forty years after Atatürk loosed his lightning, Turkey remained two nations: a minority with a go-ahead spirit, and a majority still steeped in its past. Both called themselves Turkish, and proudly so, but between them lay a chasm. Neither could understand or communicate effectively with the other. A leading politician in Ankara pictured it cruelly in a conversation in 1960, in a year when many Turks became newly aware of what their revolution had left undone.

"We have perhaps one million educated, Westernized Turks and twenty-seven million who are unenlightened," he said. "The one million, especially the younger ones, demand European comforts, bright lights, cosmopolitan living. They look down on the twenty-seven million as ignorant, dirty, and crude. They have no idea of how most of their fellow-Turks live, and they couldn't care less."

One can see and sense the disparities almost anywhere

in the Republic. The glass-and-concrete buildings of Ankara, for example, seem to be saying, in every sharp and functional line: "See how European we are!" Yet only twenty miles away, down almost any rutted side road, one comes upon a village of mud or stone hovels where families still depend upon the wooden plow, the bullock-drawn thresher, the contaminated well. A one-room white building on the edge of a village is the elementary school: one bit of evidence that there are in the government, at least, modern-minded men with concern. Sometimes a tractor, co-operatively owned, shows that mechanization has begun to reach the farms. But other signs of change are few.

The farther one travels eastward, the sharper the contrast with Atatürk's dreams. It becomes clearest in the easternmost provinces between the Soviet Union on the north, Iran on the east, and Syria and Iraq on the south. Here the landscape opens like a suddenly widened motion-picture screen. Villages look lost in the spreading emptiness around them; schools and tractors are fewer than in western Turkey. In the market towns, women flit past like phantoms, shrouded in tents of coarse cloth so that no man shall gaze upon face or form. Village children all too often show one eye already lost to trachoma, a disease of dirt and squalor. Flies feed on the sores upon their cheeks. Is this, one wonders, the Turkey that Atatürk redeemed?

Let no one suppose that the authorities in Ankara are totally indifferent to this borderland. They give it close and continuous attention for one overriding reason: the eastern provinces border for 367 miles on the Soviet Union; they are also the home of the largest remaining non-Turkish minority people, the Kurds. The east is thus militarily important and potentially dangerous. All Turkish territory east of the great curve in the Euphrates River (shown on the accompanying map) is, accordingly, a military zone; and any foreigner wishing to go there requires a permit from high officials in the capital. Militarily the east, where

Turkey ends, is well cared for. At the same time it is the place where the Atatürk revolution has most conspicuously failed to penetrate. How has it failed, and why? And what are the problems and prospects of this borderland? Such will be the subject matter of the present chapter.

Where the Revolution Stopped

By European standards—and Turks like to call themselves European—eastern Turkey is immense and underpopulated. If one includes the eighteen eastern *vilayets,* or provinces, it is as big as England and Scotland combined. In area, it is one fourth of all Turkey; in population, only about one seventh.

Two parts of this region differ from the rest in climate and terrain, in history and spirit; and most Turks do not consider them parts of the borderland. One is the coastal strip between the forest-clad Pontus Mountains and the Black Sea. Here, where half of Turkey's tea crop is grown, where the fields tilt so steeply that a farmer can tend his crops without leaning over, the soil is fertile and life benign. Copper mines near the Soviet frontier add a valuable natural resource. The sea gives it an all-season highway to the Straits and the West. In mythical times Jason and his Argonauts sailed past it on their quest for the Golden Fleece; in the present day, an excellent state-owned shipping line affords easier access to Istanbul than to most of the mountain territory at its own back door.

The second part that is untypical is a semidesert strip in the far southeast. Here camels pad silently through dusty towns; the summer heat sears the earth as in the Arab lands beyond. Here water is gold and rain so scarce that the smaller rivers sometimes dry up altogether.

The highland country between these fringes is an extension of the dry Anatolian plateau rimmed by mountains north and south. As one travels eastward, the bowl of the plateau rises; the city of Erzurum, for example, lies more than a mile above the sea, and the treeless hills beside it rise higher by another mile. Still farther east, the mountains become spectacular. The extinct volcano of Süphan, almost as high as the Matterhorn, stabs the sky above the dark blue of Lake Van; and finally, at Turkey's easternmost limit, stands Ararat, the giant of them all.

To the Moslem Turks as well as to Jews and Christians, Noah is a prophet, and the supposed resting place of the Ark is a puzzle that intrigues every generation. Nobody, of course, has ever found the remains, although in 1960 what looked like the calcified keel of a skip, in a hollow near the peak, stirred a flurry in the Turkish press. But even if it were not Noah's mountain, Ararat would excite wonder. It defies probability by lifting itself above a tableland of rocks and lava and the Turkish equivalent of sagebrush. Other high mountains, Kanchenjunga in Sikkim among them, are buttressed by mighty ranges that lead the eye toward them and detract from their scale, but they are not volcanoes. Ararat stands virtually alone, like Fuji and others of its kind. Its only companion is Little Ararat, 12,878 feet high, a puny replica toward the northeast. Big Ararat rises in an almost perfect cone, flattened only at the top, to 16,946 feet, so high that its summit is sheathed in never-melting snow, so conspicuous that from Russia in the north, from Iran in the east, it can be seen floating in the sky.

Yet one can lift up one's eyes unto Ararat and nevertheless feel cast down in eastern Turkey. Neither nature nor man has shown pity in this bleak, wind-swept country. A single earthquake in 1938 killed 23,000 in the city of Erzincan; repeated shocks have reduced the city of Kars to rubble thirteen times. As if this were not tribulation enough, invasions and wars have uprooted entire peoples in these regions since the dawn of history. Somehow it is the most melancholy of all the borderlands we know.

What makes it so is not only the harshness of its setting, but also the lot of its people. Other parts of Turkey, however poor, are better off. "The East has got a bad name," said Mahmut Makal, a young teacher, writing about the hardships of daily life in his village far to the west. "Here we are, supposed to be in the heart of Anatolia, but whenever I look at what we suffer, I shudder to think that the people in the East could have it worse." They not only could "have it worse"; they do. By almost any standard one chooses, they lag behind their countrymen.

To illustrate the lag, let us dip into official Turkish figures, remembering that "there are three kinds of lies: lies, damn lies, and statistics." The eastern Turks, to begin with, are land-hungry. Four out of ten rural families in the east wrest a living from farms of less than five acres; three out of ten is the proportion living on such small plots in Turkey as a whole. The eastern Turks, moreover, are poorer than the rest in tractors, one index of farm progress in Turkey as elsewhere. The sixteen eastern provinces had (in 1959) a total of 1,238 tractors. In West and South Turkey, on the other hand, each of thirteen provinces had more than 1,000 tractors apiece. And the single province of Adana on the Mediterranean, where cotton has become a booming crop, could boast of 5,398 tractors—more than four times the number in all of the eastern borderland. One should remember that tractors in Turkey do not usually belong to individual farmers; they are communally owned, and a farmer rents one when he needs it. Such a system would work well in eastern Turkey in spite of the small size of individual farms—if more tractors were available and their use and maintenance understood.

One can better understand the tractor shortage in the east by glancing at another index of the farmer's progress. This is the amount of credit at his disposal and the ease with which he can get it. By this standard, the farmers of western Turkey are vastly privileged compared to their eastern counterparts. Let us compare the amount of farm credit dispensed in 1960 in a dozen rural provinces of the west and a dozen of the east. With one and a half times as many people, the western dozen received five and a half times as much in farm loans.

In theory, the Turkish farmer can avail himself of two kinds of credit. First, he can get it from a branch of the government-financed Agricultural Bank—if he knows how to fill the necessary forms and if he can afford a trip to town. Second, he can get it from an agricultural credit co-operative; this is a device intended for the small farmer. Again comparing the same dozen provinces in the west and the same dozen in the east: the privileged western Turk got three times as much as the easterner from the Agricultural Bank and fifteen times as much from co-operatives. Except for two provinces, Kars and Urfa, the east of Turkey is a co-operative wasteland. The government is apparently promoting co-operatives where cash crops can produce foreign exchange. In western Turkey, European companies pioneered and developed such cash crops in the late nineteenth century. British companies invested in the growing and packing of dried fruits, Austrian companies in tobacco, French companies in hazelnuts. These crops remain profitable, and the growers have no trouble obtaining credit. The east produces few such money earners, and its farmers get little credit or none. The government was willing to expand a going concern, which already enjoyed European and American markets; it was unwilling to do the pioneering needed in the east. The neglect of the east is clear.

The borderland farmers are not only short of land, tractors, and credit; they are also sadly short of schools. Statistics on Turkish schools should be taken with a special dose of salt. "Never believe the figures put out by the Ministry of Education," said one Turkish speaker at a meeting in Ankara in 1960, during the formulation of a new education plan. Yet, even if government statistics overstate the number of schools, the latest statistics available, those of 1953, show a glaring inequality between the eastern extremities and the heart of the country. Take, for example, two eastern provinces: Van, with one single-teacher school for about every 1,500 people, and Siirt in the southeast, with one for about every 2,000. Now, in contrast, take two rural provinces far to the west. The province of Çankırı, just north of Ankara, has one school for about every 800 people; the farming province of Bilecik, nearer Istanbul, has one for about every 600. Undeniably, it is an achievement of the Turkish Republic to have brought secular schools, even too few of them, to remote villages. But if a Turk argues that all his people have equal opportunities, the official figures show that some are less equal than others. And the easterners remain the least equal of all.

What is wrong? What is the curse that lies upon this land? Virtually every developed country has had a hinterland of decay: the United States its Deep South, Canada its Newfoundland, Britain its valleys of poverty in the South Wales coal fields. But here, in up-and-coming Turkey, one finds not just a pocket of stagnation; a quarter of the entire country remains comparatively unmoved by change. Different explanations might come from a geographer, a historian, and a political scientist, each of them only partial or misleading, as we shall see.

A geographer might cite an obvious reason: the severity of eastern Turkey's climate. In Kars, nearest the Soviet frontier, January is colder, on the average, than in Anchorage, Alaska. In Erzurum, it is almost as forbidding. As for the countryside, its winters have tormented travelers and conquerors since ancient times.

Xenophon knew this eastern Turkish climate twenty-four centuries ago, and hated it. For it was through the present borderland that he and his Ten Thousand fought their way from Babylonia to what is now the Black Sea. They fought not only barbarian tribes but also cutting winds and snowdrifts. "What I want is to have a rest now from all this," said one of his lieutenants, Leon of Thurii, when they caught sight of the blessed sea, the roadway home. More than 300 years later, the Roman Lucullus wrestled with the climate of what is now eastern Turkey. During one of his campaigns there, winter fell as early as late September, according to Plutarch, "with storms and frequent snows, and even in the most clear days, hoarfrost and ice, which made the waters scarcely drinkable for the horses by their exceeding coldness, and scarcely passable through the ice breaking and cutting the horses' sinews." The army mutinied; its commander had to retire ultimately to the banquet tables of Rome. Late in the Middle Ages, Marco Polo found the cold "past all bounds," and the French friar Odoric, on his overland journey to China, reported Erzurum to be "mighty cold." But, as we saw in Hokkaido, snowdrifts do not necessarily block progress. In the Soviet Union, Scandinavia, and the American and Canadian Middle West, farmers perform prodigies in spite of a climate even more daunting. There must be other reasons for the sorry state of the Turkish borderland.

A historian might find a clue in the invasions and wars that racked this region, as they did the country north of the Hindu Kush, for thousands of years. Conquerors in endless succession have trampled its fields and pillaged its towns: Persians, Sassanids, Arabs, and Byzantines; Seljuks, Mongols, Ottomans, and Russians. Ruined forts still cling to hilltops on the old invasion routes; they bear witness to a blood-soaked past. At least one invasion left permanent scars. This was the Mongol scourge of the thirteenth century, which uprooted what had been a peasant society and replaced it with one of nomads and semipastoral farmers.

Yet the historian's explanation, like the geographer's, is too simple. Elsewhere, man has proved his recuperative powers, even in cockpits of history. The French-German border country, to take one example, has been a battleground since Caesar's day, yet it thrives as never before. Eastern Turkey has not known invasion since the aftermath of World War I. It has had time to recover, yet has not done so. The record of incessant wars does not explain why the region has not moved forward. The clue must be sought elsewhere.

A political scientist might offer a third too-obvious explanation. He might argue that the easternmost provinces have never recovered from the loss of their Armenian and Greek minorities. This used to be the homeland of the Armenian people; its place names toll in the minds of Westerners who recall the Armenian tragedy. Although some of the Armenians had farmed the highland country around Lake Van, they were primarily a commercial people. As shopkeepers, traders, or moneylenders, they were spark plugs of the economy, like the Chinese of Borneo. The Greeks along the Black Sea coast, also a commercial people, were shipped to Greece in the 1920's in an unprecedented exchange of populations. Without a doubt, the disappearance of such minorities has slowed the economic and intellectual development of the Turkish borderland. But one should remember that neither the Armenians nor the Greeks in easternmost Turkey were development-minded. When an Armenian had made enough money in an eastern Turkish town, he was apt to build himself a house in Istanbul, or set up a business elsewhere in Turkey or abroad. One can watch a similar leakage of money nowadays in neighboring Iran: wealthy Armenians in Tabriz, for example, send their cash and their sons to the capital, Teheran. From the Turkish standpoint, the disappearance of the Armenians and the Greeks has had compensations. With one major exception, which we shall discuss later, the people of the east can say proudly: "We are all Turks." The political separatism that afflicts other borderlands no longer ravages the Turkish body.

The riddle, then, remains. Neither climate nor wars nor

mass expulsions explain why the Atatürk revolution failed to budge the eastern provinces. But there are other clues. We shall look for them in three attributes of borderland life which have tended to insulate the region against the electric currents of reform. One is the omnipresence of the Army. The second is "the despotism of custom" in the life of the eastern Turkish farmer. And the third is the survival in this area of an un-Turkish minority, the Kurds. Each of these has acted as a buffer against economic and social change. Let us examine these influences, starting with the special role of the Army in the east and its effect upon the people.

The Army's Imprint

The chief reason for the Army's presence is, of course, the frontier between the eastern provinces and the Soviet Union. Instinct as well as prudence keep the bulk of the Turkish Army within easy reach of the boundary. The instinct dates back to the long-ago wars of the Sultans against the Grand Dukes of Muscovy. Wars between Turkey and Russia have been fought repeatedly for more than 200 years. In 1828, in 1854–6, and in 1877, the tsars' troops besieged and captured Kars and Erzurum; in the settlement of 1878 the Russians won the provinces of Kars and Ardahan, which they kept more than forty years. The latest of these Turkish-Russian paroxysms began in the winter of 1914–15, when the Turks rashly invaded Russia's Transcaucasian provinces. Counterattacks trapped the ill-clothed and ill-armed Turks. After a single battle in the pine forests around Sarıkamış, on the road from Kars to Erzurum, the bodies of 30,000 Turks lay frozen in the snow. In February 1916, in what Winston Churchill later called a brilliant feat of arms, the Russians again stormed Erzurum, which the Turks had thought impregnable. It was one of the last bursts of military energy from the dying Romanoff regime.

Long remembered in Erzurum was the humiliation of watching the Grand Duke Nicholas reviewing his troops outside the twin minarets of the twelfth-century *Medresseh,* or religious school, still the city's finest relic. Old-timers remember a local heroine named Kara Fatma, "Black Fatma," who recruited a guerrilla force of boys, girls, and old men and women, and fought the Russians with knives and stones. This indomitable Amazon survived until the 1950's; a monument to her now overlooks Erzurum and reminds the people, if any reminder were needed, of their traditional foe.

With such a background of enmity, is it strange that the frontier bristles on both sides? In other borderlands, northern Burma, for example, international frontiers are apt to be poorly marked. But here, all the way from the Black Sea to Ararat, the line is as sharp as the crack of a rifle, strung with barbed wire, fortified by hidden traps, guarded by thousands of sentinels night and day. The watch on this boundary never sleeps. Turkish sentry posts on stilts perch high enough for the guards to peer deep into Soviet territory. Soviet watchtowers command a strip just inside their border which is plowed but never planted. The footprints of anyone escaping or infiltrating become tell-tale marks that lead to jail.

It is not enough for the Russians to keep their Turkish frontier inviolate by man. Occasionally a Turkish animal strays across and meets the fate of a saboteur or spy. Turkish officers enjoy telling of a farm horse that somehow slipped through the wire and galloped northward. Alert Soviet sentries used the horse for shooting practice and killed it. The Turkish farmer wailed to Allah that he had lost his most precious animal.

Who was responsible? The Russians, said the Turks; the Turkish farmer, said the Russians, for it was his fault that the horse got away. The squabble led to an international conference of a sort that has become familiar on the frontier. Five Soviet officials and five Turks assembled around a conference table on the Turkish side. They haggled for ten hours while soldiers brought relays of coffee and vodka into the conference room. At issue was the equivalent of seventy dollars in damages for the horse. The Turks might as well have demanded the cession of all of Soviet Transcaucasia. Ultimately the Turkish government had to pay the farmer. Thus was Soviet honor saved and the territorial integrity of the Soviet Union reaffirmed.

Frontier-consciousness blossoms into pantomime at the spot where the Erzurum-Tiflis railway crosses the boundary, northwest of the crumbling fortress city of Kars. The railway crossing itself is an oddity. Except for one bridge in Iran, it is the only place where a railroad strikes directly into Soviet territory from a Western-allied state. Every Wednesday and Saturday a train crawls uphill from Kars and stops, with a screech of brakes and a hiss of steam, at the Turkish border post. Nobody travels on it except an occasional diplomat, for this is not one of the recognized points of entry into the Soviet Union. Yet the symbolic train crosses regularly with one coal car, baggage car, and coach, a ghost from the past when a real train used to run. Someday, perhaps, freight and passengers will cross once more; the Russians and Turks signed an agreement in 1961 to standardize the gauge and improve the roadbed on both sides.

At the frontier, the train stops again just short of a bridge over a high culvert. A Turkish lieutenant, police official, and customs guard walk to the middle of the bridge. From the Soviet side march two Russian officers and two privates in the blue-banded caps of the frontier guards. Russians and Turks salute. The Turks hand the Soviet commander the passports of the train crew. Nobody speaks. With ritual as formal as a Japanese tea ceremony, the Russian privates lift a steel rail from across the tracks. The train crosses onto Soviet soil and stops. Immediately the privates poke under each car with their bayonets, presumably to make sure that no wrecker with bombs is hiding there. Then the train, with its Turkish engine-driver, rattles out of sight, through a valley flanked by rounded hills, toward the Soviet garrison town of Leninakan three miles away. Half an hour later it returns, this time its locomotive pushing from behind. Again the salutes, the return of passports, the silence—but this time no bayonet jabs. The train is still empty.

The Turks, never solemn about this twice-weekly charade, let their foreign visitors ride the train back to Kars. To any railroad buff, the opportunity is one to cherish. One stands on the open rear platform and coasts down a gentle gradient as the engine pushes from behind. This is true range country, high and wide and lonely. It is also a bird watcher's heaven. Back in the 1840's Robert Curzon inventoried the birds in one of these eastern Turkish valleys; he noted seventeen kinds of birds of prey, seventy-four perchers, forty-two waders, twenty-six web-footed birds, eight kinds of partridge and quail—and three kinds of cuckoo. Varieties and numbers have dwindled since then, but myriads remain. Flocks of them sail alongside the train, borne on the air currents like gulls around an ocean liner. Some are sparrows, using the Turkish borderland as a flight path southward; some are hoopoes, their cinnamon heads and white-striped wings twinkling in the sun. They escort the train like guards of honor.

Twenty-seven miles from the frontier, the train slides past a clutter of ruined buildings left from World War I, among them a roofless Armenian church with its conical steeple still intact. A citadel, as colossal in its setting as Windsor Castle above the Thames, broods from a rock face and darkens the scene. Across from the citadel, flat-roofed houses encrust a hillside like barnacles. This is Kars, provincial capital and trophy of Turkish-Russian rivalry.

The loathing of Russia in Kars, and in the borderland generally, is more than mere nationalism. It has nothing to do with anti-Communism. Its ingredients include suspicion of foreigners, dislike of pork-eaters, and folk memories of a past long dead. When Turkish parents chide a child, they will say: "You'd better behave, or the *Moskoffs* will get you." A Turk in the eastern provinces does not need to be told that Russia is a hereditary enemy; he feels it in his bones. A graybeard in Kars, a tailor, was asked what he would do if the *Moskoffs* marched across the frontier. "I'd kill them," the old man said without even stopping to think. "I have seven sons, I have a horse, and I'd be the first in my family to ride it against them."

From Turkey's national standpoint, the old enmity has its uses. For the eastern provinces are poor, and exposed to Soviet broadcasts, in Turkish, which picture the Soviet side of the frontier as a farmers' and workers' paradise. Normally such propaganda might stir discontent. Among the Turks of the borderland it has fallen flat, for the simple reason that the propaganda is Russian.

It does not follow that Turkey will never resume outwardly friendly relations with its Soviet neighbors. In politics and diplomacy, modern Turks call themselves realists. When imperial Turkey was down and out in 1919, and cut off from its traditional British and French allies, it was Soviet help that enabled Atatürk to rally and arm his people. The Soviet Union and Turkey were virtually friendless except for each other. The Turkish Army continued to train with Soviet weapons until shortly before Atatürk's death. But in those years the *Moskoffs* were weak as well as friendless. They posed no immediate threat to Turkey's independence. Prophecy about Turkish diplomacy is hazardous, as the Allies in World War II discovered; the Turks remained neutral until just before the end. Conceivably they may move toward neutralism again. But one can hazard this guess with some assurance: they are not likely to be enticed by their hereditary foe. Their Army will continue to guard the border as if the very life of the Republic depended on it.

[1]

In addition to defense of the frontier, which is its first duty, the Army has a second obligation in the eastern provinces. This is to train new conscripts from all parts of the nation. The sparsely peopled east, dry in summer, frozen in winter, makes an ideal proving ground for weapons, techniques, and men. Not in Korea alone did the Turkish Brigade win its triumphs of endurance; it won them first in the windy valleys and on the barren heights of the training fields around Erzurum.

Most of this training takes place, of course, well back from the actual frontier. But Turkish commanders do not hesitate to hold maneuvers almost within sight of Soviet territory. From the lower flanks of Ararat, for example, shepherds can detect the lights of Yerevan, the capital of Soviet Armenia. Yet the straight Turkish highway that skirts the mountain is often enveloped in dust from mile-long columns of trucks carrying troops on training exercises. The dust cakes the men's faces, the Anatolian sun browns them; the combination gives them the complexion of cigar-store Indians.

Some of these Army units are motorized with light tanks and gun carriers. Some, as recently as 1960, were still horse cavalry, among the last of a vanishing breed. They train in a setting fit for gods and heroes. On summer afternoons one can catch a close-up of them by standing on a hill that faces Ararat, across an immense and apparently uninhabited valley. The clouds that hide the summit through most of the day now rise in wisps into an otherwise cloudless sky. Late in the afternoon the peak swims white and clear in the deepening blue. Silence cloaks this valley, like the silence when the earth was young, before the Flood, before the first birds sang. Suddenly one hears a thudding of hoofs. Yellow dust whirls up from the brow of the hill, and a company of troops gallops into sight on sweating horses. To watch these cavalrymen charging is to hear the trumpets of Balaklava, of

> . . . *old, unhappy, far-off things*
> *And battles long ago.*

To the farmers and herdsmen of this eastern country, the sight of soldiers has been familiar all their lives. They do not resent it as, for example, do the Shans of Burma or the Moros of the southern Philippines. For the Turkish troops in the east are their own men. If one asks a Turk to enumerate his nation's assets, he will almost always top his list with the Army. Whether or not he belongs to the modern-minded million, he honors the Army as the protector of his liberties, the defender of his soil, the insurer of his Turkishness and that of his children.

Yet, inescapably, the Army distorts his life as a citizen. He knows that the Army commander is the kingpin. The commander, not the civilian Governor of the province, holds the highest prestige. The commander, not the Governor, is the most honored nonpartisan symbol of the Republic. Whoever holds the highest uniformed rank in any locality inherits the traditional respect and obedience of eastern Turks toward their former tribal chief or pasha. The Army may not try consciously to shape the borderland, but it cannot help exerting a powerful influence upon it.

[2]

What, exactly, is the Army's influence? How does it help or hinder the people of the east among whom it serves?

It helps them indirectly in one way above all. What the Army wants, it gets, both from the civilian population and from the government at Ankara. If the Army needs a new road built or an old one improved for military purposes, neither red tape nor parsimony in Ankara can obstruct it for long. One example is the excellent west-to-east highway from Erzurum; this road holds the key to swift communications along the Soviet frontier, and the civilian government maintains it with care and skill. Another example is the smaller road that branches from this main artery to Kars. Until the mid-1950's it was an abomination of ruts and rocks. Army jeep drivers found it less punishing to avoid the so-called roadway and drive through the adjoining fields. In recent years it has been straightened, graded, graveled, and kept in repair—because the Army needed it. What the Army does not need are better farm-to-market roads; therefore these side roads, essential to the economic health of rural Turkey, are built sparingly if at all.

Education offers another example of what the armed forces can do. When the Army speeded up its mechanization, in the late 1950's, it found half its new conscripts unable to write their own names, much less to master new techniques. In a rocket-and-radar age, what is the use of a soldier if he cannot communicate? Therefore the Army, with American support, has set up schools where it gives two months of compulsory teaching to every illiterate conscript. Classroom work includes civics and health as well as the three R's. The sixteen literacy centers, teaching from 60,000 to 70,000 recruits every two months, are not, of course, confined to the eastern provinces; they are scattered all over the country. Nonetheless they bring lasting benefits to the east, which has a higher proportion of illiterates than other regions.

When an eastern boy finishes his military service, he can come home to his village not only able to read and write but also to teach his family to prevent disease, and sometimes to repair and maintain simple machinery. In many parts of eastern Turkey, discharged soldiers, products of the new training, have gone into the business of making and repairing farm tools. To this extent, at least, the Army has helped the people of the borderland. What the Army cannot do is to modernize agriculture, set up processing plants, widen social services, or produce village schools where there are none. These remain, properly, the responsibilities of the central government, acting through its provincial Governors, who are usually starved for funds.

The high caliber of many provincial Governors is another sign of the Army's indirect influence for good upon the borderland. Having to deal continually with local civilian authorities, the Army requires civilian officials who are as competent as its officers themselves. Therefore the government in Ankara seldom sends a rank incompetent to an important post in the east. It chooses its Governors there from the cream of the crop.

A Governor in Eastern Turkey may be a retired colonel like the one in the province of Ağrı in 1960, a former commander of the Turkish contingent in Korea recalled to public duty. If this official had his way, as he told visitors to his dusty capital, his first priority would be to build more schools. Or a Governor may be a professional civil servant, miserably paid yet trustworthy, and tested in the administrative routine. In the sensitive province of Kars, for example, the *vali* (Governor) in the early 1950's had climbed the ladder of public service at home and then been trained in public administration in the United States. His official home was a chilly palace built by the Russians when they owned Kars. It was grand enough for an imperial Viceroy: ceilings twenty feet high, reception room forty feet long. But this *vali's* interests and attitudes were anything but those of a proconsul. At his dinner table, lost in the vastness of his Russian home, he talked only of his hopes for the largely illiterate people of his province. If the Army had

had an indirect influence in appointing such a man to Kars, the Army had done well.

Yet even with a man of conscience in charge, the system has its drawbacks. One, as we have said, is the inability of the civilian Governor, in contrast to the Army commander, to wheedle funds from Ankara. Another is the dead hand of Ottoman tradition that reaches down into the lower levels of the bureaucracy, as distinct from the upper levels. One encounters petty tax collectors, finance officers, and building inspectors who never understood or believed in the Atatürk revolution. Their attitude is that revolutions may come and go, but officeholders go on forever. Still another drawback is the extreme centralization of government. A *vali* is appointed from Ankara; he need not be a product of his province; he may never have seen the place before. He is a mere agent of the central government, as a subordinate Army officer is an agent of his commander. Nor do the Turkish provinces elect legislatures, as in Hokkaido, to reflect the people's will and prod the central government to act. The villagers have no effective voices except their elected headmen and their elected deputy in the national capital. Local initiative and self-help are alien concepts.

The provincial Governor therefore remains a dispenser of bounty as well as an embodiment of power. His government remains paternalistic in the traditional Middle Eastern style; it also uses its paternalism to win votes in the modern Turkish style. The *vali* of Ağrı would "give" his people schools if he could; the *vali* of Kars had "given" clean water to a dozen villages, and would "give" more as funds became available. To the rank and file of the people, a Governor is too often someone remote and unapproachable: a benefactor perhaps, but too grand to understand the humble farmer's concerns.

A dominant Army and a paternalistic civilian government combine, then, to perpetuate the gulf between the small minority at the top and the mass of the people below. Young officers and Governors show clearly that they are heirs of Atatürk's uncompleted revolution. The people of the borderland, physically tough, intellectually narrow, spiritually rigid, show equally that the revolution has hardly penetrated beneath the surface. Here are the two nations we mentioned at the start of this chapter. Their separateness displays itself, plainly and painfully, in Erzurum.

The map of eastern Turkey shows only one city of this name. In truth there are two, both in the same place. Both cling to the same slope above a mile-high valley, yet they belong to different worlds. The first is Erzurum, the headquarters of the Third Army. Its sounds are the marching songs and drumbeats of a military band swinging along the main street, or the bugle calls from Army barracks high above the town. Its spirit is that of a garrison town whose men in uniform seem barely conscious of the civilian life around them.

To a Turkish officer, and still more to his wife and children, Erzurum is a place of exile: cold, cheerless, and bare, almost 900 miles from the lights and crowds of Istanbul. Who would choose to be stationed there? Yet the Army takes good care of its officers. On the outskirts of the city, colonels and their families live in new two-story houses with modern kitchens, running water and indoor plumbing, the windows gay with curtains, the balconies bright with flowers. Their children, playing around the gardens, might be models for pictures of improbably healthy youngsters in advertisements for breakfast foods. Small cars or jeeps outside the houses give the place the look of a Turkish suburbia.

On summer Sundays, the life of military Erzurum focuses on the terrace outside the Officers' Club, on the paved main street. Here officers sit at outdoor tables with their wives, sipping coffee or tea—the officers obviously an elite corps, the products of sophistication as well as schooling.

Their wives, in well-tailored suits, would not be out of place at a sidewalk café on the Via Veneto or the Champs Élysées. From the terrace with its checkered tablecloths, they look down at the Sunday strollers flowing past them on the street. Here the first Erzurum, the military center, gazes upon the second, the market town of the eastern borderland.

The strollers are townspeople, the products of an earthier world. They seldom cock their heads to glance at the terrace above them. Most of them are men, wearing the worker's cap that succeeded the fez as Turkey's national headgear. (Atatürk decreed the European felt hat as a substitute, but it never caught on; the hatbrim got in the way when its wearer touched the ground for prayers. The visored cap can be reversed, front to back, at prayer time.) Women in eastern Turkey do not usually go out in the town with their men. When they do appear, eight out of ten still hide themselves, not in veils but often in what appear to be burlap bags without shape or any hint of femininity beneath. This violates Atatürk's wish that women should come out of their shrouds. They began to do so, even in Erzurum, but under the Menderes regime, in the 1950's, taboos were allowed to reappear. Though Islam remained officially disestablished, its priests and teachers kept much of their old influence and regained much of their old powers. Anyone who had known Erzurum in 1951, and returned in 1960, could not have failed to note the reappearance of the veil, a symbol of the backsliding, in this part of Turkey at least, from Atatürk's reforms.

From the main street and the Officers' Club, dark alleys drop off to the lower part of the town. Rough with cobblestones, they are encrusted in the dirt of ages. Here one becomes a rider of an H. G. Wells Time Machine, flying in an instant back into the Erzurum of a century ago. The people living in these narrow lanes, amid rubbish and decay, are not so much a century as a world away from the

"A good Nepali farmer in Sikkim grows
more rice or maize from an acre than
any other in the Himalayas."

School in Gangtok (Sikkim) echoes to "the same popular
clamor for education that can be heard throughout Asia."

XXVI

"By 1960, about 8,000 men, women, and children were
at work on the northern road. Most of them were
Nepalis . . ." living in Sikkim.

In Afghan Turkestan: "a flock of brown and black Karakul sheep grazes on stubble of tough grass. The shepherd
turns out to be a young Pushtun from the far south near
Kandahar."

XXVIII

"An undulating thread becomes a caravan of more than a hundred camels." The Kunduz Valley in Afghan Turkestan.

"Some Afghan nomads earn their living as stockmen, who breed, pasture, and sell flocks."

"All through the year nomads are on the move on some Afghan roads and trails." These are following the ancient silk road from China as it passes through the Bamian Valley.

XXX

Tajik merchants and a scribe who takes dictation in their shop in Afghanistan.

OPPOSITE

"Almost every Afghan man or boy wears a turban and owns at least one spare. The turban of light cotton cloth measures seven and a half yards long by about half a yard wide." A turbaned merchant sells sheepskin coats in the Hindu Kush foothills.

A grizzled farmer in eastern Turkey: "From childhood to old age, his life has been a treadmill."

"Ararat rises in an almost perfect cone . . . so high
that its summit is sheathed in never-melting snow."
Kurdish nomads pass by on the Iranian side of the
Turkish frontier.

Atatürk revolution. The characteristic sound of the lower town, by day, is the clopping of horses as they pull rickety victorias, the city's chief form of public transportation. The carriages might have seen service in 1916 when the Tsar's soldiers last occupied the town. Soon after nightfall the clop-clop has stilled. The stars shine brilliantly in this high atmosphere. Because Erzurum remains in the same time zone as Istanbul, almost a thousand miles to the west, dawn breaks as early as three in the summer months. From unseen minarets, muezzins sing their praise to Allah. They compete with the whistles shrilling from dark side streets; these are the police on their patrols, notifying one another that all's well. They also compete with a high squeak, at regular intervals, like the chirp of a bird equipped with a metronome. The squeak comes from the wheels of farmers' carts, turning slowly as oxen pull them along. The oxen have been plodding all night, perhaps longer, to bring a farmer from his village, first over muddy tracks or across fields, and then, at dawn, into the bustle of Erzurum's markets.

More than anyone else, the farmer has been insulated from the revolution. Didn't Atatürk call him the master of Turkey, "more than everybody else entitled to wealth, riches, and well-being"? If so, why has he not achieved them?

The Borderland Farmer

The farmer's year in eastern Turkey consists not of four seasons but two. One, the short growing season, is also a time of preparation for the winter. The second is winter itself, the unforgiving enemy that shapes the farmer's entire life.

To give themselves warmth as well as security from marauders, the people of this highland country have always wanted a thickness of earth above their roof. The houses, of rough stone, are usually built into a hillside, so that at least a part of the family's living quarters lies snugly below the ground. Where no slope is available, the farmers pack at least a foot of earth onto their flat housetops, and stack the grain on top of it.

For warmth and protection, animals share these partly subterranean dwellings with the farm families. If a farmer is comparatively well-to-do, he quarters his animals in a stable behind the house. If not, the family lives at one end of a combined house and stable, the animals at the other. From the first hard freeze until the first grass has pushed through the snow, the animals stay indoors. The collective warmth of their breath and their bodies is the best form of central heating the farmer knows. The stable is not usually cleaned until warmer weather arrives. If one enters from the snowy outdoors, the ammonia from the urine of so many cattle makes the eyes smart and run. The family offsets these discomforts with the few amenities it can afford: perhaps a carpet on the earth floor of its living quarters, a divan with cushions along the wall, a glass window to admit a shaft of sun, and a stove in the floor for cooking *bulgur,* the cracked-wheat cereal, boiled in mutton fat, which forms the staple food.

Spring arrives late in the border provinces. The growing season lasts little more than three months on the plateau, and about two months on land that is over a mile high. Every week of this fleeting season is precious. Yet when it is warm enough to put the cattle outdoors, they must graze for at least two weeks, sometimes a month, before they can work. Those animals that have not died of disease are too weak to pull a plow. These first snow-free weeks are, of course, the time when the farmer should be plowing and sowing.

Even in these weeks the farmer's wife must start preparing for the winter. With her children, she scoops the manure from the stable, mixes it with straw, pats it into cakes, dries them on a stone wall, and stacks them in brown pyramids outside the house. For in this generally treeless land, dried dung is the only fuel for heating and cooking: an efficient fuel in the absence of any other. The search for fuel goes on through the summer wherever the animals have grazed or pulled a plow. If the children go to a village school, they must nevertheless gather fuel cakes in their off-school hours. If they have no school, this is their day-long work, so that the family shall not freeze when winter winds start blowing.

There is nothing particularly Turkish about living with the animals; rural families in parts of Europe and Asia have done it ever since cattle were domesticated. Nor is the use of dried dung for fuel solely a Turkish adaptation to a woodless land. From the Middle East to Mongolia and Tibet, fertilizer is, perforce, burned for the lack of other fuel. The soil starves for organic matter.

If eastern Turkey managed its land intelligently, it could be range country as profitable as that of Nebraska, where the climate is almost as severe. In Marco Polo's day, the grasses and herds of the borderland must have been a wonder to behold. Messer Marco reported that the eastern Tartars each summer stationed a part of their army there "on account of the good pasture it affords for their cattle." On the lower slopes of Ararat, he wrote, vegetation was so abundant that "all the cattle which collect there in summer from the neighboring country meet with a never-failing supply." Now the vegetation is scarce or gone.

The self-inflicted misfortune of the Turkish border country is twofold: its flocks and herds are too big and, partly in consequence, its pastures are barren. The status symbol of a farmer in eastern Turkey is not the weight of his cattle or sheep, nor the amount of meat or wool they yield, but simply their number. If he owns more animals than his neighbor, he feels he is the richer man.

The number of animals in the borderland is staggering.

In the province of Kars alone, a farming family in 1957 owned, on the *average*, thirty-four sheep, twenty-four head of cattle, six goats, two water buffaloes, and two horses. The number has shot upward in recent years without any corresponding effort to provide enough forage. In a sparsely peopled province like Kars, this is the true "population explosion." An official count in this province in 1954 and 1957 tells the story:[1]

	1954	1957
Sheep	987,000	1,497,000
Cattle	687,000	1,036,000
Goats	187,000	288,000
Water Buffaloes	52,000	84,000
Horses	53,000	78,000

Other eastern provinces showed increases almost as striking, although not in all kinds of animals. In some, sheep and goats dwindled, cattle multiplied. The general picture suggests an immense proliferation of animals, as if the farmers were hurrying to outdo their neighbors in the size of their herds. The period from 1954 to 1957 was one in which the Menderes government's subsidies to agriculture were in full swing. The figures may be a clue to the mystery of what the farmers did with the unaccustomed cash that jingled in their pockets in those years. One evidence of this is the sharp increase of water buffaloes, notably in Trabzon, where the number almost tripled in the three-year period. These are the most valuable of all a Turkish farmer's animals; they cost the equivalent of $180 in 1951. Only a farmer with money can afford them.

Before Atatürk, tribal chiefs controlled breeding herds and grazing lands in eastern Turkey. Now, with herds multiplying so fast, overgrazing has exhausted the natural

[1] From *Agricultural Structure and Production 1954–1958* (Ankara: Republic of Turkey, Central Statistical Office; 1959).

grasses. Alfalfa is said to have originated in Turkey, but one can find hardly a blade of it still growing in the borderland except in some cleft between rocks, a cleft too small for the snout of a bullock to enter. Turkey produces oil cake that could be used as cattle feed; instead, the Turks export it from their Mediterranean region to earn foreign exchange. Far from being an asset to the eastern provinces, the exploding animal population is dangerous, perhaps disastrous, to their earnings.

A farmer gets little from a half-starved steer, either in draft power or in meat. Yet a Turk around Erzurum usually works his bullock for seven years before selling it for slaughter; even then it may weigh only 400 pounds. Better forage on the range, plus feed in the winter, could put five times as much weight on an animal within two years. As it is, the eastern Turkish farmer, like his animals, must struggle to survive.

Watch one of these borderland Turks as he scrambles up a hillside with his herds, bound for a pasture. His leathery face, his grizzled chin, his patched and tattered clothes, all bespeak a man who has endured unending trials. From childhood to old age, his life has been a treadmill. Worse than the handicaps of climate and terrain has been his own unwillingness or inability to change. Of all the Asian farmers we have known, this Turk has the hardest lot.

How much is he entitled to blame his own government for his plight? In fairness, one should remember that successive Turkish governments had to struggle against national exhaustion in the 1920's, world-wide depression in the 1930's, and unforeseen military burdens in the 1940's. When party politics emerged after World War II, every politician was well aware that he had to do something for the farmer. But with one shining exception, which we shall examine, the "something" turned out to be no more imaginative than continued exemption of all farmers from income tax, credits that were seldom repaid, and price supports of major farm crops, mainly wheat.

The golden opportunity for an overhaul of Turkish agriculture came at the end of the 1940's with the start of American aid. The opportunity was allowed to slip for more than a decade. The blame must be shared by the Turkish government, infatuated with steel mills and factories, and by the United States government, bent on building up the Turkish armed forces and an export economy that could support them. Of the scores of American civilian advisers in Ankara in the early 1950's, only six were assigned to agriculture. If the chief of the American aid mission showed a burning interest in improving crop yields and helping the Turkish farmer, he failed to light the spark in his superiors in Washington. American and Turkish experts had worked out admirable plans for improving Turkish agriculture, but their plans were scrapped. American policy makers remained mentally stuck in Europe, tied to the priorities and techniques that had succeeded there so brilliantly under the Marshall Plan. Turkish policy makers, for their part, were bent on industrializing Turkey in the Western European image. But what was the relevance of industrial Europe's experience to a country in which four fifths of the people earned their living from the land?

After the Korean War, Turks and Americans alike turned a small part of their attention to agriculture, but only to rich cash crops in limited areas: to figs and raisins along the Aegean, tobacco and cotton along the Mediterranean, hazelnuts and citrus along the Black Sea, all of which produced foreign exchange. The interior of the eastern borderland, producing neither profitable crops nor minerals nor manufactures, was allowed to wallow along in its fourteenth-century habits.

How can one blame the farmer? How can he adopt new methods which nobody has ever bothered to show him? Atatürk had made a stab at adult education by setting up a

"People's House" in every city and a "People's Room" in every large village, with a library of sorts and at least one room for community meetings. But these were intended chiefly for political indoctrination, and the Menderes regime shut them soon after taking power. In any event, they did not meet the farmers' needs. The whole of eastern Turkey, in 1960, was without the means of communicating to the farmer what he needed to know. The government had set up three agricultural experiment stations, a cattle breeding station, three state seed farms. The missing link was an extension service to bring the benefits of research to the farmer.

Since then the government has planned a thoroughgoing overhaul of agriculture. This would provide farm extension workers and demonstration projects. If the plan is carried out—and one can never be sure in Turkey—it will require a long and patient effort of persuasion and example to make up for the arrears of centuries.

The Kurds

So far we have suggested two reasons for the grievous state of the borderland and the failure of the Atatürk revolution to affect it. The first is the government's natural preoccupation with the military defense of the east; the second, its inattention to the farmer and its inability to pull him out of his past. There remains a third explanation: the influence of the last important ethnic minority left in Turkey, the Kurds. One cannot ignore these highland farmers and herdsmen in any study of the eastern provinces, of which they form almost half the population. An Aryan people related to the Persians, they have fought every conqueror for thousands of years. Stubborn in resisting modern Turkish ways, tenacious in clutching their traditions, these people have (in Mr. Khrushchev's elegant phrase) stuck like a bone in the throats of Atatürk and his reformist heirs.

The Kurds are not solely a Turkish problem. They straddle several national frontiers. About 1,750,000 of them farm the oases and graze the hillsides of southeastern Turkey; perhaps 1,250,000 more live in adjoining Iran, Iraq, and Syria, and a few in the Transcaucasian republics of the Soviet Union. Like the Kachins of northern Burma, they used to be known and feared as brigands. They terrorized Turks and Armenians alike. The Turkish police have stamped out such shenanigans against travelers, but many Kurdish clans and families keep up their marksmanship by feuding among themselves. In the deadliness of their vendettas, they rival the Pushtuns of the Afghan hills. Kurdish men often use their boys under eighteen to carry on the work of vengeance, knowing that in present-day Turkey a juvenile cannot be hanged for murder. In most parts of Turkey, the majority of boys in the state reformatories are sweepings from city streets; in the reformatory at Erzincan, which draws its inmates partly from Kurdish country, 80 per cent are village boys.

Perhaps because Kurds fit the romantic tradition of Walter Scott's heroes, or of the Lone Ranger, Anglo-Saxons from Lord Curzon to Justice Douglas have found them personally appealing, and rightly so. Proud and crusty as individuals, suspicious of strangers but warm and generous toward any guest in their house, the Kurds have kept their sense of separateness for centuries. They show it in many ways: for example, in their national dress, which the Turks do not let them wear in the market towns. In the northern Kurdish country, the women could be transplants from the Tyrolean mountains. Their brightly flowered skirts, their blouses and bodices, might be Austrian dirndls, and the scarlet kerchiefs around their heads flash in the fields like tanagers' plumage. Farther south, Kurdish women tinkle with silver coins worn as ornaments. A sense of identity compels the Kurds to look different from the Turks around them.

Like the Shans in Burma and other ethnic remnants, the Kurds have produced separatist leaders. Encouraged by the British in World War I and by the Russians in recent years, some have flirted with the idea of an independent *Kurdistan* embracing all the Kurdish peoples. In the 1930's the Turks had to send troops into the almost inaccessible Kurdish mountains to choke a local rebellion. In the 1950's the Menderes regime courted the Kurds instead of coercing them; it allowed a Kurdish leader, Kasim Küprevi by name, to be elected to the Grand National Assembly. On the morning of May 27, 1960, when Army officers under Cemal Gursel seized power, Küprevi was arrested, along with hundreds of others of the Menderes party.

A major worry to the leaders of this smooth and bloodless coup was the thought that the Kurds might rise in insurrection. To a Turk in Ankara of whatever party, the very name strikes a sensitive nerve. They are *mountain Turks*. Let a foreigner so much as whisper *Kurdistan* and he will have committed a social error as appalling as mentioning *Armenia*. Foreigners have found it harder to get permits for travel in the Kurdish country than in any other portion of the eastern military zone. Yet the Kurds have not justified Ankara's fears. Our superficial impression, traveling in 1960 through the heavily Kurdish province south of Ararat, was one of much poverty but little tension. Many of the Kurds, without doubt, now accept the designation of *mountain Turks*. More and more of them speak Turkish in place of their ancestral Persian tongue. They appear to have reconciled themselves to being citizens of the Turkish Republic—so long as the Republic does not try to uproot their traditions.

It is their traditions rather than any desire for nationhood which the Turks find thorny to handle. The traditionalism takes two forms. One is religious. The Kurds bring mysticism and traces of spirit worship to their Moslem observances, and color them with religious fervor that has faded from the rest of Turkey. The second form of the Kurds' traditionalism is social. In the Kurdish country it is still the chief of the tribe or clan whom the people unquestioningly follow. They pay little heed to the Turkish hierarchy of provincial and local officials. A Kurd will gladly let his animals be inoculated and his village sprayed; nothing in his religion or custom stands in the way. But his tribal leader, not a Turkish government emissary, must tell him to do so. If Turkey wants to transform the Kurds gradually into a settled, taxpaying, literate minority, as it undoubtedly does, it can do this only by working through the tribal system as its instrument.

Until recently, isolation helped the Kurds to keep their hills and glens inviolate to change. No highway threatened to modernize their rugged land. In 1959, however, the Kurds acquired a new enemy: the bulldozer. The Turks began work in that year on two costly projects, intended to open the Kurdish fastness both to international traffic and to contact with western Turkey. Both projects were sponsored by CENTO, the Central Treaty Organization set up in 1955 by the ill-fated Baghdad Pact. One project is a west-to-east railway to link the Turkish rail system with Iran's north-south line. The second is a road starting just across the Tigris from Syria and running northeastward to Iran. Although the distances are small, the terrain is a road builder's nightmare. Neither Turkey nor Iran can finance their respective sections by themselves. The United States has contributed $1,350,000 for starting work on the Turkish portion, the United Kingdom £100,000 for equipment on the Iranian stretch.

To an old-fashioned Kurd, the din of compression drills and bulldozers is as hateful as the racket of a power saw in an English garden suburb. It not only shatters his peace; it sounds a knell to the seclusion that has kept the Kurds a people apart. The same thought, no doubt, occurred to the authorities in Ankara—the new road and railway should make it easier for Turkey to control and if necessary to suppress the Kurds. But highways, by themselves, cannot draw the Kurds into the mainstream of Turkish life. Unless the Turks approach these indomitable tribesmen with a greater respect for their religious and social traditions, the Kurds will remain an irritant in the body politic, an obstacle to change in the borderland.

To sum up: we have shown how and why the eastern provinces trail behind the rest of Turkey. In seeking to explain the lag, we have not found the answer either in climate or history. We have suggested other explanations: the dominance of the Army, which naturally has priorities other than economic and social development; the conservatism of the farming population; the stubborn separateness of a big ethnic minority; and, finally, the indifference of the 1,000,000 modern-minded Turks to their 27,000,000 countrymen. Must eastern Turkey forever limp behind? Has it nothing on which a vigorous government could build?

Assets for the Future

Fairly good communications link the provincial capitals of the east with the centers of national power. The main highways may not be Jersey Turnpikes, but they are soundly engineered and suited to Turkish needs. The railways cannot compete with those of France in efficiency or speed, but at least they connect the borderland with Ankara and Istanbul: one main line across the north and a two-pronged branch across much of the south. The Black Sea steamship service, as we noted, is worthy of a country with 4,131 miles of seacoast. As for air services, the state-owned Turkish airline has one of the world's cleanest safety records. Its DC-3's and Viscounts link Istanbul and Ankara with once-remote outposts such as Kars, Van, and Hakkari, until recently the most isolated corner of all. If the Turkish government should begin in earnest to develop its eastern provinces, it would not be starting from scratch.

Nor do its assets in the east end with steel rails and aluminum wings. Whatever the central government's omissions, it governs; its writ runs to the uttermost limits of the country. Public security, the basis of effective government everywhere, can be taken for granted. Brigandage has been stamped out. A visitor is safe in the lonely east. A farmer leading his creaking oxcart to market, or a shopkeeper moving a load of supplies, knows that he will not be set upon by thieves, as his father and grandfather used to be. In the Middle East, this represents an accomplishment, and the Turks can be proud of it. But public safety can be a static virtue, like the law and order of a well-run colony. What successive Turkish governments have not done is to use their writ to raise eastern Turkey's standard of living. They have failed to develop the capacities of the people. They have hardly tried—except for two remarkable attempts in the field of technical education. Both of these are worth examining, for they could bring light to a benighted region, and thus extend the Atatürk revolution. One of them is Turkey's bravest experiment in rural education, the so-called village institutes.

[1]

The village institutes, inaccurately named, were high schools designed to prepare village boys to become rural teachers and community leaders. About the time of Atatürk's death in 1938, his forward-looking lieutenants launched the experiment without either money or advice from abroad. They saw the village school and its teacher as instruments of economic and social progress in the Turkish countryside. They also knew that to bring rural children to the cities for training in village leadership would defeat the enterprise, for it would spoil them. The institutes were to turn out a new kind of village teacher, equipped to teach not only the three R's but the rudiments of modern farming, public health, manual arts, and social organization as well. In short, he would be a Jack-of-all-trades. And to influence village parents as well as their children, he would have to be a village man.

The concept was daring. In the Middle East of the 1930's, it was as revolutionary as any of Atatürk's reforms. Private funds and foresight had introduced the idea into Greece, in the form of the American Farm School at Salonika. But Turkey's was the first government of the Moslem world, from Morocco to the Indies, to make such practical training a public rather than a private concern. With its village institutes, Turkey became a pioneer in what was later to become well known as "community development" in many countries. The Turks pioneered without "foreign aid," and with a self-reliance beyond praise.

Village boys, and some girls, were chosen by examination from children in the existing five-year elementary schools. Usually at twelve, the winners then began five years of free training by the state. With their own hands they built some of their dormitories and classrooms, and fashioned some of their equipment. In the classroom they learned the usual subjects of secondary schooling: history, geography, natural sciences, music, and art, with an accent on self-expression. (Painting and drawing, in particular, broke with the traditional Turkish past, for until Atatürk's early years of power, religion had forbidden any representation of the human face or form.) Classroom study took only about half of a student's time; the other half he devoted to practical work in the machine shop or the fields. He learned to care for farm animals, to tend an orchard, to maintain a beehive, to plant and harvest crops with modern techniques.

By 1948, the end of the experiment's first decade, Turkey had twenty-one of these schools, with an enrollment of more than 12,000, mostly boys. The showplace was at Hasanoğlan, in the rolling Anatolian farmland just east of Ankara. Here the Turks displayed their government's handiwork, and that of their children, to foreign visitors. But Hasanoğlan was not a Potemkin village, a false front. Similar institutes from the Aegean to Iran attained the same high standards.

The eastern provinces, bypassed in so many other fields of national endeavor, kept pace in this one. Outside Kars, almost within sight of the Soviet frontier, amid villages where life had hardly changed for centuries, the government set up a village institute as outstanding as the rest. The dormitory was a gloomy place, for it had been built as an artillery barracks in the years of Russian rule. But the experimental farms and orchards around it were oases of greenery in a wasteland. Crops were lush, cattle sturdy, fruit trees free of blight, proving that young Turks from the poorest background could learn modern techniques. After five years of such training, they would apply their new knowledge to a new generation of village children.

The experiment went on the rocks for several reasons, some sound, some spurious. Boys and girls of exceptional talent were denied higher education by the mere accident that they had been chosen, at twelve, to attend a village institute. Morally and legally they were bound to teach in village schools for twenty years. If they wanted to go on to the universities of Istanbul or Ankara, they would have to resign as teachers and repay the cost of their five years of schooling and support. This, for a village boy or girl, was virtually impossible. How many gifted scholars, artists, and scientists Turkey lost by this system, one can only guess. One village institute boy achieved a controversial fame without going to a university; he was Mahmut Makal, whom we mentioned earlier. He wrote a book of vignettes entitled, in English translation, *A Village in Anatolia*; it shocked the Turkish conscience, angered the government, and landed him briefly in jail as a "Communist sympathizer." But Makal's rebellion was an exception. An undoubted failing of the system was its lack of an outlet to higher education. This was one of the pretexts that led the Menderes regime, in the mid-1950's, to abandon the village institutes as such, and to turn them into conventional schools.

Another pretext was the complaint of some rural parents that their children were getting a second-class education. A village-institute student had to spend at least half his time on such menial tasks as animal husbandry; a city boy could concentrate on "cultured" subjects like history, philosophy, and literature. Beyond such complaints, real or imagined, the Menderes government had a political grievance against the village institutes. It alleged that an alien ideology— namely, Communism—had taken root among students and teachers. This was a mischievous charge, unfair to the students and teachers, and unworthy of Atatürk's successors. Behind it, true enough, lay an awareness of the effect of five years' liberal education on a village boy or girl. A twelve-year-old came to the institute from a background of acceptance of the old order. A seventeen-year-old left the institute seeing the possibility of change. Sometimes he or she acquired a burning resentment. In Turkey, as in an older republic we need not name, such resentment against society is apt to be equated with Communism. The village institutes were tainted, and had to go.

Happily for the Turkish villagers, Atatürk may lie moldering in his grave, but his soul goes marching on. By 1960 there was talk of reviving the village institutes, perhaps with different rules. Graduates need not be indentured for as long as twenty years. Those of exceptional promise should have the chance of moving to a university instead of to a village schoolroom.

By and large, the system remains the most imaginative

single response to the intellectual sluggishness of rural Turkey. India, Taiwan, the Philippines, among others, train young men and women to be rural teachers and village leaders. They have forged ahead of the Turks, who were once the pace-setters in this kind of practical education. To be left behind, not only by Europeans but also by Asians, should be galling to the European-minded Turks. If they decide to resume the task, so gallantly begun, so carelessly abandoned, new techniques and attitudes will flow into the border provinces, bringing new vigor to their village life.

[2]

A revival of the village institutes will offer one hope of change; the new Atatürk University at Erzurum already provides another. Until it was founded in the late 1950's, a student from the eastern provinces had no choice but to go to Ankara or Istanbul for higher education. Even there he was unlikely to find technical education suited to his rural background. Clearly Turkey needed a university in the east, to serve not only as a resource but also as a token of confidence in its provinces bordering the Soviet Union. To show this confidence, Celal Bayar flew east, soon after becoming President in 1950, in search of a university site. The government first favored Van, on the edge of Kurdish country, in the heart of what had been Armenia. The final choice fell on Erzurum, where Atatürk had rallied his defeated and dispirited people in 1919, where soldiers had stood guard for generations against the hereditary foe.

The new university symbolized Turkey's orientation toward Europe. A Turkish architect designed its buildings in the contemporary glass-and-concrete style. Overlooking the broad Erzurum valley, they stand as a shiny token of prestige. The university has brought more than status to Erzurum. Since it came, the currents of change have quickened. When visitors asked the *vali* of Erzurum in 1960 how his city had altered in ten years, he answered: "The biggest change is that we now have students and teachers." Book-shops have sprouted on the main street. Students laden with books mix with the shepherds, farmers, and soldiers on the sidewalks. Teachers from Ankara and Istanbul have brought intellectual discussion to a community that had talked chiefly about cattle or crops or soldiering.

But before the university can serve the borderland for which it was designed, its directors will have to vault many hurdles. One is the shortage of qualified students coming up from the few high schools of the area. Until the eastern provinces build their own educational underpinnings, the university cannot fulfill its role of training their youth. Meanwhile it must accept an unhealthy proportion of students from western Turkey who have not been admitted to universities in Ankara and Istanbul. They come to the eastern provinces reluctantly and hurry home with the coveted degree, without becoming a resource to the region where they were trained.

The university faces, secondly, a critical shortage of qualified teachers. With salaries nationally fixed in Ankara, Erzurum cannot offer financial bait to entice teachers to the cold and cultureless east. It does, however, offer free modern accommodations in its faculty dormitories, equipped with central heating and other scarce conveniences.

Finally, the new university will have to wage a constant struggle to sustain its emphasis on the agricultural and mechanical arts. The Turkish government itself has tended to be lukewarm toward a change from academic to vocational education. In much of Europe and Asia, technical training is still a newfangled notion. Old-line professors frown on it in Turkey as elsewhere. They prefer the classical disciplines which they themselves absorbed in school and college. Traditional pressures may, therefore, stunt the new Atatürk University into a pale and bloodless imitation of its big-city brothers. As we have suggested, the eastern borderland constitutes a special problem, one that demands new and

adventurous treatment. Could there be any more effective
stimulant than to gear education of rural youth to the special needs of a rural society?

[3]

One cannot help seeing analogies between this Turkish
hinterland and another far away. In the severity of its climate and the relative poverty of its resources, easternmost
Turkey suggests northernmost Japan, the first of our borderlands. Both regions have suffered inattention at the
hands of otherwise wide-awake central governments. Why,
then, has Hokkaido forged ahead in the past hundred years,
while eastern Turkey remains a retarded child? Without
straining the comparisons or contrasts, one can suggest a
few reasons which Turkish governments of the 1960's
might ponder. First, the Meiji reformers of Japan lost no
time in promoting agricultural development in Hokkaido
after seizing power. They recruited the ablest foreign teachers and technicians they could find, and employed them for
ten years in opening a wilderness. Second, Japan was not
content with building roads and railroads in its borderlands,
as the Turks were; it sought to develop people as well.
When the early Meiji government introduced compulsory
education into Japan, it did not fail to extend schools and
teachers to rural Hokkaido. Thus farmers in the northern
island could absorb written instructions on technical as well
as political subjects. The Turks, too, introduced compulsory
schooling, for adults as well as children. But they lacked
the resources or the will or both to carry this impulse into
more than a small fraction of the villages in the east. Not
until the 1950's did the government contemplate a university in the borderland; the Japanese had set up theirs in
Hokkaido almost a hundred years earlier, and had stressed
practical training at a time when it was more daring than
in Turkey of the present day. On such foundations, Hokkaido supports more than 5,000,000 people, at standards

immeasurably above those of the farmers and herdsmen of the Turkish borderland. Surely the lesson is plain.

One should never say *never* in predicting the future. But there is little risk in suggesting that eastern Turkey will never become highly industrialized. Except for copper on the Black Sea coast and a trickle of oil in the far south, it lacks the fuels and other minerals, the man power, and the markets. With education and purposeful leadership, the eastern Turk could become relatively rich by raising high-grade cattle. With little outlay of capital, he could produce and process meat and dairy products for all of Turkey. He will need expert guidance at all stages, from the sowing of forage grasses all the way to the grading, marketing, and processing of meat and dairy products. A literate, productive population would lose some of its educated youth to the cities; but no matter. Enough talent would remain to make the eastern provinces an asset instead of a loss to their country. As it is, they constitute a mere colony, and a sadly unprofitable one at that.

The Turks ought to know about colonies. They once ruled subject peoples all the way from the Persian Gulf to the Adriatic. But in Atatürk's famous six-day speech in 1927, in which he reviewed his record and outlined his hopes and plans, he announced:

> . . . the new Turkey and the people of the new Turkey have nothing to consider but their own existence and well-being.

Thenceforth the Turks were to apply their brain and muscle only to their compact homeland, chiefly to the immensities of Anatolia, stretching almost a thousand miles from the Straits into Asia.

The job was never done. In the eastern quarter of the country it barely got under way. It remains for a new generation of Turks to go back to Atatürk's teachings and carry out his commands.

Postscript

THROUGHOUT this book we have been discussing change, or the comparative lack of it, in six borderlands of Asia. Now, in conclusion, let us look briefly at the process of change itself. Whether or not change is desirable, is it not bound to come? And if it rolls in, with the inevitability of an ocean tide, can it be harnessed to pull the border peoples closer to the rest of their countrymen?

When Lord Melbourne was asked to deal with any social evil at the start of the Victorian era, his answer was apt to be: "Why can't you let it alone?" Although he was not a blind opponent of change, all his instincts struggled against it. He still has his disciples; so has King Canute. In Asian border regions one still finds Westerners as well as Asians who wish that time stood still. A few missionaries, businessmen, and tea planters cannot help yearning for the tidiness of colonial days. One encounters Asians, too, who want all clocks to stop: *mullahs* in Afghanistan who cannot abide the emancipation of women; former landowners in Sikkim or Burma, bitter at having been dispossessed; Chinese merchants nostalgic for the era before Asian nationalism. In every unspoiled country—and all the borderlands in this book are relatively unspoiled—there are those who have not made their peace with this intrusive century. They are clinging to a lost cause. When children of Ainu "barbarians" hold down professorial chairs, when Moro pirates use outboard motors for their forays, when Kachins in the Burma hills form a political party, it is obviously too late to long for an earlier, simpler age.

The futility of trying to stop the clock is nowhere clearer than in another borderland which we do not know at first hand. This is India's northeastern frontier, along the McMahon Line between India and "the Tibet Region of China." Here Britain's heirs in India have been governing an assortment of rather primitive tribal groups, and doing it with the help of anthropologists as well as police and soldiers. India has made a conscientious effort to avoid upsetting traditional ways of life. Yet here is an incomplete list [1] of what India was compelled to do: to stop headhunting and the kidnapping of children as slaves; to check the smuggling of opium; to prevent human sacrifice and forbid cruel punishments; to protect land, control prices, check moneylending, and license shopkeeping; and to end the domination of the weaker tribes by the more aggressive. If all this is not upsetting ancient habits, what is?

Assuming that change must come to the borderlands, how should it be harnessed to the goals of developing nations? We have noted in preceding chapters a gap in living standards and a lack of communication between the outlying peoples and their ruling centers. To argue that the gap should be narrowed is not to suggest that a country must be shorn of diversity like a manicured lawn. A well-balanced nation needs its hills and woods and pastoral places, its space for future growth. At the same time, every nation must have urban centers of finance and trade, of learning and culture, from which the impulses of leadership can, if they are strong enough, reach out to the farthest provinces.

---

[1] For an absorbing discussion of this dilemma, see Verrier Elwin: *A Policy for NEFA* (Shillong, Assam [headquarters of the North-East Frontier Agency]: 1959).

If Asian governments want to draw the provinces closer and
narrow the gap, they can promote secondary centers of industry and culture in the borderlands. Hokkaido has its university and its processing plants for local products; Turkey
has set up its Atatürk University in the east; Sikkim's small
processing plants are adequate for its size, and its students
can get higher technical training at Shillong in Assam, not
too far away. But Mindanao, British Borneo, and the Shan
State need facilities of this kind. Once such centers have
been set up, they will be seedbeds for local leadership. Local
energizers like Governors Tanaka and Machimura in Hokkaido, or Mayor Climaco in Mindanao, can begin to speak
up for their people. Once a younger generation can be
trained *in its own region,* with opportunities *among its own
people,* the borderlanders will no longer see themselves as
colonial subjects of the central power. American aid cannot
do anything more valuable in the border regions than to
help finance this kind of belated change.

There is no need to belabor the interest of Americans,
past and present, in the borderlands: as architects of one
colony in Hokkaido and rulers of another in the Sulu Sea;
as missionaries in Burma, as investors and advisers in India
and Afghanistan, and as allies in Turkey. Only Sikkim has
escaped direct American influence of one sort or another,
but one could argue that the indirect effects of American
work with India have defied gravity and seeped even into
the high Himalayas. It is clear to us, and we assume to the
reader, that America no longer has *relations* with other
countries and peoples, but has *involvements* with them. The
involvements have been far more, of course, than political
and military.

Since the days of Adoniram Judson, the first American
missionary abroad, Americans have rarely doubted that
they had something of value to offer other peoples. The
problems have been not so much of inner conviction as of
communication. The missionaries who first carried the Gos-

pel to Asia stayed to find out, sometimes to their chagrin, that Asians can do as good a job of propagating the faith of their fellow Asian, Jesus Christ. And so the American Christian with a mission has turned more and more to teaching and healing, and done a respectable and respected job in these fields. Americans today believe they can make their major contribution in technology. Having been a recipient of technical assistance from all over the world for more than a hundred years, the United States proceeded to become not just the giver but the symbol of what was modern and magic in mechanical arts. Always second to Europeans in basic scientific discovery, Americans became pre-eminent in applying science to everyday life. This is just what the developing Asian countries need, and they have felt sure that they could acquire it easily and cheaply from across the Atlantic without abandoning what they regard as their own superior cultural heritage. Ever since 1853, when Commodore Perry landed in Tokyo Bay with a miniature railway and a telegraph line, among other marvels, to demonstrate the grandeur and glory of the American civilization, the United States has exported its technical achievements—its drums of DDT, its graduates of M.I.T., its magic formulas from "capital formation" to "self-sustained growth."

One of the important discoveries to be made in our borderland countries—and we made it repeatedly—is that the American exports of technology and theoretical economics can be as grotesque in the Asian setting as a cyclotron in a supermarket. This discovery is continually being reported back by the American technician on the scene. But it is hard for the technician to find anyone who will listen to him. The high United States government official, who might learn something from him, is too beset by big-money contracts, by Congress breathing down his neck, and by the frustrations of working with heads of Asian governments. Instead of heeding his man on the spot, he looks for guidance to the majestic American producers of automobiles, business machines, and soap. Foreign aid, to him, is a multi-billion-dollar "business."

What then have the American county agent, the sanitary engineer, the rural schoolteacher discovered in the border-land countries? We report their findings as more valuable than any of ours. They have learned that when it comes to technical tools, the United States is not necessarily the only or the best source of what Asian countries most need. For example, the Japanese have three-dollar farm implements better suited to the ox-power economy and the small field than the seventeen-dollar steel plow or the thousand-dollar tractor from Chicago. Moreover, they have seen that it makes more sense to teach single-entry bookkeeping to a Himalayan finance ministry like the Nepalese than to ship a comptometer across the cultural gap. Many of these same discoveries have yet to be made by educated Asians who are inclined to worship the comptometer and the cyclotron along with money and other status symbols.

Has the United States, then, nothing uniquely its own to offer the eager and groping Asian peoples, nothing that is both native to American soil and transplantable to the soil of the borderlands? It seems to us that the most under-valued American resource consists not of machines or money but certain ideas. They are ideas that Americans possess and hoard, often take for granted, but do not al-ways live by. They are not readily available in Europe or in Asia itself. In many ways they are the harvest of Ameri-ca's history and mixture of peoples.

One, for example, is the idea that to become "educated" is a humbling experience. Therefore the educated man can work with his hands without loss of dignity and "face." If this idea were ever incorporated into Asia's new school sys-tems, it would perhaps do as much as anything to bring the "educated" center and the borderlands closer together. In places that have been caste- or class-ridden, like India and

Japan, the old arrogance of the "educated" is dying hard, but it is dying.

Another idea is new to Asia yet relevant to borderlands: that the government official is the servant, not the master of the citizen. We can hear laughter from the wings at the suggestion that this thought, so lovingly planted in the minds of schoolchildren, has blossomed in Chicago, Boston, or Kansas City. In spite of all the weeds, the concept does manage to survive. Even those governments in Asia which are "good" and relatively incorrupt find this concept difficult to grasp and apply, so hardened are the arteries of paternalism. Borderlanders must wait a long time if they rely on the capitals for new ideas such as these. Therefore, the traditional American practice of local initiative has seemed especially useful as a third item of export. Almost as if it had long lain asleep, the idea is, in fact, catching hold in some borderlands. People are finding they can organize to get things done without waiting for government to do them. Not by advertising them, not by preaching them, but by quietly personifying them, Americans can carry ideas of this native variety to Asia. Such concepts are, to our way of thinking, the most dynamic exports the United States can send not only to capitals but, through them, to the borderlands.

SELECTED BIBLIOGRAPHY
WITH NOTES

Chapter 1

Ackerman, Edward A.: *Japan's Natural Resources and Their Relation to Japan's Economic Future.* Chicago: University of Chicago Press; 1953.
  An American geographer, formerly with the Occupation, includes an assessment of Hokkaido's minerals, forests, fisheries, and farms.

Batchelor, J.: *The Ainu and Their Folklore.* London: The Religious Tract Society; 1901.
  Legends and customs, lovingly collected by a British missionary who lived among the "departing race" from 1875 until after the turn of the century.

Campbell, Alexander: *The Heart of Japan.* New York: Alfred A. Knopf; 1961.
  A British correspondent, former bureau chief of *Time* in Tokyo, reflects present-day Hokkaido and the rest of Japan through not-too-solemn conversations with citizens.

Capron, Horace: "Memoirs. 1872–5." MS in the Library of the Department of Agriculture, Washington, D.C.
  By the director of the forty-five American technicians in Hokkaido in the 1870's; a document basic to an understanding of later history.

Cole, Allan B. (ed.): *A Scientist with Perry in Japan. The Journal of Dr. James Morrow.* Chapel Hill, N.C.: The University of North Carolina Press; 1947.

Dr. Morrow, the botanist with Perry's expedition, tells of his rambles in the countryside near Hakodate in 1854.

Cole, Allan B. (ed.): *With Perry in Japan. The Diary of Edward Yorke McCauley.* Princeton, N.J.: Princeton University Press; 1942. Seaman McCauley, later a rear admiral, kept this uninhibited account of Perry's visit to Hokkaido.

Dun, Edwin: "Reminiscences of Nearly a Half Century in Japan." MS in Library of the Department of Agriculture, Washington, D.C. An offset and supplement to Capron's "Memoirs" by his animal husbandry expert, who disapproved of his methods.

Golownin, Captain [Golovnin, V. M.]: *Memoirs of a Captivity in Japan, during the Years 1811, 1812, and 1813.* London: Colburn; 1818. A vivid journal of adventure and discovery, by the Russian officer who was the first European to see the interior of southern Hokkaido.

Harrison, John A.: *Japan's Northern Frontier.* Gainesville, Fla.: University of Florida Press; 1953. By a Far Eastern specialist at the University of Florida; a brief, clear, well-documented history of Hokkaido and Sakhalin to the downfall of the Colonial Office in 1882.

Hitchcock, Romyn: *The Ainos of Yezo, Japan.* Washington, D.C.: Smithsonian Institution, U.S. National Museum; 1892. A monograph by a respected American botanist, chemist, and microscopist of the 1880's; a detailed, firsthand study of a living society that has all but vanished.

Hodgson, C. Pemberton: *A Residence at Nagasaki and Hakodate in 1859–60.* London: Richard Bentley; 1861. The British consul describes Hokkaido in the dying days of the Tokugawa regime.

Hokkaido Imperial University: *The Semi-Centennial of the Hokkaido Imperial University, Japan, 1876–1926.* Sapporo; 1927. A commemorative volume containing a full account of Dr. William Smith Clark's term as a college president at Sapporo.

Information Office, Consulate of Japan, New York: "Japan's Park System." *Japan Reports,* Vol. VI, No. 6 (March 15, 1960).

Jones, F. C.: *Hokkaido. Its Present State of Development and Future Prospects.* London: Oxford University Press; 1958. The most useful single volume on the Hokkaido economy; the author, a Reader in Far Eastern History at the University of Bristol (England) spent three months in Hokkaido in 1954.

Lanman, Charles: *Leaders of the Meiji Restoration in America.* Re-edited by Y. Okamura. Tokyo: Hokuseido; 1931.
Contemporary accounts of the Kuroda and Iwakura missions, and of the first Japanese students in the United States.

Lensen, George Alexander: *The Russian Push Toward Japan. Russo-Japanese Relations 1697–1875.* Princeton, N.J.: Princeton University Press, 1959.
A specialist has written a spacious history that overstates the element of "push" in Russian policy.

Perry, M. C.: *Narrative of an Expedition of an American Squadron to the China Seas and Japan, Performed in the Years 1852, 1853, and 1854.* Three vols. Compiled from the original notes and journals of Commodore Perry and edited by Francis L. Hawks. Vol. I published as Executive Document No. 97 of the House of Representatives and No. 79 of the Senate, 33rd Congress, 2nd Session. Washington, D.C.; 1856.
The first volume contains the official story of the visit to Hakodate in 1854 and of Perry's negotiations there. Illustrated in color by artists with the expedition.

Spalding, J. W.: *The Japan Expedition.* New York: Redfield; 1855.
A lively and uncensored account by one of Perry's men, the clerk of the *Mississippi.*

Starr, Merritt: "General Horace Capron, 1804–1885." *Journal of the Illinois State Historical Society,* Vol. XVIII (July 1925).
A sympathetic portrait, placing Capron's Japanese years in the context of his American career.

Taeuber, Irene B.: *The Population of Japan.* Princeton, N.J.: Princeton University Press; 1958.
An American demographer shows that Hokkaido never was important as a reservoir for Japan's surplus population.

Trewartha, Glenn Thomas: *Japan. A Physical, Cultural, and Regional Geography.* Madison, Wisc.: The University of Wisconsin Press; 1945.
An encyclopedic work by a professor of geography at Wisconsin; Chapter x deals with Hokkaido.

Walworth, Arthur: *Black Ships Off Japan. The Story of Commodore Perry's Expedition.* New York: Alfred A. Knopf; 1946.
A skillful retelling of the Perry episode, by a winner of the Pulitzer Prize in 1959 (for his biography of Woodrow Wilson).

Chapter 2

Alliston, Cyril: *In the Shadow of Kinabalu*. London: Robert Hale, Ltd.; 1961.
Personal reminiscences of an Anglican missionary whose work took him to every part of North Borneo between 1950 and 1959.

Blair, Emma Helen, and Robertson, James Alexander (eds.): *The Philippine Islands, 1493–1803*. 55 vols. Cleveland: The A. H. Clark Co.; 1903–9.
Here are the historical documents pertaining to the area. Much of this basic source material makes better reading than history books.

Burbidge, Frederick William Thomas: *Gardens of the Sun: or A Naturalist's Journal on the Mountains and in the Forests and Swamps of Borneo and the Sulu Archipelago*. London: J. Murray; 1880.
The subtitle is accurate; one must marvel at Burbidge for his courage, persistence, and skill as an observer and writer.

Carpenter, Frank W.: *Report of the Governor of the Dept. of Mindanao and Sulu, P.I., 1914*. Washington, D.C.: Bureau of Insular Affairs, War Department; 1916.
An example of imaginative thinking by a colonial Governor who was ahead of his time.

Forbes, William Cameron: *The Philippine Islands*. Two vols. Boston: Houghton Mifflin Co.; 1928.
A fair and thoughtful history of America's first thirty years in the Philippines by the Boston blue blood who served as Governor General from 1909 to 1913, and in other Far Eastern posts.

Hagedorn, Hermann: *Leonard Wood, a Biography*. Two vols. New York: Harper & Brothers; 1931.
The second volume of this biography paints a sympathetic and sometimes charming portrait of Wood as military Governor of the Moro Province in 1903 and Governor General in 1920.

Hurley, Vic: *Swish of the Kris*. New York: E. P. Dutton & Co.; 1936.
A history of the Moros, told with gusto and admiration; well documented with factual material.

Keith, Agnes Newton: *Land Below the Wind*. Boston: Little, Brown and Co.; 1939.

———: *Three Came Home*. Boston: Little, Brown and Co.; 1947.

————: *White Man Returns.* Boston: Little, Brown and Co.; 1951.
Highly personal accounts of life in North Borneo during the
final years of Chartered Company rule, the Japanese occupation,
and the postwar reconstruction; by the American wife of the
British Conservator of Forests and Director of Agriculture of
North Borneo.

North Borneo, Colony of: *Annual Report, 1958.* Jesselton: Government Printing Department; 1959.
Covering all aspects of colonial administration, the report gives
valuable data about the area, combined with the flavor of life
in an outpost of Empire.

Pecson, Geronima T., and Racelis, Maria (eds.): *Tales of the American Teachers in the Philippines.* Manila: Carmelo & Bauermann;
1959.
Two Filipinas, one a senator, one a sociologist, have pieced together the tale of the Thomasites from reminiscences and other
sources.

Philippines, Republic of: *Industrial Survey Report for the Province
of Sulu.* Manila: Industrial Development Center; 1961.

————: *Mindanao Area Survey.* Manila: National Economic Council; 1961.
These are interesting preliminary surveys, designed to lead to
more solidly based development plans for the borderland provinces.

Purcell, Victor: *The Chinese in Southeast Asia.* London: Oxford
University Press; 1951.
A masterly study that includes separate sections on the Chinese
in the Philippines and in Borneo.

Rutter, Owen: *British North Borneo.* London: Constable and Co.;
1922.
An excellent account of North Borneo's history, resources, and
native tribes; its British author was at least thirty years ahead
of his time in his recommendations for training the people and
developing the territory.

Saleeby, Najeeb M.: *Studies in Moro History, Law and Religion.*
Ethnological Survey Publication, Vol. IV, Part I. Manila: Department of the Interior; 1905.

————: *The History of Sulu.* Division of Ethnology Publications,
Vol. IV, Part II. Manila: Bureau of Science; 1908.

————: *The Moro Problem. An Academic Discussion of the History
and Solution of the Problem of the Government of the Moros of
the Philippine Islands.* Manila; 1913.

In these three slender publications, we have the bulk of Dr. Saleeby's scholarly work on Moro history and lore with recommendations for American policy. Nothing else on this subject can touch Dr. Saleeby's work for precision and understanding.

Strachey, John: *The End of Empire*. New York: Random House; 1959.
A leading British Socialist ignores the stereotypes of ideology to produce a brilliant and honest study of how the British built and lost an empire.

Tregonning, K. G.: *Under Chartered Company Rule. North Borneo 1881–1946*. Singapore: University of Malaya Press; 1958.
The indispensable history of a private company's ownership of North Borneo well into the twentieth century. After writing this book, the author, an Australian scholar, became Raffles Professor of History at the University of Malaya.

————: *North Borneo*. London: Her Majesty's Stationery Office; 1960.
A postscript to the previous volume, in the vein of a travelogue with an official tone.

Wallace, Alfred Russel: *The Malay Archipelago*. New York: Harper & Brothers; 1869.
The researches described in this book led Wallace, a renowned English naturalist, to the discovery of a north-south line through the archipelago, dividing Asian flora and fauna on the west from Polynesian on the east: the famous "Wallace Line."

Ward, W. E. F.: *Educating Young Nations*. London: Allen & Unwin; 1959.
A British teacher and administrator in Africa discusses the schooling of colonial peoples; his enlightened though paternalistic ideas are as relevant to North Borneo as to African colonies.

Chapter 3

Anderson, John: *A Report on the Expedition to Western Yunan via Bhamo*. Calcutta: Office of the Superintendent of Government Printing; 1871.
The record of a daring but vain British attempt to find a new trade route from Burma into China.

Burma, Government of the Union of: *Economic Survey of Burma 1960*. Rangoon; 1960.

————: *Is Trust Vindicated? A Chronicle of the Various Accomplishments of the Government Headed by Ne Win.* Rangoon; 1960.

Cady, John F.: *A History of Modern Burma.* Ithaca, N.Y.: Cornell University Press; 1960.
An American scholar, formerly a lecturer at Rangoon, goes deeply into Burman sources, but gives scanty treatment to the non-Burman peoples. The second printing contains an unbound supplement covering the difficult 1956–60 period.

Crosthwaite, Sir Charles: *The Pacification of Burma.* London: Edward Arnold; 1912.
Britain's troubles in subduing Upper Burma and the Shan States after 1885, described by the man who became Commissioner, or chief civilian executive, in 1887.

Hall, D. G. E.: *A History of South-East Asia.* New York: St. Martin's Press; 1955.
A British scholar places the Shans and Burmans in a wider Southeast Asian historical setting.

Harvey, G. E.: *British Rule in Burma 1824–1942.* London: Faber & Faber; 1946.
Like other former British teachers in Rangoon, the author finds Britain guilty of a cardinal error in having made Burma a mere province of India.

Hoover, Herbert: *The Memoirs of Herbert Hoover.* Three vols. Vol. I: *Years of Adventure, 1874–1920.* New York: The Macmillan Co.; 1951.
The first volume contains the absorbing story of the rediscovery and exploitation of the Bawdwin Mine.

Leach, E. R.: *Political Systems of Highland Burma.* London: G. Bell and Sons, Ltd; 1954.
A British anthropologist describes the political and social organization of the Kachins and Shans.

Milne, Mary Lewis (Mrs. Leslie M.): *Shans at Home.* London: John Murray; 1910.
An Englishwoman who lived at Namkham describes the domestic life and customs of the Shans early in this century.

Nu, Thakin (U Nu): *Burma under the Japanese: Pictures and Portraits.* London: Macmillan & Co., Ltd.; 1954.
A candid record that reveals Burmese attitudes toward foreign occupiers.

Scott, Sir J. G.: *Scott of the Shan Hills: Orders and Impressions.* Edited by G. E. Mitton (Lady Scott). London: John Murray; 1936.

The foremost British chronicler of the Shans tells of "pacification" along the northern and eastern borders in the 1890's.

Seagrave, Gordon S.: *The Life of a Burma Surgeon*. With a foreword by Chester Bowles. New York: Ballantine Books; 1960.
A condensation of three earlier autobiographical volumes, with an epilogue bringing the story to 1960.

Tinker, Hugh: *The Union of Burma. A Study of the First Years of Independence*. Third edition. London: Oxford University Press; 1961.
Indispensable for its political, economic, and social history of the border peoples since they entered the Union.

Chapter 4

Davies, C. Collin: *An Historical Atlas of the Indian Peninsula*. Madras: Oxford University Press; 1953.
The history of India in maps showing, incidentally, how Indian rulers in pre-British days stopped short at the foot of the Himalayas.

Elwin, Verrier: *A Philosophy for NEFA* [North-East Frontier Agency]. Shillong, Assam: Sachin Roy on behalf of the North-East Frontier Agency; 1959.
An anthropologist in India's service describes the tribal peoples living along the McMahon Line, and suggests enlightened policies for dealing with hill peoples generally.

Fisher, Margaret W., and Bondurant, Joan V.: *Indian Views of Sino-Indian Relations*. Berkeley, Calif.: Indian Press Digests, Monograph Series, University of California; 1956.
A souvenir of the India-China love-dance that followed the 1954 agreement on Tibet; taken largely from the Indian press.

Freshfield, Douglas W.: *Round Kangchenjunga. A Narrative of Mountain Travel and Exploration*. London: Edward Arnold; 1903.
A classic of Himalayan mountaineering, with vivid descriptions of western Sikkim.

Gould, B. J.: *The Jewel in the Lotus. Recollections of an Indian Political*. London: Chatto & Windus; 1957.
The author served as Britain's Political Officer in Sikkim from 1935 to 1945, with responsibilities for Bhutan and Tibet as well.

Hooker, Joseph Dalton: *Himalayan Journals; or, Notes of a Naturalist in Bengal, the Sikkim and Nepal Himalayas, the Khasia Mountains, &c.* Two vols. London: John Murray; 1854.
After more than a century, this remains the freshest and most rewarding book about the scenery, fauna, flora, and people of Sikkim and its surroundings.

India, Government of, Ministry of External Affairs: *Report of the Officials of the Governments of India and the People's Republic of China on the Boundary Question.* New Delhi; 1961.

————: *White Paper. Notes, Memoranda and Letters Exchanged and Agreements Signed between the Governments of India and China 1954–1959.* New Delhi; 1959.

————: *White Paper No. II. September–November 1959.* New Delhi; 1959.

————: *White Paper No. III. November 1959–March 1960.* New Delhi; 1960.

Karan, Pradyumna P.: *Nepal. A Cultural and Physical Geography.* Lexington, Ky.: University of Kentucky Press; 1960.
Useful for its large maps as well as its text on a neglected subject.

Levi, Werner: *Free India in Asia.* Minneapolis: University of Minnesota Press; 1952.
A Professor of Political Science at Minnesota discusses, in Chapter vi, India's relations with the Himalayan States and Tibet.

Pallis, Marco: *Peaks and Lamas.* London: Cassell & Co., Ltd.; 1939.
A travel book of rare charm, by a writer who was equally at home climbing snow peaks and threading the maze of Buddhist symbolism in Sikkim.

Ronaldshay, the Earl of: *Lands of the Thunderbolt. Sikhim, Chumbi & Bhutan.* London: Constable & Co., Ltd.; 1923.
Travel, history, and Buddhist lore in the eastern Himalayas; the author was Governor of Bengal, 1916–22, and later the second Marquess of Zetland.

Sikkim, Government of: *Sikkim, Her Faith and Future.* Gangtok: Department of Information and Publicity; 1958.
An informative and handsome official booklet; it contains a description of the Sikkim development program, as well as messages and speeches by the Maharaja, his heir apparent, and the Dalai Lama.

Smythe, F. S.: *The Kangchenjunga Adventure.* London: Victor Gollancz, Ltd.; 1930.

Western Sikkim and its mountains sensitively described by a
(London) *Times* correspondent who tried and failed to climb
Kanchenjunga.

White, John Claude: *Sikhim & Bhutan. Twenty-one Years on the
North-east Frontier, 1887–1908.* London: Edward Arnold; 1909.
Britain's first Political Officer at Gangtok tells of his service
there, and of the history of Sikkim and Bhutan.

Chapter 5

Afghanistan, Government of: *Survey of Progress.* Kabul: Ministry
of Planning; 1960.
An annual review for the third year of Afghanistan's Five Year
Plan, with a statistical appendix. A large, paperback book of
about 350 pages, this is a praiseworthy attempt to lay a necessary statistical foundation for the future in the fields of economic and social development.

Ali, Mohammed: *A New Guide to Afghanistan.* Kabul; 1958.

———: *Afghanistan. The Mohammedzai Period.* Kabul; 1959.

———: *Afghanistan. The War of Independence, 1919.* Kabul, 1960.
The author, Professor of History at the University of Kabul,
chronicles the nineteenth-century and modern political history
of his country with a strong Pushtun bias and nationalistic
fervor; an antidote to the works of British authors.

Cressey, George B.: *Crossroads. Land and Life in Southwest Asia.*
Chicago: J. B. Lippincott Co.: 1960.
The dean of American geographers has compiled a most useful
area study, with chapters on Afghanistan and Turkey.

Douglas, William O.: *West of the Indus.* Garden City, N.Y.: Double-
day and Co.; 1958.
A traveler with rare insight into political and social problems,
Justice Douglas traversed Afghan Turkestan and eastern Turkey
during a 7,000-mile automobile journey in 1957.

Dupree, Louis: *American Universities Field Staff Reports Service.
South Asia Series.* Vol. III, Nos. 2 and 3. Vol. IV, Nos. 3, 4, 5, 6,
and 8. New York: American Universities Field Staff, Inc.; 1959–
60.
An anthropologist submits current reports on the Afghan scene.
They deal with politics, economics, and the Cold War, plus
brief history and background. The author gets around the
country and observes.

Elphinstone, Hon. Mountstuart: *An Account of the Kingdom of Caubul and Its Dependencies in Persia, Tartary and India; Comprising a View of the Afghaun Nation and a History of the Doorraunee Monarchy.* London: Longman, Hurst, Rees, Orme & Brown (etc.); 1815.

> A high officer of the British East India Company, the author was sent to Kabul in 1808 as the first British envoy to the court of the Durranis. He brought back a fresh and detailed account of the country and the people just as the Great Game was getting under way.

Fraser-Tytler, W. K.: *Afghanistan. A Study of Political Developments in Central and Southern Asia.* Second Edition. London: Oxford University Press; 1958.

> By far the best survey in English of Afghan history and politics; by a former British Minister in Kabul.

————: "Great North Road." *Journal of the Royal Central Asian Society,* Vol. XXIX (April 1942).

> A fuller account of this pioneering venture than appears in the book listed above.

Harlan, Josiah: *A Memoir of India and Afghanistaun, with Observations on the Present Exciting and Critical State and Future Prospects of Those Countries.* Philadelphia: J. Dobson; 1842.

> Part genius, part scalawag, this American "General" wrote of the borderland not only with flourish but with insight.

Holdich, Colonel Sir Thomas: *The Gates of India, Being an Historical Narrative.* London: Macmillan & Co., Ltd.; 1910.

> A servant of Empire condemns the folly of British policy that led to the First and Second Afghan Wars.

Masson, Charles: *Narrative of Various Journeys in Balochistan, Afghanistan, the Panjab & Kalat during a Residence in These Countries.* Four vols. London: R. Bentley; 1844.

> A detailed report by a Briton who "went native" to find out about the people and the country. Masson was a contemporary critic of the British decision to launch the First Afghan War.

Michel, Aloys Arthur: *The Kabul, Kunduz and Helmand Valleys and the National Economy of Afghanistan.* Washington, D.C.: National Academy of Sciences; 1959.

> An objective, up-to-date summary of the economic problems and potential of Afghanistan's river valleys. A doctoral dissertation, clearly and well written.

Wilber, Donald Newton (ed.): *Afghanistan.* New Haven, Conn.: Human Relations Area Files; 1956.

> A useful symposium by specialists on present-day Afghanistan.

Chapter 6

Armstrong, H. C.: *Grey Wolf. Mustapha Kemal, an Intimate Study of a Dictator.* London: Arthur Barker, Ltd.; 1932.
A jerky, episodic biography, probably close to the truth but so "intimate" that its sale in Turkey has always been forbidden.

Aslan, Kevork: *Armenia and the Armenians from the Earliest Times until the Great War (1914).* New York: The Macmillan Co.; 1920.
A partisan history, but less so than others on its subject.

Bryce, James: *Transcaucasia and Ararat.* London: Macmillan & Co.; 1877.
Chapters v–x of this classic tell of Ararat and the young author's ascent.

Curzon, the Hon. Robert: *Armenia: A Year at Erzeroom, and on the Frontiers of Russia, Turkey and Persia.* New York: Harper & Brothers; 1854.
The author was oppressed by the bleakness and poverty of eastern Turkey: *plus ça change, plus c'est la même chose.*

Edmonds, C. J.: *Kurds, Turks and Arabs.* London: Oxford University Press; 1957.
An authoritative account of the Kurds, with heavy emphasis on those in Iraq.

Erinc, Sirri, and Tuncdilek, Necdet: "The Agricultural Regions of Turkey." *Geographical Review,* Vol. XLII (1952).
Includes a useful survey of what can be grown, and where, in the eastern provinces.

Holmgreen, E. N.: *Agricultural Extension in Turkey.* Washington, D.C.: International Co-operation Administration; April 25, 1960.
A government report that shows, by implication, how little has been done in this field in eastern Turkey.

Kinross, Lord (Patrick Balfour): *Within the Taurus. A Journey in Asiatic Turkey.* London: John Murray; 1954.
By an observant British writer who traveled along the Soviet frontier from the Black Sea to Kars, then south to the Lake Van region.

Lewis, Bernard: *The Emergence of Modern Turkey.* London: Oxford University Press; 1961.
The first half of this history tells of the slow growth of reform from about the end of the eighteenth century; the second, of Kemalist Turkey to 1950.

Lynch, H. F. B.: *Armenia. Travels and Studies.* Two vols. London: Longmans, Green, & Co.; 1901.
A ponderous work that pictures those eastern Turkish regions where the Armenians lived.

Makal, Mahmud: *A Village in Anatolia.* London: Valentine, Mitchell & Co., Ltd.; 1954.
An annotated translation combining two books of vignettes, the first of which shocked Turkish officialdom and landed the author in jail. Makal was a village teacher trained at a village institute.

Sassani, Abdul H. K.: *Education in Turkey.* Washington, D.C.: U.S. Office of Education; 1952.
An American government pamphlet that pays due tribute to the village institutes.

Stark, Freya: *Riding to the Tigris.* New York: Harcourt, Brace & Co.; 1959.
An Englishwoman with a sense of history tells of her travels and tribulations from Van southward through the relatively inaccessible Hakkari country.

Turkey, Republic of: *Monthly Bulletin of Statistics.* Ankara: Central Statistical Office; 1954–.
These publications, in Turkish and English, supersede the more complete *Annuaire Statistique de la Republique Turque,* in Turkish and French, which was discontinued in 1953.

————: *Agricultural Census Results.* 1956.

————: *Agricultural Structure and Production 1954–1958.* 1959.
Both publications are valuable because they list land holdings, crop yields, and herds by provinces and districts, thus permitting comparisons between eastern and western Turkey.

INDEX

Abu Bakr, 93

Adana province, 280

Ade, George, 104–5

Afghan Turkestan: as highway, 219–20, 225–6, 272; as invasion route, 222–3, 272; foreign technicians in, 223, 245–6, 254, 263, 266; present-day peoples of, 224–5; refugees in, 225; Russian interest in, 225, 256, 261–4; trade through, 225–6, 236–7, 262, 264; way of life, 244; Germans in, 246; Great North Road to, 249–55; products, 255–60, 262–3, 273; industries, 255–60, 263; agriculture in, 257–9, 273; women in, 270–1; prospects of, 273; *see also* Afghanistan

Afghanistan: lack of communications, 226; constitution, 227; dominance of South, 228, 230; relations with U.S., 229, 246, 259–60, 262, 264–7; with Pakistan, 229–30, 261; with Russia, 230, 232, 239–40, 262–6, 272–3; with Britain, 232–5, 238–40, 272; period of

Afghanistan (*continued*)
isolation, 241; nomads, 241–5; trade, 242, 262, 264; education, 244–5, 247, 266–7, 271; modernization, 245–8, 261, 273; and Germany, 245–6, 257; United Nations in, 265; women's status in, 247–8, 268–71; *see also* Afghan Turkestan

Ağrı province, 293–4

agriculture: in Hokkaido, 7, 9–10, 26–7, 34–7, 39–46; in Philippines, 67, 111–14, 147; in N. Borneo, 75–6, 79, 85; among Shans, 122; Kachins, 147–8; Nepalis, 147, 181; in Formosa, 39, 147; among Lepchas, 180; under Sikkim development plan, 207, 209; in Afghanistan, 256–60; in Turkey, 277–8, 280–1, 297–303, 313–15

Ainu, 13–16, 28, 180, 317

air services: in Mindanao, 64; in N. Borneo, 64, 73–4; in Burma, 121, 163; to Himalayas, 172; in Afghanistan, 266; in Turkey, 307

A NOTE ABOUT THE AUTHORS

Ferdinand Kuhn was born in New York, and graduated from Mount Vernon High School and from Columbia University (A.B., 1925). He was on the staff of *The New York Times* from 1925 through 1940. For most of this period he was stationed in London, and was chief of the London bureau from 1937 until late in 1939. In 1941 he came to Washington as assistant to the Secretary of the Treasury, and subsequently served as deputy director of the Office of War Information. In 1946 he joined *The Washington Post,* and for seven years reported foreign affairs from the capital and abroad. Mr. Kuhn has written two Landmark books, *Commodore Perry and the Opening of Japan* (1955) and *The Story of the Secret Service* (1957). Delia Kuhn was born in New York, and was graduated from Horace Mann School and from Vassar College (A.B., 1925). From 1926 to 1931 she was Associate Editor of and contributor to *Current History* magazine, then published by *The New York Times.* From 1941 to 1953 she served the United States government as a writer and information officer in the Office of War Information, and subsequently in the Department of State and the Technical Co-operation Administration (Point 4). Since 1953 Mr. and Mrs. Kuhn have collaborated as free-lance writers and lecturers, traveling widely in Asia, North Africa, and Europe for their material, and contributing articles on world affairs to many newspapers as well as to magazines such as *Harper's, The National Geographic, Collier's,* and *Holiday.* Washington, D.C., is their permanent home.

A NOTE ON THE TYPE

THE TEXT of this book was set on the Linotype in a
new face called PRIMER, designed by *Rudolph Ruzicka,*
earlier responsible for the design of Fairfield and Fairfield Medium, Linotype faces whose virtues have for
some time now been accorded wide recognition. The
complete range of sizes of Primer was first made available in 1954, although the pilot size of 12 point was
ready as early as 1951. The design of the face makes
general reference to Linotype Century (long a service-
able type, totally lacking in manner or frills of any
kind) but brilliantly corrects the characterless quality
of that face.

Composed, printed, and bound by
Kingsport Press, Inc., Kingsport, Tennessee.
Typography and binding design by
VINCENT TORRE